To My
Loving "Woman"   NOV! 2009

HOPE
D I A M O N D

What one has to know is that
a diamond comes from a
"Black" piece of "Coal".
And it can only happen if
that coal is under
"PRESSURE."

And it does not happen over night
it takes years.

Thanks for being that
DIAMOND

JPRC

HOPE
DIAMOND

*The Legendary History
of a Cursed Gem*

RICHARD KURIN

 Smithsonian Books

Collins
An Imprint of HarperCollinsPublishers

HarperCollins books may be purchased for educational, business, or sales promotional use. For information please write: Special Markets Department, HarperCollins Publishers Inc., 10 East 53rd Street, New York, NY 10022.

Published 2006 in the United States of America by Smithsonian Books in association with HarperCollins Publishers.

The Library of Congress Cataloging-in-Publication Data has been filed for.
ISBN-10: 0-06-087351-5
ISBN-13: 978-0-06-087351-6

06 07 08 09 10 WBC/QWF 10 9 8 7 6 5 4 3 2 1

Dedicated to my daughters,
Danielle and Jaclyn

FOREWORD

The *Hope diamond is one of the* most important treasures in the Smithsonian's national collections. It is a legendary object in American culture, and one of the reasons why the National Museum of Natural History has been one of the most visited museums in the entire world over the last half century.

At the Smithsonian, we have an obligation to protect, preserve, and present to the public the artifacts, specimens and objects of art we hold in trust for the American people. The care and quality with which we do so is evident in the Harry Winston Gallery of the Janet Annenberg Hooker Hall of Gems where the Hope diamond now rests. Smithsonian scholars also research items in the national collections in order to contribute to a broader understanding of their meaning and significance. In this book, Richard Kurin traces the cultural history of the Hope diamond over four centuries and across the globe, finding it to both embody and reflect the ideas of diverse times and places. A crystal from deep underground the earth became a symbol of divine kingship; a jewel exemplifying male honor became a decorative object of romance; a stolen crown jewel became a trophy; an object supposedly laden with a curse became an icon of national pride and repute. This truly marvelous book tells how.

Lawrence M. Small
Secretary, Smithsonian Institution

INTRODUCTION

This is a book about a small stone with a big story—the Hope diamond.

The Hope diamond is blue, not a pale sky blue, but a deep, steely blue. It weighs 45.52 carats. This seems like a lot, given that most engagement rings are one carat or less. While many people imagine the Hope diamond to be about the size of a softball—or at least a baseball, it is about the size of a walnut. It is only one inch across, a bit less than an inch in width, and about a half inch in depth. This is nonetheless a very big diamond. And its blue color makes it quite rare. A blue diamond of this size and color would be valued at somewhere between $25 million and $40 million on the open market. But the Hope diamond is worth much more, its price recently estimated at $200 million!

What adds tens if not hundreds of millions of dollars to the gem's worth? Simply, it is its story. The diamond has a rich history including a legendary ancient curse attached to its origins in India. This legend was so prevalent in 1958 when the Smithsonian acquired the Hope diamond that many Americans urged the National Museum not to accept the diamond in its collections for fear that the U.S. would be cursed.

As a cultural anthropologist, I became intrigued by the way people thought about the diamond, and how the meaning they imputed to it seemed to change over the course of centuries as it moved across cultures and through different societies. This prompted a decade of research as I followed the diamond's trail to mines and ruins in India, treasure houses and battlefronts in France, castles in England, jewelry stores and mansions in the United States, and finally to my professional home, the Smithsonian.

This book seeks to understand the making of the curse legend. The curse is not ancient; it is modern. It evolved in New York, London, Paris, and Washington. It has been repeated and increasingly elaborated over the years. Young people today might think of it as an entertaining transnational "urban legend." Like some of those legends, while many of the purported facts are fictional, it provides a truthfully revealing commentary on social relationships and anxieties. Here, for the first time, the legend is pieced together and explained, not as supernatural mystery, but as contemporary folklore of the 20th century.

Perhaps more important, this book looks beyond the legend to the many other truly fascinating aspects of the cultural history of the Hope diamond. Tracing the diamond's shape, movement, and meaning teaches us about religion, commerce, and politics in India, royal and revolutionary France, the waning aristocracy in England, and the making of modern America. It even reveals a great deal about the Smithsonian itself. The diamond's tale implicates a renowned cast of characters—Louis XIV, Marie Antoinette, George IV, Napoleon, Caroline of Brunswick, May Yohe, Evalyn Walsh McLean, Harry Winston, and Jackie Kennedy, among many others. As an object of spirituality, power, bribery, jealousy, romance, revenge, greed, and pride the diamond is caught up in conflicts over colonialism, class rivalry, sex roles, religious beliefs, science, business, and national honor. While the legend certainly shines, it is this history that truly sparkles.

Richard Kurin,
Director, Smithsonian
Center for Folklife and
Cultural Heritage
Washington, D.C.

CONTENTS

CONTENTS

PROLOGUE

1

GIFT TO THE NATION

O*n Monday morning, November 10, 1958,* public faith in the U.S. government was literally wrapped up in the performance of James Todd, a 34-year-old postman—and he was late!

Three days before, Paul Haase, a former policeman working in a Fifth Avenue shipping department, had carried a plainly wrapped package on the subway to New York City's general post office. The package was addressed simply, "Smithsonian Institution, Washington, D.C., Attention: Dr. Leonard Carmichael." It weighed 61 ounces. Insured for $1 million, the postage came to $145.29.[1]

From Washington's city post office, Todd, a Navy veteran with a somewhat troubled past, was entrusted to make the delivery. Unaccompanied, and with no weapon, it was just Todd and the Hope diamond.

The method was typical of the no-nonsense "King of Diamonds" Harry Winston, the famed jewelry merchant. By sending the diamond by mail he had the whole U.S. government protecting it. "It's the safest way to mail gems," he confidently declared.[2]

Mindful of the potential publicity bonanza—or nightmare if the delivery was not consummated—U.S. Postmaster General Arthur Summerfield awaited the arrival of the package with its intended recipient, Leonard Carmichael, the Secretary of the Smithsonian. They had assembled in the recently reconstructed Gem Room of the National Museum (now the National Museum of Natural History) along with distinguished guests for an 11:30 ceremony.

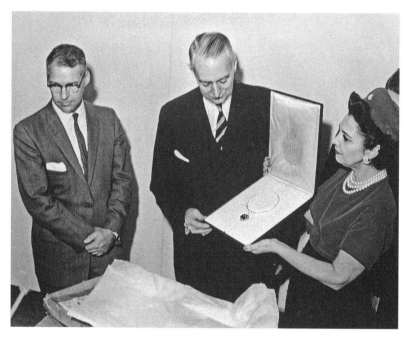

Edna Winston presents the Hope diamond to Leonard Carmichael.

Foremost among the guests was the good-natured Edna Winston representing her husband and his company, Harry Winston, Inc.—the donor and still legally the owner of the diamond, accompanied by her 17-year-old son Ronald. Others included society mavens Gwen Cafritz, Polly Guggenheim, and Nan Chase, the latter being the personal assistant of the deceased Evalyn Walsh McLean, who had owned the Hope diamond prior to Winston. George Switzer, the museum's curator of mineralogy who had pursued the donation, was ready to take possession of the famed gem. A retinue of Smithsonian guards, local police, and postal inspectors also milled expectantly.

Postman Todd put the package in his sedan and drove to the museum at 10th Street and Constitution, barely a mile away. The Hope diamond had, after a long period of negotiation and uncertainty, arrived at the Smithsonian.

At 11:45 a.m. Todd handed over the package to Carmichael who duly signed a receipt. Carmichael passed the package to Switzer,

The original installation of the Hope diamond.

who carefully unwrapped the brown paper to reveal a simple but elegant rectangular jewelry case, much to the relief of the Postmaster General and the other guests. Todd later admitted that the television cameras and all the "hoopla" had made him a "little shaky."[3]

Edna Winston held up the opened case, with the Hope diamond, mounted on a necklace, inset into a fine satin cushion. Edna's brief remarks followed the theme of her husband's official statement that the Hope diamond was a gift to the American people. "We have hopes that this will be the nucleus of a great collection to view with the wonderful works of art in our museums," she said.[4] Switzer then put the diamond into its new home in the Gem Room—a small safe that when opened could be seen by the public through a glass display window. It looked somewhat like a ship's portal, surrounded by an oversized rectangular art frame.

The Hope diamond was displayed in its setting, on its necklace, against a satin background. An accompanying sign read,

Hope Diamond, 44½ carats
The world's largest blue diamond
Acquired from the estate of Evalyn Walsh McLean, 1949
Gift of Harry Winston, Inc. 1958

The sign, as it turned out, was wrong. In fact, much of what the Smithsonian had to say about the history of the Hope diamond that morning was wrong.[5]

But it really wasn't history or science that interested either the museum or the public. Americans were fascinated by the famed curse of the Hope diamond. Just days before, the Associated Press widely circulated a syndicated story leading with "The fabulous Hope Diamond, a stone of beauty and ill fortune, is about to pass from a New York gem merchant to the Nation." The story went on to recount the legend:

> The diamond is believed to have been torn from the forehead of a Hindu idol and smuggled out of India by a Frenchman named Tavernier in 1642. Tavernier was bitten to death by a pack of dogs. Among subsequent owners: Nicholas Fouquet, a French official was executed. Princess de Lamballe was beaten fatally by a French mob. King Louis XVI and Marie Antoinette were beheaded.
>
> Henry Thomas Hope, an Irish banker, gave the stone its name and as far as is known, came to a normal end. Hope's grandson, Lord Francis Pelham Clinton, died penniless. The grandson's music hall bride from America, May Yohe, left the diamond behind her as she went off in divorce. She ended up scrubbing floors. Simon Montharides was killed with his wife and child when they rode over a precipice. Sultan Abdul Hamid of Turkey lost his throne. Subaya, the Sultan's favorite, wore the diamond and was slain. The diamond was placed on the market after the revolt of Young Turks.
>
> Mrs. McLean, wife of a former owner of the *Washington Post* and one of the capital's best-known hostesses, acquired

the Hope in 1911 for a reported $154,000. Her husband, Ned McLean, died in a mental institution. Her oldest son lost his life in a car accident and her daughter died of an overdose of sleeping pills . . . Winston bought it from the estate of Evalyn Walsh McLean. Winston has escaped the misfortunes which befell many of the diamond's earlier possessors . . .[6]

Edna Winston discounted the curse. "Not a bit of bad luck had it brought us. Instead it has been good luck for a great many people as it has traveled hundreds of thousands of miles raising money for charity," she said, referring to Hope's inclusion in Harry Winston's famed touring Court of Jewels fund-raisers.[7]

The Smithsonian, for its part, did not even mention the term "curse" in its press release, though it mistakenly acknowledged "the legends attached to the Hope date back many hundreds of years." "We wouldn't worry about the curse," said Carmichael at the time, noting, "The Hope diamond, because of its unique color, its physical properties and its chemical constitution, is an interesting scientific object."[8]

But whatever the scientific value of the diamond, there is little doubt that its popular appeal was directly attributable to its legendary curse. Enshrined in the Gem Room, it just about doubled attendance at the museum.[9] The Hope diamond had "star power." "I hope it doesn't turn out to be a jinx for Uncle Sam," opined one elderly woman.

Newsweek came out with its story about the acquisition. CURSE OF THE DIAMOND, one newspaper declared. "As of Monday, if anyone is hexed it will not be [Harry Winston] but the staff of the Smithsonian Institution."[10] A columnist wrote, "The Hope diamond has brought nothing but grief to anyone who ever owned it. Whoever accepted it on behalf of the United States did this country a great disservice."[11]

Harry Winston disagreed. His gift was motivated by the desire to do well for his nation. But others were not convinced. A gift, even if generously given and intended as a blessing, could turn out to be a curse instead.[12] Numerous letters came to the Smithsonian exhorting the Institution to reject the donation. "If the Smithsonian accepts the Hope diamond," wrote one, "the whole country will suffer."[13]

*"Bad Luck Hope Diamond Given to US," a cartoon
parody of the acquisition.*

A front-page story in the August 21, 1959 *Washington Post* gave added impetus to the idea that the gift of the diamond might be fraught with danger. HOPE DIAMOND'S POSTMAN-DELIVERER BESET BY TRAGEDY, ACCIDENT, AND FIRE, read the headline. Within a year after delivering the fateful package to the Smithsonian, James Todd had faced a string of misfortunes. Todd's leg was accidentally crushed by a truck, his wife died of a heart attack, he'd been injured in a car accident, and his dog was strangled on its leash. Finally, the story reported, the day before, his home at 6211 Field Street, Seat Pleasant had burned down.

Todd himself wasn't convinced. Asked about the Hope diamond curse he responded that he was actually very lucky that his four children had been out of the house and had thus survived the fire. "I don't believe in any of that stuff." Besides, Todd noted, "If the hex is supposed to affect the owners, then the public should be having the bad luck [not me]!"[14]

But the letters to the Smithsonian continued.

You know how disastrous the stone has been for its owners; it has brought evil to so many people that one might say some evil Hindu spirit wants to take revenge because of the fact that the stone was once stolen from a Hindu image. Why run the risk that some day your museum might be blown up and visitors might be killed.[15]

There was clearly a nationalistic spin to some of these letters. The fear reflected the tension over the "foreign" or "alien" in the Cold War period and was thematically consistent with a genre of popular science fiction movies in the late 1950s about unknown influences infiltrating and afflicting American society. As one concerned citizens' group wrote, "With our neighbor Russia able to blow our country to pieces in a few hours of missile bombardment, it would be insane to tempt fate by having anything to do with this ghastly gem."[16]

One person sent in a grainy newspaper photo of the Hope diamond with the annotation, "Look at the left side of the gem . . . There is a very definite and clear face visible within the diamond."[17] Presumably that was the face of the devil or Hindu god or other malevolent spirit.

Mailman James Todd.

The Hope diamond supposedly continued to have an effect, even while on display, as attested to by a 1983 letter,

Enclosed find two pictures of the Hope Diamond taken during my class trip in April 1978. You may laugh and find this silly, but since I took these pictures I have had more bad luck than I care to mention. I'm sending these pictures to you. I sincerely hope my luck changes for the better. . . I never realized the possibility that a curse could be carried through a picture.[18]

Letters warning of ill effects came to the Smithsonian for years. Mrs. John Schindler of Gridley, Kansas, wrote in 1964 to report on the fate of James Todd, who'd apparently moved back to his childhood home after the death of his wife.

> He started drinking and went the route with wine and women. He lost his mail job. He brought a strange woman and his four children to live in our town where his mother resides. She found them a dump to live in. The woman left in a matter of a few weeks . . . He crashed his station wagon into the front of a hardware store in another town close by while drunk. He was thrown into jail and his mother bailed him out and he left the country . . . If she knows where he is, she doesn't tell. She has the children on welfare . . . The two older boys are delinquents . . .[19]

Even decades later the legend of the curse continues unabated. Consider a 1995 *Life* magazine pictorial featuring Michelle Pfeiffer modeling the gem:

> In all but the brightest light it smolders like a huge sullen eye . . . The jewel, so the story goes, was once the eye of a Hindu idol Rama Sita. When it was stolen, Ram cursed everyone who would come to possess the stone. Indeed, fate has not been kind to those who have owned the eye of the god.[20]

The Smithsonian for its part has always denied the curse. Curator Jeffrey Post echoed his predecessors when, on the opening of the new Harry Winston Gallery in 1997, he wrote, "For the Smithsonian Institution, the Hope diamond has obviously been a source of good luck."[21]

So if the curse has no historical basis, how and where does it originate? And why does it persist?

2

LEGEND DELIVERED

The story of the curse of the Hope Diamond blossomed as an extravagant form of Parisian room service delivered by jeweler Pierre Cartier to the suite of young, rich Americans at the Hotel Bristol in 1910.

Although it is located on a rather busy and unimposing street, and is too snugly sandwiched in by surrounding buildings, the Bristol is a very exclusive place. As I stand before it in the late summer, stylish flower boxes fronting each window are flush with color. Intricate, stylized metalwork graces the balconies and decorates the facade. The glass doors, trimmed in polished brass and topped with a thirty-foot-long brass tassel, signal "expensive."

I feel out of place entering the elegant lobby. I try to project the demeanor of a Smithsonian scholar because I'd never pass as rich. I feel scruffy. But no one pays much attention. Maybe the staff thinks I'm just another eccentric foreign guest. There are reproductions of classical French paintings on the walls and sculptured heads of French kings on pedestals. The museum-quality cases exhibiting fine diamond jewelry for sale from Harry Winston, Inc. and from Cartier are most appropriate. There are *no* price tags.

It was at this very fashionable way station in September 1910 that the story of a cursed Hope diamond was first told to Evalyn Walsh McLean and her husband Edward ("Ned").

Evalyn and Ned, both in their mid-twenties, alcoholic, very spoiled, and very wealthy were vacationing in Europe. Ned McLean

The young Ned and Evalyn McLean.

was the son of the affluent owners of the *Washington Post*. Evalyn was the daughter of Thomas Walsh, a gold miner who struck it very rich. They had just driven from Vichy to Paris in a marvelous yellow Fiat coupe after gambling at casinos—Evalyn won $70,000. The trip followed their raucous honeymoon two years earlier, which, in addition to European travel included a visit to the court and harem of the Turkish Sultan, and adventurous camel and horse carriage tours in the Middle East.

Pierre Cartier knew the couple, his firm having sold them the 94¾ carat Star of the East diamond for $120,000 during their honeymoon. The Cartier Brothers—Louis, Pierre, and Jacques were in the process of expanding the family business. In the early 1900s they had begun to service rich Americans with a desire for world-class jewelry, opening up a store on Fifth Avenue in New York. Pierre, age 32, was regarded as the most businesslike of the brothers, an excellent salesman who developed fine rapport with his customers. He was especially good with Americans, having married Elma Rumsey, the daughter of a rich St. Louis industrialist.

In her autobiography *Father Struck It Rich,* Evalyn described Pierre Cartier's entrance to their hotel suite: "He carried, tenderly, a package tightly closed with wax seals. His manner was exquisitely mysterious. I suppose a Parisian jewel merchant who seeks to trade among the ultra-rich has to be more or less a stage manager and an actor."[1]

Pierre began by asking Evalyn if she knew about the Turkish Revolution. Evalyn and Ned had been in Constantinople for their honeymoon journey. They'd met Sultan Abdul Hamid and had been impressed with his emerald and his diamond-studded porcelain cups.

Pierre said, "You told me then that you had seen a jewel in the harem, a great blue stone that rested against the throat of the Sultan's favorite."[2]

Pressed, Evalyn recalled saying, "It seems to me I did see that stone." But she later wrote, "Did the Turkish Sultan Abdul-Hamid ever own it? I do not know for sure."[3]

"The woman who had that jewel from the Sultan's hand was stabbed to death," Cartier exclaimed.[4]

That caught Evalyn's attention. Cartier continued.

> The beginning of this stone's history, as we believe it, was its appearance in Europe when Louis XIV was King of France. A man named Jean Tavernier had brought it from India at a time when maharajahs and rajahs kept their wealth in jewels. In that day the world's greatest jewel markets were in the Orient. This stone when it was sold to Louis XIV was called the 'Tavernier blue diamond.' Marie Antoinette wore it, so we understand; we know positively that there was just this one big blue diamond among the French crown jewels. Marie Antoinette was guillotined and the Revolutionists seized all the wealth.[5]

The stone disappeared after the Revolution. According to Cartier, it was stolen.

McLean writes:

> By this time Cartier had me on fire with eagerness to see what treasure was sealed up in his package. But, shrewd salesman that he was, he did not open it.
>
> [Cartier] said he understood that Tavernier had stolen the gem from a Hindu, perhaps a Hindu god. My recollection is that he said Tavernier afterward was torn up and eaten by wild dogs. I might have been excused that morning for believing that all the violences of the French Revolution were just the repercussions of that Hindu idol's wrath. M. Cartier was most entertaining.[6]

Cartier recounted how the diamond had later appeared in London in the possession of the Hope family. Lord Francis Hope's fortune as well as his marriage dissolved. The diamond was sold to Selim Habib and the Turkish Sultan.

Evalyn could wait no longer. "Let me see the thing," she implored.[7]

Cartier unwrapped the package with great flourish, revealing the Hope diamond.

> Cartier told me things he did not vouch for; that it was supposed to be ill-favored, and would bring bad luck to anyone who wore or even touched it. Selim Habib is supposed to have been drowned when his ship sank after he had disposed of the gem. We all know about the knife blade that sliced through Marie Antoinette's throat. Lord Hope had plenty of troubles that a superstitious soul might seem to trace back to a heathen idol's wrath . . . There were others too.

Wrote McLean, "You should have heard how solemnly we considered all those possibilities that day in the Hotel Bristol."

"Bad luck objects," I said to Cartier, "for me are lucky."

"Ah, yes," he said. "Madame told me that before, and I remembered. I think, myself, that superstitions of the kind we speak of are baseless. Yet, one must admit, they are amusing."[8]

Despite the alluring story, Evalyn and Ned did not purchase the diamond. Evalyn was disappointed with the setting.

Though temporarily dissuaded, Cartier must have sensed Evalyn's interest, for later that year he sailed for New York carrying the diamond. He again visited with the couple, this time in Washington. The Hope diamond had been placed in a new setting. Cartier also brought with him documentation of the diamond's history. After a series of meetings, Evalyn and Ned agreed to terms for the purchase of the Hope diamond on January 28, 1911. Cartier valued the purchase at $180,000. The agreement included the condition, "Should any fatality occur to the family of Edward B. McLean within six months, the said Hope diamond is agreed to be exchanged for jewelry of equal value."[9]

The story of the cursed diamond, as presumably told by Pierre Cartier and interpreted by Evalyn Walsh McLean, circulated quickly and widely. The *New York Times* reported the sale on its front page on January 29. J.R. M'LEAN'S SON BUYS HOPE DIAMOND read the title, with an ominous subtitle, CREDITED WITH BRINGING ILL-LUCK TO ITS POSSESSORS. Other papers picked up the story. A German newspaper added details connecting the diamond to its own Duke of Brunswick, and noted that the "belief in the 'bad luck-carrying' stone is old, and has lasted into our time."[10]

Cartier's tale had all the characteristics of a legend. It was regarded as a long-lived tale, widely known and passed down over time. It purported to be factual, but self-referentially admitted that some of those facts might seem fantastic and even fictional. Given the personalities, it was endowed with special significance. Indeed, it became instant folklore early in the era of modern mass communication. And, with the press's eager cooperation, it was amenable to continual elaboration. Whether to be taken seriously or as entertainment, Cartier's tale engaged the McLeans and a much broader public.

THE EAST

3

TAVERNIER'S QUEST

artier's tale turned instances of bad luck associated with the diamond into a curse—supernatural retribution exacted by a foreign god for a wrongful theft. For McLean and Cartier, this god was simply a Hindu idol. In subsequent accounts, specific, suspect gods and divine figures—Rama Sita, Shiva, Vishnu, Kali, and even the Buddha, have been named.

Pierre Cartier identified Jean-Baptiste Tavernier as the original transgressor, the person who had first gone to India and stolen the gem. Cartier, of course, knew better; he'd read the Tavernier journal. Yet he was prepared to subordinate knowledge to profit. Tavernier's story and the insight it provides into East-West relationships is far more interesting than the tale told at the Hotel Bristol.

Tavernier was indeed the gem merchant who sold to Louis XIV (1638–1715), King of France, a large blue diamond that was eventually cut to form the Hope diamond.

Tavernier was born in Paris in 1605. His father, Gabriel, was a mapmaker who had fled Antwerp in 1575 along with his brothers to avoid the religious persecution of Protestants. Tavernier was born at a propitious time in France. King Henry IV had in 1598 issued the Edict of Nantes, establishing the legal toleration of Calvinism in Roman Catholic France. Under the Edict, Protestants gained civil and educational rights, including the ability to hold government office. This legally, if not socially, ended three decades of intermittent conflicts between Catholics and Protestants, and provided opportunities for Tavernier and his family in government service and business.

As a youth, Tavernier apprenticed to a jeweler and later in life, at the age of 55, married the daughter of a jeweler. Diamonds intrigued him, as did maps in a Europe attentive to exploration and discovery. At the age of 15 Tavernier undertook the first of his voyages to the Near East. But his goal was India—at that time the *only* well-known source of diamonds in the world.

The source and means of obtaining Indian diamonds was the stuff of fable. Tavernier was well aware of Marco Polo's account widely available throughout Europe. The famed 13th-century Venetian traveler reported that diamonds are only found in the Indian kingdom of Motupalli, where there are mountains with

certain great and deep valleys, to the bottom of which there is no access. Wherefore, the men who go in search of diamonds take with them pieces of flesh, as lean as they can get, and these they cast into the bottom of a valley. Now there are numbers of white eagles that haunt those mountains and feed upon the serpents. When the eagles see the meat thrown down they pounce upon it and carry it up to some rocky hilltop where they begin to rend it. But there are men on the watch, and as soon as they see that the eagles have settled they raise a loud shouting to drive them away. And when the eagles are thus frightened away, the men recover the pieces of meat, and find them full of diamonds which have stuck to the meat down in the bottom. For the abundance of diamonds down there in the depths of the valleys is astonishing, but nobody can get down; and if one could, it would only be to be incontinently devoured by the serpents which are so rife there.

There is also another way of getting the diamonds. The people go to the nests of those white eagles, of which there are many, and in their droppings they find plenty of diamonds which the birds have swallowed in devouring the meat that was cast into the valleys. And, when the eagles themselves are taken, diamonds are found in their stomachs.[1]

Polo also noted that Indian diamonds "are found both abundantly and of large size. Those that are brought to our part of the world are only the refuse, as it were, of the finer and larger stones."

While Polo visited the port town of Motupalli in about 1290, there is no evidence that he actually journeyed to the diamond valley or witnessed the diamond gathering processes. Instead he based his account on the legends of Sinbad, the sailor hero of the Arabian Peninsula and Persian Gulf, compiled in about 800 A.D., and tales of Alexander the Great, stretching back more than a thousand years before. Even though the Macedonian world conqueror ended his 326 B.C. expedition at India's ancient historical border, the Indus River in present-day Pakistan, the account is similar to Polo's save that the birds are vultures, not eagles, and the meat is especially fatty. There is also a variation reminiscent of the tale of Medusa. The gaze of the snake is deadly. In order to retrieve the diamonds, Alexander and his men use mirrors, holding them in front of them as they advance. The snakes gaze at their own reflection and die.

The story of Sinbad's second voyage provides another twist. The sailor is deposited in the Indian diamond valley by the mythical roc, a huge eagle-like bird said to carry elephants in its talons. Sinbad endures his time with the serpents, grabs some diamonds, and finally makes his escape by wrapping himself in the sheep flesh cast into the valley by the diamond gatherers. The roc comes, plucks him out of the valley and carries him to freedom.

❊　❊　❊

Tavernier was intrigued, and India, thousands of miles away, beckoned. He made six voyages there between 1631 and 1668 in order to obtain and trade diamonds. The hardships he faced were daunting, though more practical than mythic. Transcontinental travel in the mid-1600s was arduous, dangerous, and rare. With no government sponsorship or portfolio, left to his own wits and resources, Tavernier had to arrange conveyance and accommodations, exchange cash, secure credit, and protect himself and his diamonds. Though he certainly enjoyed luxury, Tavernier had to endure difficult voyages aboard small ships and hard journeys in caravans. He survived a shipwreck and imprisonment. In India itself, he traveled perhaps 20,000 miles over the years, mainly in small oxen-drawn carriages, bullock carts, on horseback, and on foot. He developed the knowledge to negotiate taxes, customs, and tolls as he crossed the boundaries of regional kingdoms. In the heat, he journeyed by night. Rest was at traveler's lodges maintained by regional authorities. These were sometimes fairly elaborate, but usually offered only the most basic of amenities—food and shelter. Tavernier enjoyed the protection, society, and sometimes

Sinbad's Valley of the Diamonds.

the wrath of his customers and clients. Arriving in a place, he was just as likely to be threatened as fêted. But so successful was Tavernier in the diamond trade that he was honored and lauded by a variety of major and minor rulers in Europe, the Persian Gulf, and Arabian Peninsula, India, and Southeast Asia.

In Tavernier's time, the Kingdom of Golconda was at the center of the diamond trade in India. Golconda was located in India's southern midsection, the Deccan Plateau, straddling two major rivers, the Krishna and the Godavari, which flowed toward the Indian Ocean. Polo's Motupalli was a town on the coast.

Jean-Baptiste Tavernier in his Oriental robes.

Golconda was also the name of the capital, a rich, amazingly cosmopolitan city ruled by a Persian Shi'a Muslim King or Sultan that attracted European travelers, traders, physicians, and artisans. The ruins of Golconda, now a historic site, are adjacent to the modern city of Hyderabad. William Methold, an Englishman who served as the Dutch factor in the early 17th century, described Golconda as

> A citie that for sweetnesse of ayre, conveniencie of water, and fertility of soyle, is accounted the best situated in India, not to speake of the Kings Palace, which for bignesse and sumptuousnesse, in the judgement of such as have traveled India, exceedeth all belonging to the Mogull or any other Prince, . . . a King, who in elephants and jewels is accounted one of the richest Princes of India.[2]

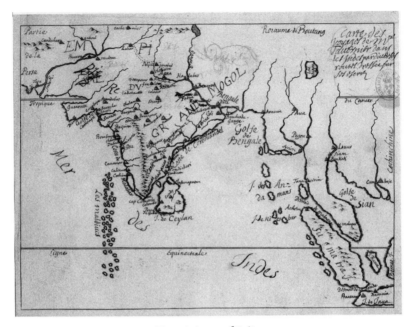

Tavernier's map of India.

Golconda was protected by a city wall and hosted a diamond market. Tradesmen and artisans in the city turned raw diamonds into jewelry.

The fortress-city itself contained no mines. Indeed, the mines referred to as those of Golconda were to be found in the kingdom's hinterland a hundred miles away. The famous, large, and colored diamonds presumed to come out of the Golconda mines are stunning, and may have included the Koh-i-Nur, Darya-i-Nur, Dresden Green, Empress Eugenie, Florentine, the pink Hortensia, Nassak, Nizam, Orlov, Pigot, Regent or Pitt, Sancy, and Star of the East.

Methold described a Golconda diamond mine, which he visited with two Dutch officials, but never identified by name. The mine was reportedly a new one, only recently developed after a goatherd had stumbled upon a diamond in the rough. It was located at the foot of a great mountain, in barren country adjacent to the Krishna River, 12 leagues from Masulipatam. The mine consisted of pits dug directly into the earth. This was unlike European mines familiar to

Methold which were built underground and supported by timbers. Miners, he said, could recognize from viewing and smelling the pit rock whether it contained diamonds. Hence some pits were dug only a few feet deep and abandoned, others to a depth of 10 or 11 fathoms.

A Brahmin named Rai Rao governed the mine on behalf of the Sultan. Methold reported 30,000 people working at the mine. They and their dependents, along with tradesmen, food suppliers, and others populated a town of about 100,000 two miles away. Sections of the mine were rented out to merchants involved in the diamond trade. They paid an annual fee for the right to mine, but as was long-held custom, had to submit to the King any diamond mined that was over 10 carats in weight. According to Methold, the Sultan's governor employed guards and spies to make sure no big diamonds escaped the King. Punishments for stealing diamonds due the King were severe. But Methold heard about a diamond of forty carats that escaped the watch of the King's agents.

Methold also heard that the mine was shut down temporarily in 1622 and all workers dispersed in an effort to restrict production. Apparently the King of Golconda, Sultan Abdullah Qutb Shah, feared that the ambassador to his court from the powerful and rival Sunni Mughal empire to the north would insist on receiving three pounds of diamonds demanded as tribute to the Emperor Jahangir. Rather than pay tribute, he shut down the mine. Two years later he leased the mine to four Hindu entrepreneurs for an annual fee of 260,000 *pagodas*—a very large sum of money.

When Tavernier first visited Golconda City in 1642, it was ruled by the same Sultan. The most active mine in the Golconda region was Kollur, also spelled "Coulour."[3] Tavernier traveled by different routes to this mine several times, once in 1645, again in 1653, and perhaps also in 1660. On his first trip, he traveled 71 *cos* from Golconda, a *cos* being an Indian measure equal to the distance a cow's bellow is heard. Tavernier converted this measure, and the *gos* (equal to four *cos*) into French leagues. He crossed the Krishna River to arrive at the village of Kollur and a short distance away, the mine.

While other Europeans, notably Methold, had visited mines in preceding decades, it was Tavernier who actually brought home diamonds, and so it was his later writings, immensely popular in France and quickly translated into English and German, that provided the first broadly read description of the diamond mining operation.

Tavernier found that once a place for digging was selected, the Hindu miners would perform a worship ceremony on the spot. After a feast, the men would excavate the earth with pickaxes to a depth of 10–14 feet. Women and children would carry the rubble to an adjacent mud-embanked pit or *bund* built for the purpose.

Rubble deposited in the *bund* would be soaked with water so that everything became a soupy mix. Watery clay would be drained out of the *bund* periodically, and the mix dried, leaving small stones and sand. Women and children would then winnow the dried remains so that the fine sand would be blown away. The coarser remains would be returned to the *bund* and raked. Then workers used large wooden pestles to pound the remains, winnowing them again, and scrutinizing what was left. In the end, hundreds of eyes would pore over the bits of stone and gravel for a diamond. Suspected diamonds would be soaked in mud-built washing tanks. The work was painstaking and

Tavernier at a Golconda diamond mine.

tedious. Given production figures from revenue records, and estimates from a 1677 report, it is likely that this labor would produce a few thousand stones a year, some 30 percent less than 1 carat, many with imperfections, and most of inferior color and quality.

Miners were paid little for their efforts; they lived in a "temporary" shantytown of some 60,000 men, women, and children. There were no amenities. When a diamond was found the workers would perform another ceremony to thank the god or goddess for the good fortune.

Raw diamonds were turned over to other workers who, as Tavernier observed at Kollur, used hand-powered, bow-operated diamond dust-covered disks lubricated with oil to cut the rough gems in order to remove obvious flaws. The merchants, who held the rights over the mines, would then price them and send them to the diamond market in Golconda City for more careful artisanal faceting and sale. Despite the provision that diamonds larger than 10 carats were supposed to be sent to the Sultan, sometimes large diamonds were surreptitiously held back. As Tavernier reported in his memoirs, he himself bought some of these.

In the course of his travels, Tavernier acquired a magnificent heart-shaped, rough-cut 112³⁄₁₆-carat diamond. He described it as *"net et d'un beau violet,"* or a clear and beautiful violet—the term "violet" at that time meaning intense blue. Upon Tavernier's return to France in 1668, Louis XIV, the French "Sun King," invited the traveling gem dealer to tell of his adventures and also to sell him diamonds. Louis XIV bought Tavernier's *"beau violet"* diamond, 46 other big and medium-sized diamonds, and 1,102 small diamonds for a total price of 893,731 French *livres*. The violet diamond was the most expensive in the lot, and was itself valued at 220,000 *livres*, worth approximately $1.8 million today.

In addition to the cash, Tavernier received the promise of a title. This came the following February, as he was made a baron. Using proceeds from the sale, he bought land in Aubonne, Switzerland, a

Protestant area, a purchase likely motivated by the renewal of religious conflict in France. He wanted a safe place to enjoy his honors and good fortune.

In Aubonne, Tavernier dictated his memoirs to several scribes and writers, among them playwright Samuel Chappuzeau, who complained about the baron's undisciplined ways and work habits and the insults he had to bear from Tavernier's wife. But Chappuzeau had little choice—King Louis XIV had prevailed upon him to help complete the work.

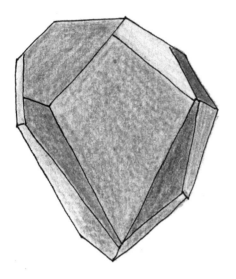

Tavernier's Violet.

When published beginning in 1675, Tavernier's memoirs were quite popular. *Nouvelle Relation du serrail du Grand Seigneur* was the first, followed by *Les Six Voyages de Jean-Baptiste Tavernier* appearing the next year. An illustration of the violet diamond and the other important diamonds sold to Louis XIV was included in Tavernier's account of his "Voyages des Indes."[4]

Tavernier did not indicate directly in his text how he'd acquired the violet diamond. Apparently, a page of notes was supposed to accompany the chart. Tavernier had dictated this page to one of his scribes, but it may have been one of the pages reportedly sent to the printer late. Unfortunately, despite a search of libraries and rare editions in Washington, New York, Paris, London, and Geneva, this missing page has yet to turn up.

There is, however, strong evidence for Kollur as the original site for the mining and acquisition of the diamond.

For one, the style of the diamond indicates a gem cleaved or cut in a rough manner to eliminate large flaws—consistent with the techniques used at the mines, not the marketplace in Golconda City. When the cut of the violet diamond is compared to some of the

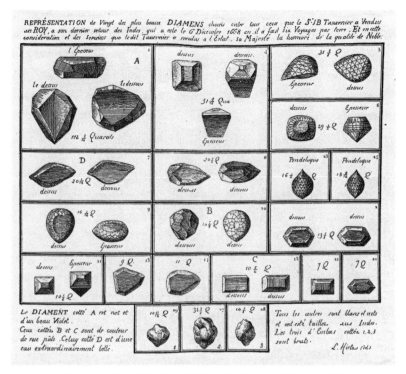

Diamonds sold to King Louis XIV—the Violet is "A," upper left.

other large diamonds sold to Louis XIV, the differences are quite obvious. Marketplace gems are more symmetrically cut with more surfaces, reflecting a more refined, calculated approach to faceting than was done at the mines.

Secondly, Tavernier himself reported that Kollur had a reputation for producing both large and colored diamonds. He had visited three other mines—one in Rammalkota in 1646, one at Soumelpur, and one along the Krishna River, but failed to note any similar reputation there.

Finally, Tavernier provides an indirect clue about the violet diamond's origin in his book. Several of the other diamonds he acquired are depicted in a plate, labeled table 4, that follows the chart documenting the sale to Louis XIV. In that table, Tavernier refers to "no. 6" as follows, *"C'est un autre diamant que j'achetais l'an 1653 à la mine de Coulour."* ["This is another diamond that I purchased in the year 1653 at the mine of Kollur."] But there is no *other* diamond in the illustration described as coming from Kollur. Thus, it may be that the antecedent reference of *"autre"* is none other than the beautiful Violet. If so, it was purchased at Kollur in 1653.

How did Tavernier acquire the diamond? It is unlikely it was from one of the mineworkers. Punishments stipulated for thievery were severe, and ranged from flogging to death. The level of cooperative work and oversight would make it difficult for anyone to chance upon a stone alone and conceal it from others. More so, the probability that the diamond was cut at the mines leads to the conclusion that the sale was sanctioned at some level.

The merchants at the mines were Hindu Gujarati middlemen. One of them could have made the sale, but they would have risked stiff penalties had it become known that they were double-crossing the Sultan and his agents. According to Indian historians, the governor of the mine had a reputation for corruption. But the most likely candidate is Mir Jumla, the prime minister and leading general under the Sultan of Golconda. Mir Jumla was responsible for the overarching supervision of the mine.

Originally from Persia, Mir Jumla was a professional soldier who took up service in the Golconda sultanate. He fought battles for Golconda against the armies of surrounding kingdoms. He had to fend off Mughal forces, and engage those of Europeans, particularly the Portuguese. Mir Jumla was regarded as corrupt by adversaries and even allies. He courted the Mughal rulers of the north while serving the Golconda Sultan. He solicited bribes from petty rulers in the Deccan. He also formed a relationship with Tavernier and other Frenchmen in India.[5]

As prime minister, Mir Jumla held a monopoly of first right of refusal for all gems sold by Golconda's merchants. He met with Tavernier often over several decades, trading scores, if not hundreds of diamonds and other gems.

In the early 1650s Mir Jumla was accumulating huge amounts of diamonds and cash. In one meeting with Tavernier in 1652, Mir Jumla was said to possess 10 bags of diamonds, each weighing four pounds. Unbeknownst to Tavernier, and presumably most others, Mir Jumla was preparing to defect to the Mughals. The Mughal emperor Shah Jahan, and his son, Aurangzeb, the Viceroy of the Deccan, desired to take over the Golconda kingdom and its rich mines. Aurangzeb was secretly working with Mir Jumla. When Mir Jumla left the service of the Golconda Sultan in 1655, he was said to have taken with him more than 408 pounds of diamonds. Among them was the 787½-carat diamond that came to be known as the Great Mughal.

If he bought or traded for it in 1653, Tavernier held on to the violet diamond for 15 years. He kept it in spite of having his ship sunk, being imprisoned, and finding himself in the middle of armed conflict. Tavernier had broad and continual dealings over the years and at times possessed very large diamonds. Yet for some reason, this fair violet one held his attention. It was the largest diamond he kept for any length of time, and given its color, the rarest.

The Kollur mine was closed hundreds of years ago—certainly by the mid-18th century—and the population dispersed. There are no listings in contemporary gazetteers. Kollur does not appear on any commonly obtainable map. Valentine Ball, a British geologist and English language-version editor of Tavernier's journal, had relocated the site in the late 1880s based upon Tavernier's reckoning of his travels. Ball gave coordinates for the Kollur area, and located it on a general map in the section of the Krishna River country.

I did locate a roughly drawn map in the Bibliothèque Nationale in Paris, presumably made in 1679 based upon Tavernier's account. Others are not of sufficient scale to locate the actual mines. Kollur was indicated on a very poor latter-day copy of a map that I happened upon at the old Golconda museum near the mausoleums of the Sultans. The legend indicated it dated from "about 1670." This allowed for computations using Tavernier's diary to locate the general area, but not enough to actually locate the site.[6]

In the course of my research in Hyderabad and old Golconda

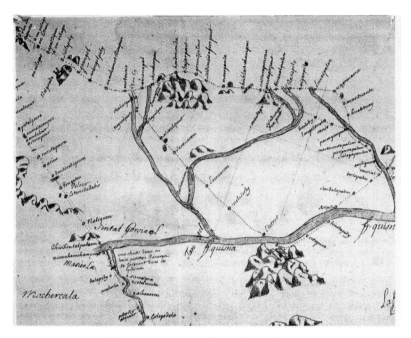

Tavernier's routes to the Indian diamond mines.

City, I met Govindas Mukendas and Satish Shah, a father and son team, descended from the Gujarati merchants who managed the financial affairs of the mines and the sales of diamonds. They still owned the land and the ruins of an ancestral house in Golconda dating from the times of Tavernier and the sultanate. The father was a mine owner and incredibly knowledgeable lay historian, the son an energetic and enterprising gemologist. They both claimed to have visited Kollur. They had pictures and a map marking the diamond pits to prove it.

Using the various maps, I headed for Kollur starting from the medieval 14-foot-high masonry road posts on the outskirts of Golconda—mentioned by Tavernier as the gateway to the kingdom's mines, and extant today. Tavernier had reported one trip from Golconda to Kollur via caravan as follows:

> From Golconda to the mine of Coulour or Gani, it is 13¾ gos, which amounts to 55 of our leagues. From Golkonda

to Almaspinde, 3½ gos; Almaspinde to Kaper, 2; Kaper
to Montecour, 2½; Montecour to Nazelpar, 2; Nazelpur to
Eligada, 1½; Eligada to Savaron, 1; Savaron to Mellaserou, 1;
Mellaserou to Ponocour, 1¾. Between Ponocour and
Coulour or Gani there is only the river to cross.[7]

On the road, by car, almost 350 years later, I traveled by miles, not
gos. The contemporary town names were familiar enough. Kaper
was now Malkapur, Montecour was now Mungod, Eligada had become Mirialguda, and Mellaserou was now Melacheru. It took
almost two full days to go about 120 miles along Indian highways,
potholed roads, mud roads, and no roads—it had taken Tavernier
seven days by oxen cart.

The area is known as the "sickle," where the Krishna River takes
a big bend. Viewed from above, it would be a large undulation of the
serpentine river. Past the villages of Chityala and then Gollapeta
was Kollur. Its houses are made out of slabs of stone, the refuse of

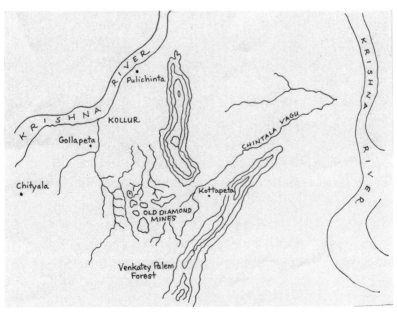

Map of the Kollur diamond fields.

Medusala Mountain.

mining operations. Translating between Urdu and Telegu, local villages led me through the brush to a site a few miles away, the hillside area of the mines.

There is not now much to see. According to Ball's English translation of Tavernier's journal, the gem merchant had crossed the river and looked at the large mountains in the form of a "cross." With some imagining, the vertices of the top of a cross could be discerned, but there was certainly no full cross. Perhaps trees and other vegetation had covered up rock faces that may have been bald in Tavernier's time. The mountain face looked long, narrow, and curved, and indeed, a year later when I consulted a French version of Tavernier's journal, the connection was more obvious. He reported the mountain as shaped not as a "cross," but as a "crescent" (*"hautes montagnes qui font une forme de croissant,"* he'd written). To me it actually looked more like a baked croissant, but alas, such had not yet been invented by Tavernier's time. The mountain is, on the map, named Medusala, a striking cognate with Medusa, the snake-haired Gorgon of Greek

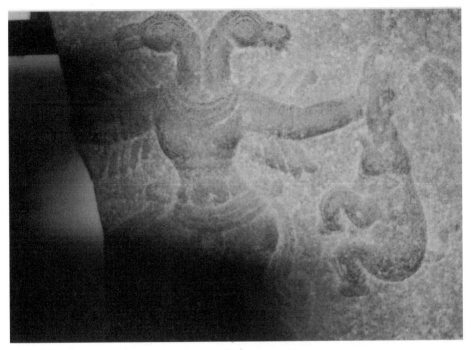

Sculpture of Gandabherunda.

mythology. Was this the diamond valley of Alexander, Sinbad, and Marco Polo?

I encountered a number of snakes; one even reared up and seemed to attack my vehicle, and another slinked across my path. The sky abounded with vultures, though no eagles—and no diamonds were visible in the rough.

Local villagers did not know if their ancestors had in fact worked the mines—they said authorities had moved people around quite a bit so there would be no generational memory of where the mines were located. It made sense. Why would state authorities and ulers—whether the Golconda sultans or the British Raj want thousands of people to know the exact location of the diamond mines, places where those people might return to dig and raid?

Villagers didn't know any of the old work songs, if there were any, nor did they have a body of mining lore. This is not what a folklorist wants to hear. They did, however, note a widespread belief that elephants were once located on the top of the mountain ridge. They had no tales of catapulting sheep, goat, or elephant carcasses and rocs—though nearby I did find several representations in coin, sculpture, and textile of Gandabherunda—a mythical two-headed bird-god. In one, this fabulous creature holds elephants in its talons; in another it wears a blue gemstone on its breast.[8]

Guided by a couple of villagers, I make my way along the hillside. The soil is sandy, indicating alluvial deposits of the river. Vegetation is scrawny and decidedly unfriendly—thorns on scrub and bramble tear my clothing and cut my hands. It feels like a wasteland, and in the summer the temperature and humidity must be intolerable. There is no environmental hint of riches buried below.

Gandabherunda wearing a blue gem.

We follow the Mukendas map and find pits of stone refuse; piles of stone striated with the marks of pickaxes and other implements, some earthen formations indicative of the mud *bunds* and earthen washing structures used in the old technology. These are the remains of the famed Kollur diamond mine. Now unworked since the 1700s, the Indian government has closed off the area surrounding the mines, calling it a national park—the Venkataya Palen Forest Reserve. The government allows no mining—though I found evidence of some limited, likely unsanctioned, recent activity. The allure of diamonds is still there, and the local experts, Mukendas and Shah, are convinced that with the application of modern technology, large diamonds like the Koh-i-Nur or another Tavernier Violet may be found.

4

GOLCONDA'S WEALTH

Tavernier's violet diamond came to the West as a result of the massive growth of trade links between India and Europe. Indian diamonds had been known in Europe—Roman trading outposts in the Deccan had sent them westward in the first century A.D. Others trickled in over the centuries. In Tavernier's time, during the age of European exploration, a new form of mercantile globalism was taking hold. It predated Western empire building in Asia, and was intimately connected to colonization in the Americas.

Tavernier was one of a small number of Europeans trafficking in the transcontinental trade of luxury goods during the mid-17th century. He traded gold coins, ornaments, watches, and luxury goods from Europe, pearls from the Persian Gulf, and diamonds from India, along with various gemstones from Sri Lanka and Southeast Asia. He visited markets, ports, and customs houses through which passed the international trade of his day—Paris, Constantinople, Aleppo, Alexandria, Basra, Hormuz, Mashad, Shiraz, Isfahan, Surat, Goa, Agra, Golconda, Batavia (now Jakarta). He conducted business with dozens of rulers, and witnessed firsthand the great construction of Versailles in France, Isfahan in Persia, and the Taj Mahal in Agra. More than just an aficionado or treasure hunter, Tavernier helped develop and standardize global trade in diamonds. In doing so, he became a carrier and translator of Indian and European cultures, enabling their interaction and interpenetration.

✳ ✳ ✳

Much of the luxury trade in the 14th and 15th centuries went through Calicut, a port of the Malabar region on India's west coast. Fronting the Arabian Sea, Calicut was larger than Lisbon at the time. Calicut exported the riches of India—spices, precious stones including diamonds, incense, sandalwood, silk, and cotton. Imports came from much of the known world—gold, silver, copper, iron-ware, satin, silk, carpets, opium and porcelain from China, horses from Persia, pearls, vermilion, copper from the Middle East, damask, glass beads and glassware from Venice. Venetians, Chinese, Arabs, and Indians participated in this early developing global economy.

The Calicut trade reached Europe by shipping either through the Persian Gulf or the Red Sea, and then offloading goods and transporting them overland through Arab and Turkish lands until they reached the Mediterranean, where they would be re-loaded on ships setting sail for home ports. The route was expen-sive, difficult, and risky, and Europeans looked for a way to minimize these problems. Direct sea routes between Europe and India were the solution; after all, that was the original purpose of Columbus's exploration. After a century of exploratory voyages down the west coast of Africa, Portugal's Vasco da Gama sailed around the Cape of Good Hope and landed at Calicut in 1498.

Da Gama faced two problems when he arrived. First, the poor-quality goods he carried did not interest the Indians and other Asian traders—nothing matched the richness of India's natural and man-ufactured treasures. Second, Muslims were the dominant power both on shore and at sea. These obstacles were overcome in surpris-ingly short order. Europeans developed superior battleships to coun-ter Asian military advantages. On the commercial front they found a new source of wealth—American silver, which paid for trade goods with India beginning in the 16th century.

Da Gama's voyages led to the establishment of a Portuguese outpost in India: Goa. They were followed a century later by the English, who in 1600 founded the East India Company and established a presence in

Fort St. George (that grew into Madras, now Chennai), Bombay (now Mumbai), and Fort William (later Calcutta). The Dutch established their outposts in Surat, Cochin, Masulipatam, and in Ceylon.

These outpost ports, called "concessions," were established with the approval of Indian rulers and local officials for trade, not colonial conquest. Trade with India was first largely driven by the desire for spices. Textiles, of much better quality than available in Europe, and with acquired English names like "muslin," "calico" (from Calicut), "chintz" (from a local dyed or patterned material called *chint*) proved another popular item. Europeans learned that they could not only sell these back home, but could also use them to trade for spices in the East Indies. European mercantile agents, like Methold, were known as "factors." They organized groups of Indian weavers from villages, usually located within miles of their outposts, into production units for making exportable textiles. These textile production units came to be known as "factories"—the modern origin of the term, exported back to Europe.

Knowledge of the great diamond wealth of southern India arose through the reports of European travelers at the beginning of the 16th century. They provided firsthand observations about the abundant presence of diamonds, their display in India's royal palaces, in Hindu temples, and in Muslim treasuries. These accounts captivated European merchants and monarchs who heretofore thought of diamonds as exceedingly rare. The sheer amount of Indian diamonds available for export drove new demands among European royalty. Fortunately for Europe's rulers, silver bullion from America was entering the economy and could now be used to pay for diamonds from India. Ironically, as European explorers searched America for El Dorado, the legendary city of gold, they actually discovered a city of diamonds in India—Golconda.[1]

Golconda, originally meaning "fortress on a hill" in Telegu, the language of the regional Hindu population, was one of a number of Muslim kingdoms taking shape in the 16th century. In 1565 its leader, Sultan Ibrahim Qutb Shah, defeated the Hindu Vijayana-gar kingdom. That kingdom—reported by European travelers of the time to be a paradise on earth and to have a capital city bigger than Rome—earned its prosperity through its diamond mines and famed diamond market.[2] The mines now fell under the control of Golconda.

Shah established a new diamond market in his capital. Merchants from Arabia, Persia, and Turkistan visited and took up residence in rest houses in the newly built Karvan-e-sahu (cognate of the term "caravan") neighborhood. Bania immigrants from the Gujerat region provided the business acumen to run the diamond trade. Artisans, cutters, and jewelers populated the city and its wealth grew. Golcondans named their children after gems, *Moti* for pearl, *Hira* for diamond, and poeticized their good fortune:

> *Diamonds, rubies, jaspers, silver and gold*
> *Sapphires, agates, blackstone, and coal*
> *Topaz, marble, and the beautiful hyacinth*
> *Glass, jade, iron, salt, zinc, and arsenic*
> *Mines of such elements lie buried in the land of the Deccan*
> *Wealth of great proportions lie underneath our feet.*[3]

Tavernier described how merchants placed their gems on flat black stone "tables" sunk into the ground. I came across several of these as I explored the modern ruins of the city. Buyers and sellers sitting cross-legged face-to-face would then each put their right forearms together in their sleeves or under a cloth. They would exchange squeezes of the whole forearm and the fingers to indicate amounts to be paid in a way no one else could observe. A squeeze of the arm might be equivalent to 1,000 rupees, two squeezes, 2,000 rupees, and so on. Grasping four fingers could indicate 400 rupees, three fingers 300 rupees. A representative of the Sultan would weigh and grade the diamonds to assure quality control.

Tavernier, anxious to correctly value his diamonds, devised a

Ruins of Golconda.

formula still used today, albeit in modified form, where the price of a diamond increases geometrically in proportion to its size. For size, Tavernier used the Indian measures of *"rati"* (probably related to the word "carat"—customarily attributed to the weight of a carob seed) and *"mangelin."* As Tavernier's journal indicates, he had to translate and compute these measures into a variety of other Indian, European, and Asian ones.

Tavernier and other merchants continually had to calculate exchange rates for precious metals and coinage. They relied on a strong understanding of the "market" and the global gem trade. Tavernier, for example, points out the impact of South American emeralds on Asian markets as they came to be imported via the Manila trade!

The cosmopolitan Golconda court patronized Muslim, classical Hindu, and local Telegu culture. Mosque building, civic architecture, urban improvements, and the decorative arts flourished. Ibrahim's son and successor, Mohammad Quli Qutb Shah, composed religious poetry using gems as metaphors for spirituality, wore diamond ornaments incorporating Hindu themes as well as a turban, feather aigrette, and diamond *sarpanch,* or head stone. Diamond jewelry took on a particular "Golconda" style. The Golconda settings called for shallow cuts, preserving the bulk of the diamond.

Europeans were interested in acquiring raw diamonds. By the late 16th century, diamonds began to compete with pearls in Europe as the gem of choice among royalty. The Portuguese *Carreira da India* vessels shipped raw diamonds in *bizalhos,* containers for about 300 stones ranging from ¼ carat to 10 carats or more. In the years 1599 to 1601, some 60–80 *bizalhos* were shipped—amounting to about 18,000 diamonds per year!

Raw diamonds went from Goa to Lisbon. Portuguese entrepreneurs built up a network of merchants in the early 1600s that connected diamonds coming into Lisbon to jewelers in Antwerp, Amsterdam, London, Hamburg, Frankfurt, Riga, Rouen, Paris, and Naples for cutting and setting. This network distributed diamonds to the royal houses of Europe. By the 17th century, diamonds predominate over pearls in European adornment as reflected in royal portraiture, and are fitted into the crowns, ornaments, and jewelry of kings, queens, and other nobility across the Continent.

The Portuguese in India displayed diamonds and adapted some Golcondan ideas of ornamentation, sending back to Europe a distinctively Goan style of decorative art. In the Goan museum is a painting

Nizam of Hyderabad wearing Golcondan diamonds.

Turbaned Portuguese governor.

of the 16th century governor of Goa, Jorge Cabral. Depicted in European clothing of the time (1549–51), he wears a turban with a feather aigrette, and a blue gem on his forehead, quite like his contemporaries, the sultans of Golconda. It is an early example of Europeans imitating and adapting Indian forms of ornamentation.

Not only did diamonds move between India and Europe, but so too did the ideas about them.

5

COSMIC GEM

Indians discovered diamonds thousands of years ago and thus had a long time to think about their significance. Drawn into the Indian diamond market, Tavernier confronted and adapted terminologies and ideas, some of which he brought back to Europe.

Golconda's merchants and gemologists classified diamonds in a variety of ways, some of which might seem strange to contemporary Westerners. Indians, well aware of the fact that raw diamonds come in a variety of shapes, described them as having gender. Male diamonds have many angles, straight planes, and are bright. Female diamonds are more cylindrical, less angular, and have more lines and spots. Neuter diamonds are triangular, thin and elongated. Indian merchants assessed the clarity of diamonds in determining their price. Clarity was described in terms of the diamond being like "clear milk," "clear honey," or "cream," and probably inspired Tavernier's assessments of diamonds being of the "first water," the "second water," and so on—in order of increasing murkiness and decreasing price—a system still known among Western jewelers.

No one in Tavernier's time knew where diamonds really came from, what they were made of, or how they'd formed. It wasn't until the late 19th century that scientists understood that Tavernier's Kollur diamonds were created through normal geological processes.

All diamonds are made of the element carbon—the same substance that forms coal, soot, and graphite. Most scientists now believe that Indian diamonds formed from primal, inorganic carbon some 90–160 miles below the surface.[1]

There, deep under some of the oldest sections of the planet's crust, bits of carbon were subject to tremendous pressure and high temperature. Some of this carbon crystallized with adjacent atoms, sharing electrons and forming covalent bonds in interconnected tetrahedral structures—the strongest type of molecular attachment. These crystals, mainly split-pea and tiny pebble-sized diamonds, took prismlike, octahedral, cubical, and even spherical shapes. Some crystals had a milky translucence, with numerous cracks, fissures, and imperfections. Often, bits of detritus from surrounding rock got trapped within the crystalline structure, forming what is called an inclusion. Sometimes traces of other elements mixed with the carbon to give the stones green, brown, yellow, even black color, or much more rarely, pink, red, and blue colors. Nitrogen makes some diamonds yellow, boron—about one atom per million of carbon—makes the Hope blue.

Hundreds of millions of years ago, under the surface, molten lava filled subterranean caves, liquefying the rock and rubble. When the temperature stayed below 2,700°F., the diamonds in these subterranean caves did not melt—they floated in a molten magma sea. When the pressure of the hot, molten mix built up, there was a volcanic eruption. Tons of magma containing the few bits of diamond rose to the surface at 6 to 18 miles per hour, traveling through pipelike shafts or vents in the earth's rock mantle. Reaching the surface, the magma exploded and then cooled into giant boulders and smaller stones, encasing the rare diamonds. Those stones, in effect, represent a biopsy of the world below.

About 40 to 50 million years ago a huge island and its underlying tectonic plate collided into Asia, becoming the Indian subcontinent. The crash speed was only about 2 inches per year. But the power of the grinding landmasses, given their terrestrial and subterranean size, was tremendous. The collision uprooted a section of the planet. The surface was driven down, bedrock up, shooting miles into the sky and forming the tallest mountains in the world—the Himalayas.

The volcanic vents or "pipes" were located in the island's midsection, the Deccan Plateau. The massive mountains created a new weather system—the monsoons. Rains washed the plateau, forming and re-forming streams and rivers, two of the larger being the Krishna and Godavari. Flowing through India's midsection, these rivers carried the rock-encased diamonds eastward—sometimes as the alluvial flow of river sludge and dirt and pebbles, sometimes in building-sized boulders borne by torrential floods. The rubble journeyed downstream until the force of the water subsided, or until it came to rest against outcroppings of hills and mountains.

The flow and flooding of the Krishna River was cyclical. As the river receded into its valley, or pursued a new course, it left volcanic refuse on the earth's surface. Continuing eruptions and alluvial deposits followed over the years, leaving layers and layers of new earth. In a region to be known as Golconda, a mountain—Medusala—stood as a detour for the river. Floodwaters would lap at its hillside, or flow around it. It was along this hillside that alluvial deposits of encased diamond stone were built up and weathered over millions of years, eventually becoming the Kollur minefields.

Although a number of volcanic pipes have been located in the Deccan region, no one has identified the specific pipes that carried the blue diamond to the surface. But people did discover the alluvial deposits where, in rare cases, erosion wore away encasing stone, revealing its treasures. Tavernier was well aware of this, as was Marco Polo, who in addition to the diamond valley account wrote:

> There are certain lofty mountains in those parts; and when the winter rains fall, which are very heavy, the waters come roaring down the mountains in great torrents. When the rains are over, and the waters from the mountains have ceased to flow, they search the beds of the torrents and find plenty of diamonds.[2]

Mostly, the crystals remained hidden and sealed within. Then finally, as at Kollur, the diamonds—Tavernier's intense blue among them—completed their natural journey, to begin a new one in the realm of men.

The Kollur diamonds emerged within a society where scholars and sages had their own understandings of diamonds.

One of the most anciently rooted ideas about diamonds, or *"vajra,"* as they have been called for millennia, is traced back to the *Rg Veda,* the oldest of written Indian Sanskrit texts dating to 1500–1200 B.C. In this compilation of incantations and verbal formulae is the declaration: *Indra is thunder. What is thunder? The vajra* (diamond lightning).

Indra is a god, the ancient Indian equivalent of the Greek Zeus and the Roman Jupiter. He rides an elephant and wields the diamond thunderbolt to destroy enemies and demons, to ward off evil, and to defeat the malevolent forces of nature.

Ancient Indians knew lightning was powerful, could be projected over great distances, and was incredibly focused. To fling his lightning, Indra uses a scepterlike *vajra,* said to contain a large diamond at its focal point encapsulating enormous energy. His lightning opens the belly of the cloud serpent, releasing rain needed to fertilize the earth. Born of the thunderbolt is Yama, who, coming from the sky to the earth, is the first man. He is also the first to die, thenceforth becoming lord of the underworld.

Vajra *with diamond focal point.*

Only the most powerful of the gods was able to open the diamond and then direct its force to the clouds or to earth to generate life, or against enemies to squelch it. Indeed, the English term "vigor," implying as it does strength and even sexual prowess, is etymologically related to the Sanskrit word *"vajra."* Diamonds, in the Vedas, are thus conceived of as frozen *lightning,* or *solid energy,* containing within them the power of life and death if released by some supernatural being.

Though ancient and Indian, this idea resonates in Western culture. George Kunz, an eminent American gemologist, noted how "a diamond is congealed sunshine."[3] A contemporary physicist might see the formation of diamonds with the application of heat and pressure over time as representing the transformation of tremendous kinetic energy into material form. And in several popular films including *Diamonds Are Forever, Batman and Robin,* and *Congo,* diamonds are used as the source to project superconcentrated death rays.

Indians figured that diamonds—hard, relatively indestructible, and flush with concentrated energy—needed to be handled carefully and used wisely. Among Buddhists, diamonds become objects of meditation, a means of focusing energy inward by destroying worldly ignorance. "Diamond masters" crafted a whole religious practice—Vajrayana, the Way of the Diamond Thunderbolt—around the symbolic elaboration of the diamond's power represented by "third eye" gemstones on Buddha statues, thunderbolt scepters, and mantras or sacred verbal formulae.

Sometimes Buddhist iconography illustrates the fierce use of the *vajra.* Yamari (the Buddhist version of Yama) rides a buffalo, carrying a noose and a mace with a skull topped by a *vajra.* He may be depicted wearing garlands of skulls and dancing upon bloody mutilated victims who symbolize evil, temptation, and other vices. Though such representations in

Buddhist meditation on the vajra.

Yamari uses the vajra *to destroy evil.*

Tibetan *thangka* paintings and in brass sculpture might appear gruesome at first glance, one must realize that the destructive power of the
vajra is specifically channeled *against* evil. The Dalai Lama and many
Tibetan Buddhist monks continue to use the *vajra*—called by its
Tibetan term *"dorje"* for meditative purposes.

The power of diamonds comes from their perceived source. In
some versions of the Indra myth, bits of divinely endowed bone
come to earth with the thunderbolt. The bone bits are alive—they
are seeds for the "growing" of diamonds on the earth. In other stories, the celestial bones are those of an esteemed sage or *rīshi*. Indians
recognized the symbolic equivalence of bone as the hardest element
of the human body and diamond the hardest element of the celestial body—it is a way of connecting humans and the cosmos. This
is evident in tales about Indian gemstones, which are taken to be
bits of the sun, moon, planets, and stars fallen to earth. Again, this
seemingly startling Indian idea resonates with metaphoric Western
ones. For example, in the early 20th century, the former French ambassador to the United States, Jules Jusserand, called the Hope

diamond an "ominous unearthly stone"; three decades later the *Washington Post* referred to the Hope as a "tiny fragment of midnight sky, fallen to earth and still aglow with star gleam."[4]

In falling from the sky, gems generally end up buried underground. In order to "grow" they are guarded and even possessed by snakes—hence the popular depiction in the Golconda area of cobras with diamonds in their hoods.[5] Finding diamonds is a matter of locating the places where such celestial stones or divine bones fell to the planet. Coming upon a cache of snakes—as the old diamond valley legend suggested—may be a clue.[6] Some Indian gemologists argue that the snakes are metaphorical, and represent the serpentine rivers of the Deccan Plateau. Wise ancients built temples along those rivers in the places where diamonds were to be found, so that according to this gemological geography, diamonds might be found at the hood of the snaking river, in its mouth, along its trunk, and at its tail.[7]

The relationship between gemstones and their users is elaborated as the folk gemology of India, termed *"nau ratna,"* or "nine gems"—a conceptual framework that may have originated in the ancient Middle East and flourished in Golconda, among both the Hindu and Muslim population. In *nau ratna* theory, gems originate from and embody the power of living celestial bodies. Rubies come from the Sun and are associated with the center of the cosmos and the god Surya; sapphires come from Saturn, associated with the god Varuna and the west. Diamonds come from the planet Venus and are associated with Indra and the east, and so on. Taken as a whole, the gems constitute the interrelated powers of the cosmos. All humans are born under a particular constellation of celestial bodies, which thus help define their characteristics and determine their fate. The job of Brahmin priests and astrologers is to determine which planetary influences are consonant with a person's birth and other characteristics, and which are antagonistic. One wears appropriate stones to absorb the rays—and thus mitigate deleterious rays from bad "stars"—and promote the rays and effects of good ones. As one Indian jeweler who had lived in Michigan for many years before returning to Hyderabad told me, "You know it's kind of like a force field."[8]

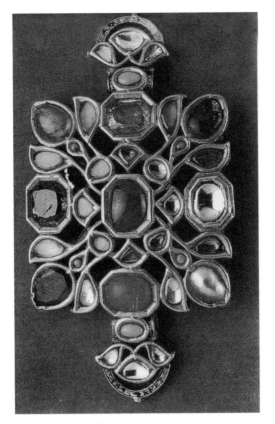

Nau ratna *jewel.*

As Tavernier noted, gods and goddesses at Hindu temples in the Deccan Plateau are bedecked with jewels. These jewels, donated by royalty, but also by wealthy people, provide a means of gods to promulgate "good rays" and take "bad rays" out of universal circulation. Gods—known as *deva* or "shining ones," project "good rays" through a process of gazing known as *darshan.* They also have a greater ability than humans to tolerate "bad rays"—essentially absorbing and transforming them into positive ones. The jewels on godly crowns and other ornamentation must be of the correct size and in the correct position to be effective. If jewels are wrongly made, mispositioned, or stolen, the god, temple, and its constituents may not have adequate protection.

The same logic applies to humans. Kings and queens need gems to help them rule effectively and not be overcome by malevolent forces and energies, whether from cosmic sources or carried by the black tongues and evil eyes of rivals and subjects. Rulers, because their responsibilities are onerous, need to wear many large gems. Other wealthy and powerful people also may be able to obtain gems to protect themselves, though most do with smaller stones. The poor have to settle for colored glass imitations commonly available in the bazaar. The destitute get no protection at all.

During Tavernier's time, jewelry and ornamentation styles in Golconda attempted to properly exploit the inherent power of gemstones—particularly diamonds. The bigger the gem the more protection afforded. Flaws, cracks, and spots in gems allow deleterious rays to seep through. Cutting, grinding, and cleaving them off eliminates such flaws. But too much cutting could damage and even drastically reduce a diamond's natural protective properties. For that reason, as Tavernier observed, Indians valued size over shine or sparkle even though they had a diamond-cutting technology on par with or better than Europe.

Raw diamonds don't sparkle—most don't even shine unless their crystalline shape is just right; they must be cleaved or faceted and polished to do so. The Golconda *kundan* (flat) and *pachi* (raised) styles called for shallow cuts, preserving the bulk of the diamond by only eliminating flaws, not for giving the gem a regular geometric shape. The simple cabochon was preferred, and the result was a gem that an American, these days, would probably take as roughly cut glass. Tavernier observed that Indians cleaved diamonds, but only to eliminate flaws. Indian jewelers to this day speak of "keeping the life in the stone."

Some of those same Indian beliefs characterized ancient European thinking about diamonds—not surprising, given the trading links between Rome and the Deccan region that reached their height in the 2nd century A.D. A Roman verse declares:

The evil eye shall have no power to harm
Him that shall wear the diamond as charm.
No monarch shall attempt to thwart his will,
And even the gods his wishes shall fulfill.[9]

In Rome, diamonds were generally mounted as natural crystals, valued primarily for their hardness and strength, not their appearance. The term "diamond" itself derived from the Greek *"adamas,"* meaning unyielding or unconquerable.[10]

In his *Natural History,* the Roman Pliny opines that the diamond has the greatest value among the objects of human property, and is known only to kings and even to very few of these—presumably as a sign of their indestructibility.

Romans were reluctant and possibly unable to cut and facet diamonds with any degree of precision, other than removing flaws. This fueled the centuries-held European belief in *acheiropoietos,* that something of nature, not made by human hands, retained a certain natural power. Any fashioning of rough diamonds through cleaving or polishing was a sure way of reducing their power. Hence, diamonds were valued for their magico-religious powers.

This idea started to change by the 15th century or so, as the Renaissance in Europe brought forth new ways of conceiving light, and new applied sciences like optics. Eyeglasses, magnifying glasses, and telescopes—as well as the worlds they opened up—were the result. Among the consequences was the development of new gem-cutting techniques, fueled by increased diamond supply from India. Those new European styles started filtering back to India through the presence of Italian, Venetian, and French masters in sculpture, furniture, jewelry design, and other decorative arts hired to craft forts, courts, mausoleums, and monuments for the Mughals and other regional rulers. European approaches to diamond cutting conflicted with the Golconda style—as Tavernier reported in his meeting with the Mughal Emperor Aurangzeb. Tavernier writes that he held in his hand the diamond termed "the Great Mughal." It had been a massive raw diamond of 787½ carats. A Venetian gem cutter, Hortensio Borgio, ground and cut it down to a stylish 280 carats. This infuriated the Emperor, who, sparing the Venetian's life, nonetheless fined him 10,000 rupees for so reducing his diamond.

❉ ❉ ❉

I ndians placed colored diamonds within their cosmo-gemology. The term *varna* literally means "color," but also refers to social caste. Accordingly, Indian classical texts as well as gem merchants in Tavernier's time referred to clear (white) diamonds as *brahmins,* or those of the priestly caste, as they supposedly promoted knowledge and sanctity. Red diamonds were *kshātriya,* or of the warrior caste and associated with glory; yellow diamonds with the *vaisya,* or business caste and wealth. Blue or blue black (*nīlā*) or gray "frog colored" diamonds were termed *śudra*—the servile laboring castes. Higher caste diamonds were more expensive than lower caste ones.[11] The different colored or caste diamonds were also associated with gods: white with Varuna, yellow with Shakra, and blue with the Hindu god of death, Yama.

Blue diamonds were not well regarded. "Blue diamonds are to be avoided" is the translation from a Sanskrit text on the medicinal qualities of gems.[12] Another warned readers about certain diamonds:

> Those with spots in the shape of crow's feet; those marked by lines; those of cylindrical shape; those with spots; those with cracks or rent asunder; those of flat shape; those of coarse texture; and those of blue color.[13]

According to the text, "a diamond having good qualities yields weal and wealth; otherwise it becomes a source of sorrow."

In making his sales and trades, Tavernier was clearly interested in large male diamonds of good waters. He may have relatively easily and cheaply acquired the large violet diamond with Mir Jumla's acquiescence because the latter, even though he was a Muslim, may have believed it would be hard to sell or gift to a compatriot a diamond associated with the god of death and ill-regarded. Tavernier, for his part, never recorded any such misgivings.

THE WEST

6

THE FRENCH BLUE

Tavernier *returned to France a hero.* The French poet Boileau
wrote of him:

From Paris to Delhi, from sunset to sunrise
This famous traveler ran more than once.
From India and Persia he kept the company of kings.
And on the shores of the Ganges we follow him.
In all places his honesty was his biggest asset.
In public and in front of our eyes he presents
The rarest treasure that the sun brings to life,
He has not brought back anything so rare as himself.[1]

Tavernier met with Louis XIV and his influential Controller General of Finance, Minister Colbert, on December 6, 1668, at Versailles and sold his violet diamond along with more than one thousand others he'd brought from India. The transaction is reported in the royal accounts and in the works of Colbert. The diamond was described as *"un grand diamant bleu forme de cœur, court, taillé à la mode des Indes, perquant 112 ks ³⁄₁₆,"* a large blue diamond in the shape of a heart, thick, cut in the Indian style, weighing 112¾ carats. Given the size and the rare color, the sale was quite noteworthy, and reported abroad in the English publication *Philosophical Transactions.*[2]

Tavernier's success spurred French commercial activity. Compared to the Portuguese, and even the English and Dutch, the French were very slow to become involved in the India trade. In the late 16th century, at the urging of a returning traveler, the French King Henry IV had authorized a 30-boat expedition to India, but it failed to materialize. Others, including Tavernier, took off on their own, and in 1664 a tract was published in Paris urging the formation of a French trading company for the East Indies on par with the efforts of other European powers. The force behind the report was Minister Colbert. His suggestion was adopted. The crown invested in *La Compagnie des Indes Orientales,* and Louis XIV presided over the first meeting of the shareholders in 1665. Colbert was elected director, and plans were made for a trade mission. Excitement about Tavernier's diamonds, and the subsequent publication of his well-read, bestselling travelogues created additional impetus and support for the French company—though Tavernier was not directly involved and seems to have calmed his wanderlust, enjoying his baronial estate in Aubonne near Lake Geneva.

In 1684, the 79-year-old Tavernier was approached by Frederick William, the Elector of Brandenburg in German lands, about establishing an embassy and a commercial trading company in India. Tavernier was a strong choice to negotiate with the Mughal Emperor for a German trading concession. He was nominated as Ambassador and appointed to the honorary offices of Chamberlain to the Elector and Counselor of Marine. Three vessels were to accompany Tavernier on his new voyage to India.

Jean-Baptiste Tavernier.

Tavernier first had to put his house in order. In 1685 he sold his Aubonne estate for 138,000 *livres,* presumably to use as his own investment in the trading venture. He apparently had some trouble in completing all his business, and during the interim, the Brandenburg scheme collapsed. But things had changed in France. Louis XIV had revoked the Edict of Nantes. France was now officially Catholic, and Protestants like Tavernier would be disadvantaged in terms of official appointments and opportunities. With his baronial estate sold, and prospects in France limited, Tavernier decided to set out on a seventh journey to India to recoup losses and glory. He traveled to Copenhagen in 1688 where Jacques d'Agar painted his portrait. He arrived in Russia in February 1689, carrying a passport granted by the King of Sweden. He presumably died shortly thereafter. In the late 19th century, his grave was rediscovered in an old Protestant cemetery near Moscow, with the name "Tavernier" preserved in full, but the date somewhat obliterated as "16 " with the last two digits worn away.[3] Contrary to Cartier's assertion that he'd been torn up and eaten by wild dogs, no evidence of how Tavernier died has been found. I did, however, find his homestead in Aubonne, on a street named in his honor.

There is no indication that Tavernier stole the violet diamond or any other diamond from the eye of a Hindu "idol" as Cartier suggested to the McLeans. Tavernier was respected by Indian and Persian rulers, fellow merchants, and many European colonial authorities as a knowledgeable and honest gem dealer. Even though some of Tavernier's fellow French travelers and explorers reported on his flaws, none ever suggested he'd committed any diamond theft. Stealing a diamond from a Hindu temple seems far-fetched, much too risky, and antithetical to Tavernier's cordial modus operandi.

Tavernier did report that he visited many Hindu temples in Mathura, Tirupati, Jagannath, Benares and other well-known sites. He witnessed many displays of gems in temples, or "pagodas," as he called them. He described seeing diamonds used for the eyes of "idols" such as "Ram Kam" in a temple near Benares.

It is easy enough to imagine how Cartier or others could have gotten the idea about cursed gemstones. In one passage Tavernier describes the temple of Kesora at Jagannath and relates a tale of a supernatural occurrence connected to an attempted diamond theft:

> The great idol has two diamonds for his eyes and a pendant from his neck which reaches to the waist, and the smallest of these diamonds weighs about 40 carats . . . It should be remarked that jewelers who come like others, are not now permitted to enter the pagoda, since one of them, intending to steal it, who allowed himself to be shut up during the night, extracted a diamond from one of the eyes of the idol. As he was about to leave in the morning, when the pagoda was opened, this thief, they say, died at the door, and the idol performed this miracle as a punishment for sacrilege.[4]

If Tavernier was negatively affected by the violet Indian diamond, he showed no evidence of it. Indeed to the contrary, Tavernier wrote:

> I have taken such good care of myself that I have never been inconvenienced by the least headache, or by a bloody flux, which is the ailment that carries away many people. That which in my opinion has contributed most to my health is, that I do not think I have ever grieved on account of any misfortune which has happened to me.[5]

If Tavernier was cursed, he didn't know it.

According to the records of the French court, Tavernier's diamond was placed in the King's cabinet of curiosities between 1669 and 1673. On the orders of the King, the diamond was recut and reshaped by court jeweler Sieur Pitau in 1673. In the 1691 Inventory of the French Crown Jewels, the diamond is described as "a very big violet diamond, thick, cut with facets on both sides in the shape of a heart with eight main sections or faces, clear and of a lively water, weighing 67⅛ carats, set in a pin of gold with enamel back, and of an estimated value of 400,000 *livres*."

In later inventories, the diamond is referred to more formally as the Blue Diamond of the Crown, or what historians call simply, the French Blue. Its 1691 declared value would be the equivalent of about $3.6 million of today's dollars. The gem was set in gold and apparently Louis wore it in two ways—as a brooch and hanging around the neck suspended on a light blue ribbon.

Reducing a diamond without internal flaws, like Tavernier's, to just over half its weight would have been deemed wrong and wasteful in India and anathema in pre-Renaissance Europe where uncut diamonds had been associated with magical power and bestowed upon kings and religious leaders. However cutting Tavernier's diamond into a more symmetrical shape with patterned planes or facets in order to reflect light made perfect sense in 17th-century Versailles. The world had changed, and the ways of altering diamonds for particular new ornamental purposes reflected that change. The fact that the diamond's value more than doubled with its cutting and faceting (and actually close to tripled—given a 1689 currency devaluation) while being reduced almost by half in size, is indicative of the value placed on shining diamonds.

P itau's recutting of the Tavernier into the French Blue was part of an aesthetic-philosophical movement to manipulate light for its greater dissemination. The diffusion of light is a central conceptual tenet of later Renaissance art and an aesthetic goal that resonates with several major themes of late 17th- and 18th-century Europe.

Louis XIV is termed the "Sun King," often depicted with symbols suggesting that rays of light emanating from him illuminate society, or bathe people in his glory. This image is consistent with the widespread belief in divine kingship. In the domain of philosophy and political thought, a new perspective begins to unfold; it is termed *enlightenment,* the increase and diffusion of knowledge throughout society as a force for good. Louis XIV sponsored the creation and expansion of the Académie Française, the Royal Academy in Rome, the Royal Botanical Gardens, the Royal Observatory, and Royal Academies in Dance, Music, Painting and Sculpture, Architecture, and Science. He even appears in plays, and in *La Nuit* dresses as the Sun itself. "Light" becomes a symbol of knowledge, beauty, goodness, and munificence.

In visiting Versailles it is easy to see how Louis XIV's palace served as a living example of how the decorative arts enhanced the diffusion of light and thus signal these symbolic attributes of kingship. Everywhere I looked mirrors, chandeliers, inlay, cut, ground, and polished glass abound. It is dazzling to the eye. Clearly, advanced knowledge of optics and technical know-how were applied to glass cutting. Key to manipulating the play of light is the patterning of planar surfaces, which enables glass to shine and sparkle.

Tavernier's Violet came to Versailles as a diamond whose natural surfaces were flattened and smoothed in an irregular way likely through cutting or grinding and polishing. Obeying the King's order to reshape the diamond, Pitau had available to him a variety of design styles that had developed over the last three centuries in Europe; these would come to be known as "cuts." Pitau also had a repertoire of techniques for shaping a diamond: cleaving—splitting the gem by striking it along a plane of cleavage to form a straight or flat surface; cutting or bruting—grinding and scratching a gem through abrasive movement to form a facet or planar surface; and polishing—smoothing a facet through continuous abrasive action. All of these techniques used diamonds to cut other diamonds, as no other substance could. Refashioning a diamond, then as now, calls for a good deal of knowledge and the tools necessary for precision movements.

The European art of reshaping diamonds probably began in

earnest in the 14th century in Venice and perhaps a bit later in Paris. Early European-fashioned diamonds include table cuts—a single flat surface across the "top" of the gem, and point cuts—polished sides of a pyramidal-shaped diamond coming to a point at the "top." John the Fearless, Duke of Burgundy, possessed table-cut stones, supposedly presenting some of them as gifts at a dinner for the King of France in 1407. Diamonds in a 1436 painting of John de Leeuw, the jeweler to the Duke of Burgundy, by the Flemish artist Jan van Eyck, includes the subject holding what appears to be a small cabochon or simply polished diamond between his thumb and forefinger. And diamonds embellishing the court goblet made for Philip the Good (Duke of Burgundy, 1419–67) include cuboid and point-cut gems, apparently with facets not only in the crown (at the "top" of the diamond), but also in the pavilion (the lower, "bottom" portion of the diamond).

Some of these diamonds may have been fashioned by cleaving, though there is a good deal of disagreement among gem historians. Several believe that gem cutters of the 14th century discovered the fact that diamonds have "grain."[6] Cleaving a diamond entails splitting away a piece of the stone so that it falls off along the grain. Cleaving allows for a quick means of ridding a rough diamond of imperfections and achieving a workable mass for more elaborate fashioning. It also results in two or more stones, often called the main stone and a lesser satellite stone.

The cleaver secures the stone so that it cannot move—typically setting it in some form of beeswax or resin cement attached to a wooden baton or dop stick and then anchoring it. The cleaver closely and carefully identifies the grain and marks, in ink, a cleaving line on the surface of the diamond. Another diamond is then used to scratch a kerf or groove into the diamond along the line. This assures a clean cleavage. A blade edge—generally steel—is placed in the kerf and used as a wedge. The cleaver then firmly smacks a mallet once against the blade, splitting the diamond. An awkward hit or a light hit would ruin the cleavage; the failure to adequately identify the grain and cleavage plane would result in a badly fractured gemstone. Much is at stake in cleaving the diamond; every blow has the potential to inflict heavy financial loss. After the first splitting, the cleaver would then heat the resin and remove the diamond. If another cleaving was called for, he would need to reposition the main gem for a subsequent splitting, repeating the risky process.

Prior to the 15th century, most of these European gems were more likely fashioned by a process called "bruting." Gem cutters basically ground one diamond against another to cut in each a faceted surface. Cementing each diamond in a holder, the two diamonds would be tediously rubbed against each other, the friction producing diamond dust as the surfaces were worn down. The two diamonds would be reset in their holders numerous times, so that the variously planed facets of the stones could be scraped out, one by one. The dust would be saved and used as an abrasive in its own right to polish surfaces, and hence give them a smooth, reflective finish.

The turning point in the development of diamond-cutting technology is supposed to have occurred in the mid-15th century— variously 1454 and 1476. A Jewish diamond worker, Louis de Berquem (Loderwyck van Berkem), working in Bruges, in Flanders, now Belgium, is often credited with the European discovery of the technique of using diamond dust with olive oil as lubricant on a rapidly rotating grindstone to cut and polish diamond facets. The attribution of this innovation is made in the 1661 publication *Les Merveilles des Indes orientales et occidentales,* an account written by a descendant of the de Berquem family, Robert, some two centuries later.

This grinding process is perhaps first described in writing in 1568 by Italian goldsmith and Renaissance artisan Benvenuto Cellini, who fashioned diamond jewelry for Pope Clement VII. The diamond is secured, cemented into a weighted armature or clamping device. One surface of the gemstone is exposed and held (somewhat like a stylus on a record player) against a rotating steel wheel impregnated with diamond dust and olive oil. The grinding wheel is turned by either hand or foot-treadle power. The application of olive oil is key in the process, as the grinding of diamond dust against diamond produces a great amount of heat that can damage the gemstone. The exposed surface of the diamond is worn down. The diamond is then repositioned and re-cemented with a new surface facing the wheel. It is ground again, cutting and faceting the gemstone.

The same use of the diamond-dusted, olive oil–lubricated wheel allows for the polishing of the finished stone in order to even out rough surfaces and increase the gem's luster. The process is demanding and requires constant, focused attention. Albrecht Dürer noted this, writing that jewelry workers of the period "kept their noses to the grindstone."

The legendary de Berquem is said to have became famous for cutting gems for the French King Charles VII (1403–61) and for Charles the Bold, Duke of Burgundy from 1467–77. Using his technique, he was able to form regular, symmetrical facets, elaborating upon simple, table-cut diamonds. These diamonds were able to reflect about 30 percent of the light reaching their surface. This is still rather primitive by today's standard, but it was a major innovation of the time. De Berquem's students went to Paris and to Antwerp and Amsterdam where they played seminal roles in establishing long-standing communities of Jewish diamond workers.[7]

De Berquem is also connected to two important precedents in diamond use. One grew from his purported role as the jeweler for Jacques Coeur and Agnes Sorel. Coeur was a wealthy international trader who became chief financial adviser to Charles VII, patron and friend to Sorel, the King's mistress. Coeur's ships were connected to a pre-Vasco da Gama network that brought luxury goods to France. Because of Coeur, the Parisian elite could enjoy linens, sables, pearls, ostrich feathers, coral, incense, tea, spices, dyes, and gems from around the world, including very rare diamonds originally from India. Now, utilizing de Berquem's new techniques, diamonds could be fashioned into eye-pleasing jewelry. Coeur, whether by whim or grand design, came up with the innovative idea of having a diamond necklace, gold brooches set with diamonds, and a diamond belt buckle made for Sorel. Sorel was not particularly beautiful, at least in the surviving portraits. But wearing her diamonds and pearls, she became known as the "Dame de Beauté." Heretofore European women had not worn diamonds; nor had diamonds been associated with beauty. While most jewelry for the elite, whether men or women, was composed of pearls—as would be so for another two centuries—diamonds had made their mark. Due to Coeur and Sorel, Paris became an early center of the fashion business. Sorel's diamonds became part of the royal jewels of France after her death.

The second development concerns de Berquem's work for the Duke of Burgundy, a wealthy and powerful rival, ally, and relative of the French King. Many of the earliest cut diamonds embellishing jewelry and decorative items are found in the Burgundian collections. Their line of succession came to an end in 1477 with the death of Charles the Bold. His eldest daughter, Marie, married Maximilian von Hapsburg, the Holy Roman Emperor. Among the groom's gifts to the bride was a diamond ring. Apparently, as the legend goes, the ring was placed on the third finger of her left hand, so as to rest upon the vein of love that was connected to the heart, as first explained by Bishop Isador of Seville. This incidence did not develop into a widespread custom, as diamonds at that time were much too rare for betrothals and weddings beyond even a small segment of the aristocracy. There is a record of only a few marriages following this practice for hundreds of years. While it did connect diamonds to marriage, it was not until some 400 years later that the tradition of a man giving a woman a diamond *engagement* ring is firmly established.

By the 1500s, technological innovation in diamond cutting coupled with increased supply from Golconda invited creativity in European styles. Cutters developed the rose cut, a domed pattern of angled facets—sometimes 12, sometimes 24—on the top of the gem that gave it the appearance of an opening rose. They reflected more light than the simple table cuts, but being flat on the bottom, lacked any fire or sparkle. Variations developed for double-sided rose cuts, and with thicker stones, a rose-cut crown with facets in the pavilion or lower part of the diamond. These cuts allowed the diamond to reflect light off its outer surfaces and also to take light into the gem and refract or bend it off its interior faceted surfaces, and send that out as well. European buyers highly valued such cuts that "opened up the diamond" to release more light.

By the end of the 16th century, there was an excess of flat and dodecahedral-shaped diamonds from India on the market. New and more inventive cutting patterns were required. Among them were the baroque rose cut, the bead, briolette, and Sancy. In the 1620s a cut appeared that was later named the Mazarin, after a Parisian cardinal and diamond collector who was later a customer of Tavernier. The cut was cushion-shaped. It had a girdle or defined middle border. Above the girdle at the top of the diamond was the crown, consisting of a square table and 16 symmetric facets. Below the girdle was the pavilion, with 16 symmetric facets culminating in a centered culet at the very bottom. The style allowed for considerable internal refraction of light.

The effort to maximize the movement of light through a diamond reached its pinnacle by the mid-17th century with the widespread standardization of the brilliant cut.[8] This is essentially the form of diamond cut we see today. The brilliant cut has a girdle or middle belt of limited width—not so narrow as to be sharp, not so thick as to throw off other angles of refraction. The facets and proportions of the brilliant cut are quite precise. Above the girdle is a crown of 33 facets including a typical octagonal-shaped table. Below is a pavilion of 25 facets including a centered culet at the bottom, making 58 facets in all. The main angles of both the crown and the pavilion are 45°. The ratio of the height of the diamond above the girdle to that below is 1:2. For maximum reflection of light, 29 percent of the bulk of the diamond needs to be above the girdle, 71 percent below. The table typically takes up 56 percent and the culet 8–10 percent of the gem's horizontal area.

The brilliant cut took full advantage of the octahedron crystal

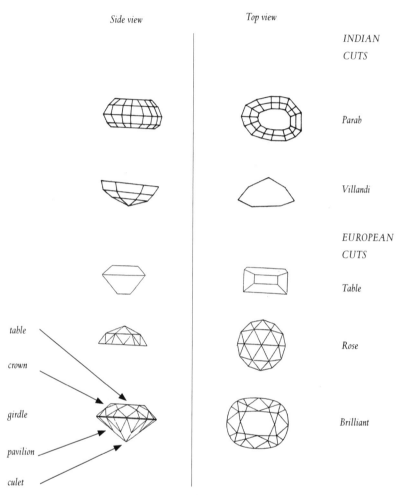

Side view   *Top view*

INDIAN CUTS

Parab

Villandi

EUROPEAN CUTS

Table

table

crown

Rose

girdle

pavilion

Brilliant

culet

Basic types of diamond cuts.

shape. The upper table cut allowed light to pass into the lower reaches of the diamond and to be reflected and refracted off the angular surfaces so as to disperse light and give the gem "fire," a term for the sparkling brilliance of diamonds. The disadvantage was that the cut tended to dramatically reduce the weight of the raw diamond, often by half.

More than anything else, the brilliant cut made diamonds

sparkle. This outstanding feature was quickly replicated, so much so that the term "brilliant" itself became synonymous with diamond. More than a century later this quality was enshrined in a poem still recited today—"Twinkle, twinkle, little star, how I wonder what you are, up above the world so high, like a diamond in the sky."[9]

The new brilliant cut stimulated demand for all sorts of diamond jewelry among European royalty. Faceted diamonds came to decorate much of Europe's Crown Jewels in France, England, Russia, and the Austro-Hungarian Empire. Older diamonds and those cut in India were recut in the new brilliant style. Diamonds represented the wealth of monarchs and royalty, and as such, the wealth of their nations. They thus decorated the symbols of royalty: crowns, maces, and thrones. And while queens wore diamonds, they were worn as much or even more by kings.

P rior to the reign of Louis XIV, Paris maintained small family workshops for the cutting of diamonds. A 1584 law allowed French cutters no more than two grinding mills; in 1625 they could add an additional one if desired. Because France did not have a strong presence in India, it was not at the center of the diamond trade nor cutting enterprise. That, however, was to change with the coming to the throne of Louis XIV in 1643.

Diamonds became a way for Louis XIV to shine. When he initiated his reign, the French Crown Jewels were valued at 938,000 *livres*— about $8.5 million in today's dollars. Cardinal Mazarin and the Queen Mother left him their diamonds; Louis himself obtained most of the others, bringing the

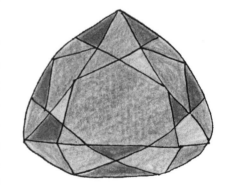

The French Blue.

value of the Crown Jewels upon his death to over 11,442,000 *livres* according to the 1691 inventory—over $100 million today. Some 109 diamonds were over 10 carats in size; 273 weighed between 4 and 10 carats.

Kings and other nobles, as well as Popes, used their diamond wealth as an asset, borrowing against their holdings, pawning their gems to raise armies, ships, munitions, and to give as bribes or favors. It was only in times of great prosperity and peace that a sovereign or ruler could expect to retain, let alone add to, the Crown Jewels. Those kings and nobles who lacked diamonds had to rent them for coronations. The great accumulation of diamonds under Louis XIV illustrated his prowess vis-à-vis his peers, for the French Crown Jewels became the most valuable in all of Europe.

The cutting of diamonds in the relatively new brilliant style matched the rhetoric of the Sun King.

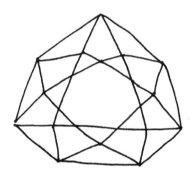

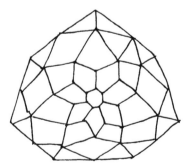

Top and bottom views of the faceting for the French Blue.

Pitau's shaping of the French Blue took this style as his inspiration, but created a variation—termed by some "cushion" and others "stellar"—as a way of avoiding the elimination of the bulk of Tavernier's stone. The Indian gem was asymmetric—long and wide, but not proportionally thick enough for the standard brilliant cut. Pitau retained much of the diamond's original asymmetric shape, so it came out triangular or heart-shaped rather than round. This resulted in a table of seven sides, not eight, with the seven-fold symmetry then played out through the faceting.

The recut stone could not, however, realize the proper ratios of above-the-girdle to below-the-girdle length or bulk. According to the analysis of

French gemological historian Bernard Morel, Pitau made 63 facets in the blue diamond. This is a bit more than the standard 58 for the brilliant. Unlike the brilliant that has more facets above the girdle than below, Pitau made 27 facets above the girdle and 36 below. Pitau added numerous horizontal culet facets below the girdle to compensate for the squatness of the diamond. These facets created the refractive surfaces in the pavilion, allowing for the dispersal of light. This made the blue diamond shine, though not with the fiery character of a standard brilliant. Nonetheless, it was a most impressive diamond.

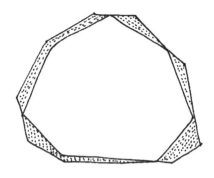

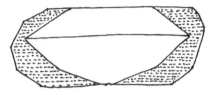

Cutting the French Blue from the Tavernier Violet.

There is no record of any satellite stones being produced from this cutting, although gemologists have long speculated that it might have been possible.

L ouis XIV established a room on the south side of the Versailles marble court to exhibit his diamonds and other gems. It was not only accumulation that interested the King. Louis XIV loved to wear diamonds, and he appropriated the Crown Jewels for his use. He had two complete sets of diamond coat and waistcoat ornaments. Hundreds of jeweled buttons, decorated buttonholes, and other ornaments graced these garments. He used diamond ornaments for his hat, garters, and shoe buckles. His sword was enriched with diamonds—the hilt alone valued at 224,000 *livres*. Louis XIV was also the first to introduce the use of gemstones in the insignia of Orders of Chivalry that had previously been made of plain or enameled gold and silver. He ordered the cross of St. Esprit to be decorated in diamonds. The diamonds reflected light, and with it the power, wealth, and prestige of the Sun King.

Among the Crown Jewels was a variety of spectacular women's jewelry: a necklace of 45 diamonds, a set of earrings with large diamonds valued at 500,000 *livres,* and so on. But Louis XIV's queen, Marie Thérèse of Austria, was of rather modest temperament, and wore very little of the Crown Jewels.

Though King Louis XIV did not give his queen many diamonds, he did bestow jewels as presents to some of his mistresses. At the time of Tavernier's visit, the King's favorite was Madame de Montespan. She was the King's penultimate in a series of preeminent mistresses during his rule, having come into favor beginning in 1667. Athénaïs de Montespan liked to wear jewelry. She was also successful in getting pregnant—at least seven times in nine years with the King, which may have accounted for her jealousy vis-à-vis potential rivals. In 1679, a scandal swept Paris. Montespan was accused of procuring poison in an effort to harm such a rival and of association with a satanic cult. By 1681 she fell out of favor with the King and was replaced by the woman who had been taking care of her children, Françoise d'Aubigné, generally known as Madame de Maintenon, but also pejoratively called "the great man's old crone." Maintenon was born a Protestant Huguenot, but later became a zealous Catholic. She secretly wed the King in 1683 and maintained a strong influence over him and his court for the rest of his life. She was a somewhat dour character, with no zest for elaborate adornment. Indeed, she limited the King's proclivity toward the ostentatious display of gems. It was in part due to her influence that the Edict of Nantes was revoked, leading in 1685 to the emigration of some 200,000 Protestants, and probably the departure of Tavernier.

During the course of his reign, Louis XIV presented important visitors, ambassadors, friends, and courtiers with gems. He lent jewels to other nobles, to princes and princesses, so they too could share in the light of his kingship. But there is no indication that anyone save the King wore the Blue Diamond of the Crown, and he only rarely.

Louis XIV ruled for 72 years, dying in 1715 at the age of 77. As part of the Crown Jewels, the blue diamond passed to his successor, the next French King, Louis XV, who found a more dramatic use for the Indian gemstone.

7

INSIGNIA OF THE GOLDEN FLEECE

A *key to the history of the Blue diamond* is the Insignia of the Order of the Golden Fleece, an extraordinary jewel and one of the most expensive ever assembled.

L ouis XV was only five years old in 1715 when he found himself the successor to the French Crown upon the death of his great-grandfather, Louis XIV. The kingdom was powerful and prosperous. France was Europe's most populous state, and was endowed with its greatest military and economic resources. But Louis XV turned out to be neither a strong nor visionary leader and did little to quell the appetite of the feudal aristocracy or the clergy in appropriating the benefits of society—wealth, land, and office. He failed to satisfy the growing aspirations of the bourgeoisie, the city dwellers and town folk, intellectuals, businessmen, and artisans who were at the forefront of developing a modern economy and the enlightenment ideas to match it. Louis XV's ideas instead were rooted in a royal past.

In 1745, Louis XV became a knight of the *Ordre de la Toison d'or,* or the Order of the Golden Fleece. Knighthoods of the 18th century were of little practical consequence, though they signaled solidarity among aristocrats and between monarchs. Each knightly order had its insignia—a medal, badge, sash, ribbon, or other adornment that the knights would wear when meeting for stately and other important occasions. These were literally "decorations" and status symbols—for kings to both receive and bestow.

The historical insignia of the Order of the Golden Fleece was a stylized chain worn around the neck as a collar, from which was suspended a golden rendition of a ram's fleece. Members of the order could, if they desired, procure more elaborate versions. On December 29, 1749, Louis XV commissioned court jeweler André Jacquemin to design a special *Toison d'or,* or Golden Fleece.

Jacquemin assembled hundreds of gems for the piece—diamonds, rubies, sapphires and topazes—keeping track of each. He relied on the cutting work of Jules Guay, an artisan who had done work for Madame Pompadour, mistress of the King. The resultant jewel, two years in the making, was known as the *Toison d'or de la parure de couleur,* or colored version of the Golden Fleece. It contrasted with the *blanche,* "white," or plain version. It was a stunning royal insignia, worn from a red ribbon, only by the King, and most prominently featured the French Blue.

A basic drawing of the *Toison d'or* first appeared in

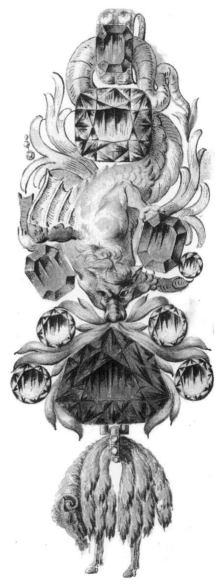

Jacquemin's drawing of the Golden Fleece

Jean Henri Propser Pouget's *Traité des Pierres Précieuses* published in 1762. More than a century later, Germain Bapst, an authority on the French Crown Jewels, published more detailed drawings made by Hirtz based upon Jacquemin's templates. About 5 inches long, the *Toison d'or* symbolized the Greek legend of Jason and the Golden Fleece. The French Blue was the largest diamond in it, with the heart-shaped diamond pointing up. Above the French Blue was set the marvelously crafted 105-carat ruby spinel known as the *Côte de Bretagne* in the shape of a dragon. The ruby formed the head and body of a dragon whose tail was composed of 200 small diamonds curled around a large 42-carat brilliant cut diamond and culminated with a 24-carat hexagonal diamond that attached to the ribbon. The wings of the dragon were set with scores of diamonds. The dragon was surrounded by palms formed by more brilliant diamonds. Flames of gold enriched with topazes issued from the dragon's mouth and encircled the French Blue. Below the French Blue and suspended from its setting were 86 small white diamonds set in the shape of a ram—evoking the fleece.

In the inventory of the French Crown Jewels taken in 1774, the *Toison d'or* was valued at 1,290,000 *livres,* approximately $7.3 million in today's dollars. The French Blue alone was valued at 1,000,000 *livres,* making it the second most valuable of all Crown Jewels.

Why Louis XV would have desired such an elaborate insignia of the Order is not explicitly known; one reason might be that he was a direct lineal descendant of Philip III, known as Philip the Good, Duke of Burgundy, who founded the Order of the Golden Fleece in 1430. Another might be that he found the story of the Order fascinating and what it stood for consistent with his own perspective on pre-Revolutionary France and Europe.

The Order of the Golden Fleece had been explicitly established to revere God, maintain the Christian faith, honor the noble order of knighthood, and engage in chivalrous deeds. Philip was the wealthy leader of a duchy made prosperous by trade with the East. At a time when Europe was still occupied and threatened by Muslim Turks and Moors, Philip sought to unify its rulers under a common banner—and perhaps make the Orient's treasures more accessible.

Closer to home, he wanted to gain some moral traction in his fight against Joan of Arc and his cousin, the newly crowned King of France, Charles VII. Philip had sided with the English in a battle for the French throne. The English offered him membership in the most prestigious of the English knightly orders, the Order of the Garter. This required an oath of allegiance to the English monarch who functioned as the sovereign of the Order. Philip III turned that down, not wanting to appear disloyal to France. But having his own kingly ambitions, he didn't want to submit to the royal claims of his cousin either. In 1429 an army of French loyalists led by the spiritually inspired peasant girl Joan of Arc defeated the English at Orléans. Accompanied by Joan, Charles went to Reims for his coronation as King of France. A few months later, Philip, in reaction, instituted the Order of the Golden Fleece.

The Order directed its knights to uphold the Church, fight against its enemies and protect it from heresy. The Order provided Philip III the moral means, indeed the chivalric means, to justify his opposition to Joan of Arc.

Just months after the Order was instituted, Philip's Burgundians captured Joan and sold her to the English, who then turned her over to the Church for trial and conviction as a heretic and witch. Whereas Joan would claim divine inspiration in her battles against the English, Philip would claim divine motivation for saving the Church through the Order. While Joan's visions were declared diabolical by the Church court, Philip's were blessed by the Pope. In 1431, male chivalry and entrenched power trumped female assertion, nation-building, and popular sentiment.

The Order of the Golden Fleece was initially limited to 24 knights and soon expanded to 30. Philip served as Sovereign of the Order. The primary insignia of the Order was established as a ram's fleece worn as a pendant from a collar. The collar consisted of 28 fire steels and 28 flints emitting sparks. The fire steels are in the shape of two Burgun-

Sculpture of Louis XV with the plain version of the Golden Fleece.

dian "Bs" interlaced face-to-face. The flints were composed of gray and white enamel, giving off gold rays or flames or showers of sparks. Naming the order after the Golden Fleece recalled the story of Jason and the Argonauts. Some of the knights thought the association too pagan for a Christian order, but the name stayed.

Philip and King Charles reconciled in 1435. Paris was recaptured from the English the next year. Relative peace and prosperity followed, trade expanded, de Berquem cut diamonds, Jacques Coeur and Agnes Sorel had their day. The English were finally expelled from France by 1453; Joan of Arc was posthumously vindicated in a formal trial in 1456.

In ensuing generations, the French Crown seized Burgundy, bringing to an end its existence as a Duchy. Failing a male successor, the title of the Sovereign of the Order of the Golden Fleece passed into the hands of the Hapsburgs, rulers of the Holy Roman Empire. The Order became a prestigious one under the Hapsburgs, as they ruled much of Europe. In the early 1700s, conflicts between the two great royal houses of the Continent, the Hapsburgs based in Austria and Bourbons based in France, over succession to the Spanish throne and Burgundian inheritance rights resulted in a schism in the Order. By 1721, the Order of the Golden Fleece had formally split into two separate institutions, the Spanish (Bourbon) and the Austrian (Hapsburg), each selecting new knights, installing a Sovereign, and holding occasional meetings.[1]

Louis XV represented the opportunity to reconcile this schism between the two great royal families of Europe, and the Golden Fleece became its symbolic representation. As King of France, Louis

XV was the predominant Bourbon ruler. He had also inherited the title of the Duke of Burgundy through his grandmother's Hapsburg family. Inducted as a knight of the Golden Fleece into both the Spanish and Austrian orders, Louis XV could, at least symbolically, fulfill Philip the Bold's dream of uniting European rulers in a noble purpose—albeit in Louis XV's vision that seemed to be limited to the continuity of royal privilege.

Louis XV initially had a standard plain or white version of the insignia of the Golden Fleece made upon his induction as a knight. This version, worn either from a neck ribbon, or as a military-like medal on a red ribbon, resembles forms of the Golden Fleece found among the Russian, Spanish, Austrian, and German royal collections.

But the plain version could not express the importance of Louis XV's standing at both the confluence and pinnacle of European royalty. The colored version of the insignia of the Order of the Golden Fleece, replete with the great French Blue and packed with literally hundreds of sparkling brilliant-cut diamonds, aptly reflected the grandiosity with which Louis XV perceived his own standing.

The iconography of the colored insignia of the Golden Fleece tells a decipherable story, but not so much about Jason.

In the Jason tale, the hero must obtain the Golden Fleece guarded by a fierce dragon in order to claim his rightful kingship. He learns the secret of getting past the dragon—which is to sing it a lullaby. He then steals the fleece, but betrays his partner and would-be wife, and suffers a tragic end.

In the colored version of the *Toison d'or,* the jewel's motif is actually more suggestive of Marco Polo's tale of the diamond valley in India. The diamond-winged red spinel dragon hovers over the diamond—not the fleece. The dragon's diamond fire breath surrounds it. The fleece, like the meat tossed into the valley, adheres to the blue diamond, pulling it away from the serpentine creatures.

The *Toison d'or* reflects the transformation in the themes and technologies of modern royal jewelry. With an increased supply of diamonds, more stones could be used in jewelry. As the boundaries of European interests had moved farther eastward, to China and India, motifs moved beyond those of the Renaissance. And as the means of cutting and polishing diamonds had been refined, jewelers could use their sparkle and shine to create the illusion of movement and flow. Complex ensembles of diamond flowers and fountains, wings and plumage were the result.

While starting with the Greek Jason myth for its imagery, the court jewelers for Louis XV must have looked farther afield. Given the known origins of the French Blue, designing the jeweled tableau as an Indian story must have seemed most appropriate.

The jewel also reveals its own, European frame of reference in presenting the "East." This is not unlike French silk weaving that invents chinoiserie—a stylized way of representing purportedly Chinese themes and motifs in a thoroughly French way. The ruby-red spinel dragon is clearly one-headed, not like the many-headed hydra-dragon construed by the Greeks. Madame Pompadour supposed it to be cut in the style of the eastern Orient. But in both Chinese and Indian mythologies, the dragons or dragonlike serpents are not usually depicted with wings. They do not breathe fire. Neither the Indian *naga* serpent nor the Chinese *lung* are particularly malevolent. In fact, Eastern dragons may be good, kind, and intelligent. European dragons, perhaps due to the influence of Christianity, are presented as evil, greedy, and loathsome. Interestingly in both Eastern and Western legends, dragons guard gold and jewels, often underground or in caves.

The *Toison d'or* thus sets out its own European construed mythology—where the mock Eastern dragon is outsmarted by Western human ingenuity; Eastern supernaturalism is tamed or averted by Western know-how. Ironically, a century later, another artistic creation would reverse the relationship.

8

STOLEN CROWN JEWEL

Marie Antoinette loved diamonds, and so she was well suited to become Queen of France when her husband, Louis XVI, succeeded to the throne in 1774 at the age of 20. She wore diamonds at her wedding, and was criticized for obtaining costly diamond jewelry and holding lavish balls while the common people of France lived in poverty. She preferred light settings and ensembles of diamonds where the design, rather than the individual gems, were highlighted. She was particularly fond of matching sets of necklaces, earrings, pendants, and head wreaths. Importantly, as a contemporary noted, she was accorded use of most of the Crown Jewels,

> The great crown diamonds, including the Regent, the
> Sancy and the Mazarins were set negligently in an aigrette
> of heron's feathers, or as drops of water on garlands of
> flowers. As a result, most of the stones in the women's
> ornaments among the crown jewels were taken from
> their settings and used in an ever-changing number of
> settings . . . The Queen had added some of her own jewels
> to the crown jewels . . . and it became impossible to
> distinguish the state jewels from those of the Queen.[1]

But the Queen's run of the Crown Jewels did not include the French Blue. Louis XVI was also inducted into the Order of the Golden Fleece and inherited the amazing colored version of the insignia containing the French Blue. There is a single documented case of the blue diamond's removal from its setting. That came in 1787, not for the Queen's adornment but rather for a scientist's experiment. The Grandmaster of the King's Wardrobe handed the blue diamond to Mathurin-Jacques Brisson for physical testing. The latter was conducting studies on specific gravity, and using the French Crown Jewels as a sample for his measurements. Brisson weighed the gemstone at 260 grains and computed its specific gravity, comparing it to other colored diamonds in the unparalleled collection.[2] Its return to the Golden Fleece was also recorded.

In the mid-1780s, Marie Antoinette was implicated in what came to be known as the "diamond necklace affair." Although she was not directly involved, her attributed lust for a necklace of 647 brilliant diamonds made her a target for satirists and critics. The scandal exposed the greed, myopia, and shallowness of French royalty and undermined the King and Queen in popular opinion. Napoleon later blamed the French Revolution in part on this scandal. Louis XVI was of course also to blame. He was an ineffective King during trying times. He failed to grasp the scope of popular discontent with the privileged nobility and the clergy. He was a poor leader and did little to solve a growing social, economic, and political crisis.

As a prelude to revolution in France, the Bastille in Paris was stormed on July 14, 1789. A few months later, a violent mob marched on the Versailles palace. Marie Antoinette and Louis XVI, protected by the Marquis de Lafayette and his contingent of revolutionary national guardsmen, were evacuated to nearby Paris. They became virtual prisoners of state. The French Constituent Assembly passed a law giving the King the right only to use, not own, Crown property—including the Crown Jewels. Following the King's failed escape from Paris in June 1791, the Crown Jewels, including the Order of the Golden Fleece with the French Blue were confiscated for fear that Louis XVI and Marie Antoinette would use them to buy their freedom. An inventory of the Crown Jewels was carried out; the French Blue is listed and valued at 3 million livres—the equivalent of more than $18 million today.

The jewels were sent to the Garde Meuble, also known as the Royal Warehouse—a building that contained historical armor, furniture, tapestries, and other Crown possessions. It functioned both as a storehouse and a museum. Under the direct control of the National Assembly, the jewels were put on public display once a week.

The revolutionary movement in France was unsettling to others in Europe. The Hapsburgs, rulers of the Holy Roman Empire centered in Austria, the Prussians, and nobility in German areas bordering France worried about revolutionary fervor and anarchy spreading to their own populace. French émigrés—disgruntled aristocrats—were flooding neighboring regions, excoriating their noble cousins to correct revolutionary wrongs. Though uncertain of each other's motives, the Prussians and Austrians formed an alliance by the spring of 1792 to turn back the French Revolution and restore Louis XVI and Marie Antoinette to the throne.

Insurrection broke out in Paris. The Commune of Paris, urged on by Georges-Jacques Danton, Jean-Marie and Manon Roland, and other revolutionary leaders stormed the palace; Louis XVI was imprisoned. Disorganization, mutiny, and retreat characterized the French reaction.

Prussian King Frederick William II and Austrian Emperor Francis II selected Carl Wilhelm Ferdinand, the Duke of Brunswick, to lead their troops. On July 25 the Duke issued a Manifesto to the people of France declaring that he would lead an invading army in order to restore the monarchy. He promised no harm would come to those French who supported the King and the reestablishment of order. Resisters and rebels though, would be punished "according to the most stringent laws of war, and their houses shall be burned or destroyed." His warning to the residents of Paris was extremely stern:

> if the least violence be offered to their Majesties the King,
> Queen, and royal family, and if their safety and their
> liberty be not immediately assured, they will inflict an ever
> memorable vengeance by delivering over the city of Paris to
> military execution and complete destruction, and the

rebels guilty of the said outrages to the punishment that they merit.[3]

The Duke of Brunswick was widely regarded as one of Europe's most successful generals. He was, however, a somewhat confounding personality, more cautious than bold in military maneuvers, apparently more liberal than autocratic in political outlook. The Brunswick duchy was located in the northern central region of German lands, near Hanover, the seat of the ruling house of Great Britain. The region was heavily involved in trade and quite prosperous. The Brunswick family home was in Wolfenbüttel, where an ancestral Duke, Anton Ulrich, had aspired to build a "northern Versailles." The Duke's wealth included treasure troves of Renaissance paintings, jewels and gems, and exquisite furnishings, in addition to extensive lands and a world-class library.

Carl was connected to the highest rung of European aristocracy. His uncle was Frederick the Great, King of Prussia. He was often allied with Catherine the Great of Russia; his daughter was resident in her court. His wife was the sister of George III, King of Great Britain. George III offered him the command of the British forces to subdue the American Revolution—a commission he declined because he thought British forces were insufficient to retake the wayward colony.

Carl became the Duke of Brunswick in 1780, succeeding his father. In 1786 the Duke led a Prussian army into Holland, reestablishing the authority of the Prince of Orange.

Carl Wilhelm Ferdinand, Duke of Brunswick.

In 1792, Brunswick could not

refuse the commission given him by the Prussian and Austrian rulers. The Manifesto was mainly authored by a French émigré, and forced upon the Duke. "That unlucky manifesto! I shall repent it to the last day of my life. What would I not give never to have signed it," he later confided to his aide.[4]

Some revolutionaries in France regarded the Duke of Brunswick as empathetic to their cause. Earlier in the year, the Revolutionary Government, with the support of King Louis XVI and the revolutionary Girondins and Jacobins, had offered the Duke of Brunswick the supreme command of the French army. Though the Duke turned it down, he expressed his support for French reforms. He had no sympathy for the émigrés and was opposed to the despotic rule of the aristocracy and clergy. Even after the Duke's July Manifesto was issued, Jean-Louis Carra, a colleague of Danton, a scholar, scientist, a journalist for a revolutionary gazette, and a member of the National Assembly wrote,

> There is nothing more stupid than those who believe, and
> would like to make others believe, that the Prussians
> intend the destruction of the Jacobins . . . The Duke of
> Brunswick is the greatest soldier and statesman in Europe.
> Perhaps all he lacks now is a crown to make him; I do not
> say the greatest king in Europe, but certainly the true
> redeemer of European freedom. If he does reach Paris,
> I would wager that his first act will be to visit the Jacobin
> Club and don the red cap of liberty.[5]

Carra knew Brunswick personally. They'd met in 1782. The Duke had given Carra a gift. Carra had dedicated a book to the Duke, and held him in extremely high regard.

In August, Brunswick hastily assembled his troops—a 34,000 man Prussian army, supplemented by thousands of émigrés and Hessians. He thought they were ill prepared, and that an autumn invasion might get bogged down as winter approached; he wanted to wait until the next spring. He distrusted the Austrians and had little respect for the military prowess of his cousin, the Prussian King. Yet he was pushed to begin the invasion to retake France quickly. By the end of August he took control of the French border and by mid-September had arrived in the hill country between the Bionne and Auve Rivers, near the small hamlet of Valmy, about 100 miles from Paris. Here, Brunswick was joined by a force of 15,000 Austrian troops. It was at Valmy that the fate of the French Revolution would be decided.

F rance was in a revolutionary state, with normal relationships disrupted and confused. Its economy was in tatters. On August 16, the Minister of the Interior had suggested to the National Assembly that the Crown Jewels be sold in order to back the nation's paper currency, and thus gain a measure of fiscal stability. But events were to intrude upon that plan.

At this time, the Crown Jewels were locked up in the Garde Meuble, or Royal Warehouse. The displays to the public were suspended in light of revolutionary massacres that had gripped the city during the first week of September.

The Royal Warehouse of the time was located in a large building on the Place Louis XV—just weeks before it was renamed Place de la Révolution. The huge church of St. Marie Madeleine was being built up the street. Currently, the building, now housing the Ministry of Marine, is in the center of the city on the Place de la Concorde, but in 1792 the city was much smaller, and the Royal Warehouse was near its border, with shanties, fields, and forests nearby. At night, there were no street lamps, only two lanterns attached to the side of the building.

Thierry de Ville d'Avray was the chief conservator for the treasures and responsible for their security. He was killed on September 2, and succeeded by Citizen Restout, who had the 50-page inventory of the Crown Jewels made the year before. They were valued at 24 million *livres,* or about $90 million in today's currency. The Crown Jewels were kept not on the ground floor, but one flight of stairs up, in locked cabinets in a chamber, the doors to which were locked and bolted, with wax seals affixed.

Restout too worried about the security of the Crown Jewels; he wrote several letters to Santerre, the Commander in Chief of the National Guard and Adjutant General Doucet in early September requesting help. Restout had only a dozen men to guard the building. He wanted 60. He complained about the quality of the guards, writing "Is it through negligence, forgetfulness, or deliberate malice that the guard is often left without relief for forty-eight or even sixty hours at a stretch?"

Paris was in turmoil. Different groups competed for control in a time of national and municipal confusion. The Commune of Paris, Roland, the Minister of the Interior, Danton, the Minister of Justice, the revolutionary Committee for Public Safety, and the National Guard all exercised some degree of policing authority to limited success. The September Massacres—a revolutionary killing spree encouraged by the Commune of Paris—led to the wholesale and in many cases gruesome butchering of some 1,500 prisoners, aristocrats, clergy, and "enemies of the revolution" during the first week of the month. Bands looted. Some, dressed in uniform, impersonated revolutionary officials and police, conning citizens to give up their gold and valuables for the defense of the Commune in light of Brunswick's Manifesto.

Restout received no help.

In the late night of September 16, an officer of the National Guard, Camus, and his patrol observed men looting the Royal Warehouse. There were men on the street and others up on the first floor open-air colonnade, obviously taking things out through the windows and passing them down in a basket. A ladder was propped up against the building. Instead of directly challenging and arresting the men, Camus led his men around the building to wake up the caretaker, who then roused Restout and the guards. The party marched up the internal staircase to the locked chamber to see if it had been disturbed.

The wax seals had not been broken, and a debate ensued about whether the group should nonetheless enter the room. All this wasted about thirty minutes, and by the time Camus and Restout finally entered the room to discover the obvious theft of jewels, most of the thieves were long gone, though two of them were detained.

The police were called and arrived at about two in the morning. Roland, the Minister of the Interior, was called. He arrived at four o'clock and dismissed the police, asserting that the theft was a matter for a government commission.

The next day, members of the National Assembly were surprised to learn that most of the Crown Jewels had been stolen. Only a fraction—about 600,000 *livres* worth, remained. All the major jewels—the Regent, the Sancy, the Golden Fleece with the French Blue, and hundreds of others were gone. Outrage was directed at Roland for lack of security at the Royal Warehouse. Roland defended his position, saying he was responsible not only for the Royal Warehouse, but for the entire nation.

In the days and weeks that followed, the theft sparked numerous additional accusations about responsibility. More thieves were apprehended, but no supposed ringleaders. Several trials ensued, and in some cases, punishments were exacted; in others, thieves went free. Historians have tended to agree with the leading chronicler of the event that "the theft of the Crown Jewels is one of the enigmas of history."

According to the trial testimony, the plot was almost comical. It was supposedly engineered by Paul Miette, 35, a resident of Belleville, and an inmate in Paris's La Force Prison who had been convicted of fraud. Apparently, he convinced some other inmates, who themselves had been imprisoned for looting, to rob the Royal Warehouse. Miette told these fellow prisoners how badly guarded the building was, and how easily a theft could be performed. He seemed to have convincing inside information about the storage of the Crown Jewels and the lax security arrangements.

Miette recruited an initial group of ten inmates including Cadet Guillot from Rouen, who in turn involved several acquaintances to

assist in the robbery. Miette led a
first group out of La Force and
across town to the Warehouse.
Their first assault occurred on
the night of September 11. Using
a ladder, they were able to get up
to the outdoor colonnade on the
first floor. The windows were
not barred, as they should have
been. They cut a window with a
diamond glass cutter and gained
entry. They then opened windows to the colonnade for the
easy movement of thieves and
goods. They made sure to secure
interior doors, and proceeded,
quietly, for fear of being discovered by guards.

They made their way to the
Crown Jewels. Many of the jewels had formerly been displayed

Garde Meuble.

in glass cases. But given security concerns, they were now mainly
locked away in boxes held in the drawers of locked cabinets. The
King's decorations, likely including the Golden Fleece, were held in
a walnut casket, too big to go into the drawers. Instead, it rested on
a table in the middle of the room. The thieves managed to open the
locks of the cabinets and loot the drawers and the casket. On that
first night the thieves could only carry a fraction of the jewels, and
left with their booty.

Two nights later several of the thieves, joined by other
acquaintances—perhaps a dozen in all—returned to the scene.
This group was led by a man named Meyrand. They followed a
similar course as the initial group, and took more gems. On the
night of September 15, a third group, led by Deslanges, continued
the thievery.

The next day, key members of the three groups met at a café owned by a man named Retour to divide their booty. Animated arguments ensued. Douligny suggested that many jewels still remained, and so a fourth visit was planned for that night.

By this time, having so successfully looted the Royal Warehouse, the thieves had become careless. The group expanded outward to friends and girlfriends of the conspirators, so that many involved did not even know one another. The late night theft turned into a party, as the robbers brought with them food and wine to celebrate their good fortune in the very midst of the Royal Warehouse.

The raid this night was carried out in a most indiscreet way, with the thieves literally tossing valuable items—statues, swords, and decorative bells, out of the window and onto the street below. For their meal and revelry, the thieves lit candles, opened bottles of wine, and feasted. Apparently, so their story went, two Parisians who'd just happened to be walking by were threatened or cajoled into joining the group on the spot. Two of the other thieves were supposedly later to be revealed as police informers, though one was found in possession of stolen property.

It was during this theft and celebration that Camus and his patrol came upon the robbers and alerted the police and Minister Roland.

Some of the Crown Jewels were recovered almost immediately; others returned to Paris anonymously, and after several years. One of the conspirators located jewels buried along the Allée des Veuves (Avenue Montaigne). An anonymous letter to the Commune of Paris led police to some of the stolen jewels. The prize among the jewels, the famed 137-carat Regent diamond, was supposedly located in an attic. Other diamonds were located in a house owned by a man named Tavenal. Many of the jewels went missing. The 53-carat Sancy was years later identified in the possession of the Demidoff family in Russia. The Golden Fleece was surely broken up, for the red-ruby spinel dragon was later found in Germany, and after disappearing a second time, was mysteriously returned to France—where it now rests in the Louvre.

Some of the thieves were caught—17 were arrested. Depositions were taken. Twelve were found guilty and condemned to death, but only five were executed. Their scaffold was built outside the Royal Warehouse in the Place de la Révolution, where two were beheaded in October, and others thereafter. These executions served as the direct precursor for the guillotine that would behead the King and Queen months later in the same square. As many as 34 people involved avoided capture and prosecution.

Charges and countercharges surrounded the theft. A prosecutor blamed Marie Antoinette, who was allegedly conspiring to regain the jewels she loved and needed. Others saw in the theft a counterrevolutionary plot to undermine the government by depriving it of its wealth. Revolutionary leader Jean-Paul Marat blamed aristocrats. Jacobins blamed Girondins.

It is possible to suppose that the theft of the French Crown Jewels was exactly as it appeared to be—a bungled robbery during chaotic times, planned and executed for the sake of looting.

Germain Bapst, a late-19th-century historian of the French Crown Jewels, asserted, albeit with no evidence, that the Golden Fleece with the French Blue was taken by Cadet Guillot in the initial robbery on September 11. Supposedly, Guillot immediately left Paris for Nantes and then went on to Le Havre, after which he sailed for London. Bapst alleges that Guillot had the Golden Fleece broken up in London, with the French Blue then cut into two pieces. The diamond and Guillot then disappeared from history.

Bernard Morel largely agrees with Bapst, asserting that Guillot left Paris with several of his fellow thieves from Rouen—Gobert, Auguste, Salles, and Fleury-Dumoutier. They carried with them not only the Golden Fleece but other gems as well. Guillot kept the lion's share, while splitting up the rest of the loot and heading for London. Salles and Fleury-Dumoutier were later apprehended in France for other crimes.

Various gems of the broken-up Golden Fleece came to light in ensuing decades. According to Morel, Guillot sold the smaller diamonds in the Fleece one by one in London, although the fate of the French Blue is unaccounted for. Indeed, according to Morel, Guillot returned to the Continent in 1796, trying to sell the Cote-de-Bretagne.

Incredibly, he was put into a debtors' prison by one of his coconspirators. Guillot's supposed risk taking and lack of wealth make it unlikely that he had disposed of the blue diamond.

Madame Manon Roland had another explanation for the theft. She accused Danton—the Minister of Justice and leader of the Revolution—as the lead conspirator, and named as his coconspirator her own husband—Jean-Marie Roland, Minister of the Interior.

Manon Roland contended in her diary, written during her later imprisonment, that Fabre d'Eglantine, Danton's principal aide, had visited her the day after the theft was discovered. The visit struck her as quite strange and totally out of character—she'd been out, and he'd waited for hours in order to see her. When she returned, he came up to her apartment uninvited. She writes:

> Though I did not so much as offer him a chair, he stayed
> for an hour and a half, bemoaning the previous night's
> robbery—which he said, deprived the nation of such solid
> wealth—in highly hypocritical tones. He asked if no one
> had the slightest knowledge as to who might have done the
> deed, and expressed amazement that nothing had leaked
> out about in advance.[6]

She then, according to her diary, told her husband, Jean-Marie, "One of the men who robbed the Royal Warehouse was here this morning to find out whether he was under suspicion." She named Fabre d'Eglantine and said,

> So bold a move can only have originated with our master of
> audaciousness—I mean Danton himself. Whether this will
> ever be proved in the formal sense, I don't know; but I am
> absolutely sure it's true.[7]

Historians Robert Christophe and Stanley Loomis took this claim seriously, and argued that Danton orchestrated the affair and

conspired with Roland to have the
jewels stolen expressly for the purpose of bribing the Duke of Brunswick—inducing him to retreat,
thus saving France and the Revolution. In this view, d'Eglantine's
visit to Madame Roland was a way
of probing her to see if her husband
had revealed any of the plot to
her—a test of whether he would
maintain his silence in the wake of
public outcry. Danton had organized the plot to look like a common, disorganized theft, but in
reality, he directed, perhaps through
d'Eglantine, some of the key orga-
nizers.

Conspiracy advocates point to
the suspicious circumstances of the
theft. Miette and his colleagues
were prisoners in La Force. They

Georges-Jacques Danton.

needed some latitude to plot the theft while incarcerated. They also
had to be freed. While they could have escaped or been released in
the chaos following the September Massacre, prison officials—who
reported to Minister of Justice Danton—may have been ordered or
encouraged to let the plotters go.

In the aftermath of the theft public suspicion immediately fell
upon Maître Camus, whose patrol had discovered the break-in, but
bungled the apprehension of the thieves. Camus was no ordinary
National Guard patrol leader. He was a lawyer, a writer and member
of the Academy of Letters, a former deputy of the Constituent Assembly, and a newly elected member of the National Convention
that would shortly meet to decide on a new government. Camus
was widely accused of negligence, if not complicity in the crime. In
reaction, he had a poster printed—REPLY TO THE TRUTH ABOUT THE

ROBBERS OF THE ROYAL WAREHOUSE—denying any complicity. Copies were displayed all over Paris.

Others saw Camus as a friend of Danton, doing his bidding. Camus, it was charged, had purposefully stayed away from patrolling around the Archives for the first three days of theft. He had only patrolled on September 16 because he thought the thievery was done. Once the patrol had observed the robbery in progress on that night, Camus had no choice but to follow through, though he did so in a manner that enabled almost all the thieves to escape.

Advocates of this conspiracy theory argue that the plot was necessary because neither Danton nor others could publicly suggest that the Duke of Brunswick and the Prussian army be bribed in return for halting their march toward Paris. The very admission that such a bribe was necessary to defend the Revolution would have been devastating. It would have undermined the assertion that the French army was strong enough to defeat the invaders. It would have undermined public faith in the moral authority of the revolutionaries—how could they secure their goal by bribing aristocrats? Cashing in the Crown Jewels would meet with public repudiation—how could the revolutionary leaders squander the newfound wealth that now belonged to the people? For Danton, the plot solved both a military problem and a political one.

Organized by Danton and his underlings, the key thieves would raid the Royal Warehouse and turn over the more valuable diamonds and gems to his agents. Other items could be kept for services rendered. Danton supposedly arranged things with Camus so that no one would be caught. He'd also secured Roland's passive participation, lest an aggressive investigation afterward turn up evidence of the plot. But given the stakes, Roland would surely understand. However, the conspiracy frayed as it got out of hand. Too many people had become involved. Disputes among them led to more outrageous raids than were needed, occasioning the forced action by Camus. As for the jewels, some were taken haphazardly for personal gain; they had to be recovered and those thieves apprehended and punished. Some of the jewels, including the French Blue, were taken by Danton's agents—and these had to get to Valmy.

9

REVOLUTIONARY BRIBE

W as the French blue used by Danton to bribe the Duke of
Brunswick to "throw" the French Revolution?

The French revolutionary government, as splintered as it was,
tried negotiating with Brunswick as he invaded France. Meetings were held with Billaud-Varenne, who is rumored to have offered
Brunswick money to turn back. The negotiations failed.

At Valmy, Brunswick commanded the combined armies
of Prussia and Austria, augmented by the French émigrés and
others—some 60,000 troops in all. They initially faced a French
force of 36,000 led by General Charles François Dumouriez. Dumouriez had served Louis XVI, and also been Minister of Foreign
Affairs and Minister of War under the provisional revolutionary
governments, and most recently, replaced Lafayette as commander
of the army. Dumouriez called the battle France's "Thermopylae,"
referring to the famous ancient Greek battle where a small, overwhelmed band of Spartans sacrificed their lives to give Athenians
time to build up their forces to turn back the invading forces of
Persia. If the French force lost, the way would be clear for the
Duke's rapid march to Paris.

From about September 10 or so, Brunswick maneuvered his
troops in the area to outflank the French and illustrate to Dumouriez and his generals the futility of their position. Rather than a

frontal assault, Brunswick thought he could place his troops in such a strategic position so as to convince the French to retreat.

On September 14, Brunswick sent one of his chief staff aides, Massenbach, to meet with Dumouriez with the object of securing the retreat of the French. Dumouriez, himself a bold, energetic, and vigorous commander, refused to see him. Massenbach instead met French General Duval, but purportedly to no avail. Brunswick nonetheless held the advantage, and various actions of the French, including preparations seen by Massenbach, convinced the Duke that the French would indeed retreat.

Brunswick thus held off from an attack, despite the fact that his army was well prepared for it. At Valmy, one of the chroniclers accompanying the Prussian army was the great writer Johann Wolfgang von Goethe, then in his forties and just at the beginning of a famous career.

Goethe reported in his diary, "our troops were most eager to pounce upon the French, officers as well as men were most ardent in their desire that the General [the Duke of Brunswick] should instantly make the attack."[1]

Goethe, who didn't particularly get along with the Duke of Brunswick, nonetheless had "unbounded confidence" in his prowess as a general. Had Brunswick moved swiftly in the period from September 14–18, he might have defeated the French army. Yet he did not.

Instead, French General Kellerman, summoned to the front by Dumouriez, had a chance to bring his army of some 18,000 into position. This now put both sides at about equal troop strength.

The two sides jockeyed for position between the high ground and the rivers over the next few days. Nothing decisive occurred. Representatives from the two armies met several times.

At one point the King of Prussia, present on the battlefield and outranking the Duke of Brunswick, became convinced that the French were retreating. He overruled Brunswick and ordered Prussian troops forward to cut off the supposed French route of retreat. This immediately put the Prussians in danger of being surrounded, for the French were not retreating. Brunswick was disgusted by the inexperienced King's intervention, and had to reverse his order. Other interventions by the King frustrated Brunswick.

There were no engaged infantry battles to speak of, though there were heavy artillery shellings, among them a notorious cannonade on September 20 with Kellerman's French troops crowded together adjacent to the now famous hilltop windmill at Valmy—a scene immortalized in the familiar painting of Horace Vernet. According to Goethe, some 10,000 cannonballs fell; Dumouriez cites double that number. The cannonade brought a "hammer beat" that "fired our blood" and "poured melted lead into our eardrums," reported one of Goethe's companions. Goethe himself termed the effect "*Kanonenfieber*," or cannon fever.[2] But the ground was soft, and the cannonballs landed in the moist mud and clay of the battlefield rather than ricocheting around and causing major casualties. "The earth literally trembled, and still there was not the slightest change in the positions," wrote Goethe.[3] Indeed, the toll was extremely light. The French lost somewhere between 300 and 500 men, the Prussians 184. Many more had died of dysentery during the invasion.

The Cannonade at Valmy.

It was clear to Brunswick that a full battle was futile. Brunswick took a firm hand with the Prussian King and proclaimed his decision not to fight. The Prussian and Austrian army then organized its retreat, meeting with French commanders.

Contemporary accounts by military observers found the withdrawal suspicious. Many agreed with Goethe's assessment that an aggressive Prussian-Austrian attack in the period September 14–18 would have defeated the French. A report prepared for the King of England noted that the Prussian and Austrian armies were about to attack the French at a pivotal moment when "a suspension of army was suddenly proclaimed."[4]

Another, "authoritative" account reported that:

> from the highest general to the lowest soldier [of the Austrian and Prussian combined army], the same ardent desire to be led directly to the enemy animated all; and had not reasons of a superior weight prevailed on the King [of Prussia] to desist from an engagement, we should certainly have obtained the most glorious victory.[5]

Decades later, Goethe recalled sitting around a campfire on the evening of the decisive disengagement and telling a group of discouraged Prussian officers, "From this place and this time forth commences a new era in world history and you can all say that you were present at its birth."[6]

If the Prussians succeeded they would have stopped the French Revolution. Instead, the day after the retreat at Valmy, the French National Convention abolished the monarchy. On September 22, the Convention declared it "Year 1 of the new republican age." Declarations of support for other revolutions throughout Europe followed.

French troops went on the offensive, invading German territories. Dumouriez led his troops to the Low Country, defeating the Austrians and taking much of Belgium and the Netherlands. The Prussians turned their attention to the conquest and annexation of

Polish lands. In January 1793, Louis XVI was executed. Marie Antoinette followed him to the guillotine nine months later.

Counterattacks by the Austrians and the Prussians reversed French territorial gains, but not the Revolution itself. France was able to aggressively defend its new national integrity, and indeed in the years that followed, marginally increased its territory at Prussian and Austrian expense. By January 1794, the Duke of Brunswick renounced his commission as the commander of the Prussian army, citing a lack of coordination between Prussian and Austrian forces. Valmy had proved decisive. The Revolution was secure.

S tanding next to the windmill at Valmy, overlooking the battlefield of long ago and plotting out the position of troops arrayed during those fateful dates of September 1792, it is hard for me to image why the Prussian and Austrian forces would have retreated unless Brunswick simply did not want to engage in the battle with the French.

French nationalist historians sympathetic to the Revolution have traditionally argued that the French troops at Valmy were not a ragtag band of revolutionaries, but highly trained and well equipped. Their morale was high, and they were fighting for the ideals of the Revolution. No such strong ideals motivated the Germans. Facing the fierce French resolve, Brunswick rightly judged that he was in for a tough fight, and decided to retreat.

German historians, no less nationalistic, have pointed to other reasons for the retreat. There was no difference between the adversaries with regard to valor or zeal. Rather, some have argued, differences between the experienced Brunswick and the less-experienced King of Prussia resulted in a lack of clear command and strategy that ultimately made engagement too risky. Others have pointed to the fact that Valmy was not as important as the French later made it out to be. Rather, for the Prussians, Valmy and the invasion of France to save the King was a strategic feint for the real campaign to take Poland. Indeed, this is precisely what happened, as Prussian troops gobbled up Polish territory immediately following the retreat. This left Prussia's uneasy ally, the Austrians, to defend their holdings in the Netherlands, and become preoccupied in battles with the French.

Other commentators offer another, technical reason. The French had developed one of the finest artilleries in Europe, while the Prussians emphasized cavalry and infantry. At Valmy, the French artillery had proven superior, and hence the battle illustrated the victory of the cannon over the musket.

According to one historian, the Duke of Brunswick, later reflecting on the campaign supposedly said, "No one will ever know the real reason for the defeat at Valmy."[7] There was, however, a very strong suspicion. The retreat at Valmy provoked immediate charges of treachery, especially from the French émigrés within the Duke's army. Bribery emerged as an explanation—the rumor was that he'd received some 5 million *livres*. Others opined that he received some of the stolen French Crown Jewels, the French Blue the most prominent of them.

In Paris, Danton wanted to forestall Brunswick's invasion, at any price. Danton sent military man Westermann to Dumouriez as his liaison, but also, according to conspiracy theorists, as someone who knew that a plan was afoot to bribe the Duke. Danton also is supposed to have informed Colonel Egalite, an aide to Dumouriez, that they had nothing to fear from the Duke. All this assumes some kind of prior communication with the Duke in the period leading up to Valmy.

In Paris, the Commune appointed Tallien and Carra, respectively loyal to Roland and Danton, as delegates to the headquarters of General Dumouriez. They reportedly left Paris on September 17, but it could have been earlier. Carra is supposed to have carried the stolen French Blue and other gems in his saddlebags. It would have taken them a long day's horse ride or so to get to Valmy, and contemporaneous accounts place him there days later.

Not so "secret" meetings were held between senior staff of the two opposing armies at Valmy. Most concerned food and water supplies and neutral corridors. Some involved more serious negotiations. One, between the cabinet secretary of the Prussian King and Dumouriez, supposedly secured the French commander's assurance to Brunswick that he would provide safe treatment of King Louis XVI once he'd returned to Paris. Another session was held with the Prussians and Carra and Tallien. These continued through the end of September and even into early October in order to affect the peaceful retreat of the Duke's army.

The bribe, as might be expected, if it did occur, is not documented in the memoirs of either Dumouriez or Brunswick's chief aide, Massenbach.

At the front, Goethe had his suspicions. Reporting on his conversations with Brunswick he told his companion, "While the Grand Duke talked of Dumouriez coming over to our side, I pictured one of his [the Duke's] soldiers calling him a traitor and blowing his brains out with one shot of his musket."[8]

One account notes that Dumouriez and the other French generals had such admiration for Brunswick's military prowess that they considered bribery as an appropriate means of neutralizing him. Danton too advocated bribery as a legitimate tactic of the Revolution. He declared in a public speech, "Where cannons fail to force an entry, we should try infiltrating with gold."[9] The revolutionary government even established a 50 million *livre* secret contingency fund for such purposes.

If the bribe was made, the question remains whether it was decisive or merely helped to seal a decision already made. If Carra left Paris soon after the initial theft of the French Blue on September 11, he would have had ample time to negotiate the bribe and forestall the Duke's prebattle advantage precisely at the time it would have mattered most. Brunswick, neither itching for a fight nor trusting his King or Austrian allies, might have been receptive to such a deal. There is even the possibility that others sent by Danton communicated ahead of time with Brunswick and Dumouriez, so that both armies would bide their time at Valmy, essentially waiting for the French Blue and other booty to arrive. Alternatively, if there was no pre-knowledge, and the Duke had already lost his strategic advantage on the battlefield before Carra arrived, the diamond bribe would have provided an incentive for the Duke to follow through on a sound military decision—that the armies had reached a stand-off. Rather than face massive casualties and achieve no decisive result, the Duke could retreat with his troops intact and the French Blue in his pocket.

If the French Blue was at Valmy, its immediate history after the retreat is unknown. Some historians cite an inventory of Brunswick's jewels left at his death in 1806, which supposedly included a very large blue diamond—minus a 45-carat piece. But amply researched records of the Duke do not mention either a Golden Fleece or such a diamond. He also may have disposed of the French Blue before his death.

The conspiracy did not end at Valmy. Danton saw to the punishments and exile of the conspirators in the months that followed. Several were executed—the first, Louis Lyre, was cited for theft on September 11, 13, and 15. Others, though sentenced to death, were actually sent to the Beauvais prison and then given a fresh trial, after which they were given short sentences and left to enjoy the fruits of their robbery. Douligny was pardoned and went to Brest; Camus was sent to Belgium—out of reach of any government inquiry. Supposed ringleaders Miette, Meyrand, Deslanges, and Cadet Guillot were never apprehended.

In 1793, Fabre d'Eglantine denounced Roland as being part of the group responsible for the theft, along with other Girondists. Madame Roland was imprisoned and executed. Her husband committed suicide thereafter. Carra, too, was condemned for his more moderate positions; his declarations the year before in favor of Brunswick proved especially damning. He was found guilty on October 31, and executed.

Dumouriez drove the Austrians out of Belgium and invaded the Netherlands. The Duke of Brunswick suggested that the French general be bribed to defect.[10] Dumouriez was defeated in March 1793, and shortly thereafter deserted the French cause. He wandered around Europe and eventually settled in England.

Danton too did not survive. Faced with military setbacks in 1793, he advocated a somewhat conciliatory course in foreign affairs—a more moderate policy than his radical colleagues on the ruling Committee of Public Safety. Danton opposed the excesses of the Reign of Terror. By 1794 he and his followers were charged with conspiracy to overthrow the government. His trial was a sham, and he was guillotined. As with Louis XVI and Marie Antoinette, no one at the time suggested anything having to do with a cursed diamond as leading to his gruesome end.

10

CAROLINE'S LEGACY

T he French Blue disappeared from history after the 1792 theft; no certain evidence documents its travels or existence for years. Two alternatives have been raised. One has a Royal Warehouse thief making off with the diamond to the French coast and setting sail for England. Many French jewels headed to London in the wake of the Revolution—so much so that they depressed the market for some twenty years. After that the diamond is supposed to have been lost, stolen, and hocked by a chain of shadowy figures—none of whom has been proven to have existed. It may have been recut either quickly or alternatively after some years either in London, or possibly Amsterdam.

The other richer and more circumstantial evidentiary alternative is to countenance the bribe to the Duke of Brunswick and follow its possible trail from there.

T he Duke of Brunswick, returning home from Valmy, had to contend with the Prussian King, Austrian allies, French émigrés, and most difficult of all, his daughter, Caroline Amelia. Caroline was born in 1768 to Carl Wilhelm Ferdinand and his wife, Augusta Hanover, the beloved older sister of King George III of Great Britain. Caroline was a very spirited young woman. In her teens she was suspected of improper sexual dalliances, with a particular penchant for men in uniform, as well as lesbian tendencies—then termed "the German disease." She was headstrong, independent, somewhat ill-mannered and ill-educated for the times given her station in life. She was considered physically attractive by some, plain by others. Most of all, she was her own untamable person—regarded as uncouth, playful, mixing with her "inferiors," and out-spoken.

Duke Carl Wilhelm and Duchess Augusta had a hard time finding an appropriate husband for Caroline. Her quirky personality and high aristocratic status, coupled with the political needs of the Duchy, restricted the European matrimonial field. By 1794 she was getting dangerously old for marriage and merely biding her time at home.

Meanwhile, in England, King George III had his own problems with his eldest son, George. Born in 1762, George was given the title of Prince of Wales as heir to the throne. The young man drank, cavorted, and gambled himself into trouble and almost insurmountable debt. Pampered by his mother, and disliked by his father as a wastrel slacker, George was exceedingly self-indulgent and fond of excessive extravagance. In 1785, Prince George, without his father's needed permission, secretly married the twice-widowed Maria Anne Fitzherbert, his Catholic lover. This was illegal for an Anglican aspirant to the throne; Prince George stood to lose his claim to succession. The marriage was annulled.

Looking for stability for their respective children, King George III and his sister, Duchess Augusta, concocted the idea of marriage between these two unmanageable cousins.[1] To the Duke of Brunswick, who knew both his impetuous, spirited daughter and the libertine Prince, the marriage seemed risky, but worth pursuing. Charlotte, the Queen of England, objected strongly to the marriage, as did others, but to no avail. The union was encouraged by Parliament, which promised to cover the Prince's incredible debts—over £500,000—equivalent to about $40 million today, and to increase his annual allowance from £60,000 to £100,000 upon the marriage.

A marriage proposal came in early 1794. The Duke of Brunswick loved his daughter dearly and was worried about how Caroline would fare in British courtly life. He expressed such thoughts to James Harris, the Earl of Malmesbury, who, as an emissary of King George III, came to Brunswick (Braunschweig) in 1794 to participate in a proxy wedding, and bring the Princess back to England. Malmesbury spent weeks with the Duke and his family as fighting between French and other troops blocked his return route through the Low Countries to England.

During his time in Brunswick, Malmesbury too saw the looming problem between the future royal couple. He tried to prepare Caroline for her life with George. Knowing George's reputation for a fastidious "toilet," he instructed Caroline in various matters of personal hygiene, urging her to wash more carefully and change her coarse petticoats more often.

Malmesbury was also to bring back gifts from the Brunswicks to the Hanovers, including, as he reported, without particulars, several items of jewelry. Jewels, though, probably would not have helped the mismatched pair. Caroline, met upon arrival in England by George's latest mistress, Lady Jersey, and others, was indiscreet about her prior dalliances, unwittingly giving her rival information to feed to George and poison his relationship with his betrothed.

George and Caroline first met with only Malmesbury present. The latter reported that Caroline knelt before George who then embraced her and without saying a word left the room. The Prince then said, "I am not well; pray get me a glass of brandy."[2] The Princess, for her part, was astonished. She asked Malmesbury if the Prince was always like this. She also noted that the Prince was quite fat, not at all like his fine portrait.

The wedding took place in St. James Chapel a few days later, on April 8, 1795, with the Archbishop of Canterbury presiding. Standing in for the Duke of Brunswick, King George III gave away the bride. Both Prince George and Princess Caroline were put off by and disappointed with each other. George thought Caroline coarse, bad-mouthed, foul-smelling, silly, and unpredictable. She found him a haughty, fat drunkard, distracted by his own amusements and sexual dalliances. Their relationship only worsened over time. They are supposed to have bedded only within the first week or two of the marriage, if that, with George heavily fortified by drink. Amazingly, they did produce a lovely daughter, Charlotte, born on January 7, 1796, nine months to the day following the wedding. A story, likely apocryphal and speculative, and attributed to Mrs. Fitzherbert, has it that Caroline was already pregnant with child from her lover, Prussian Prince Louis Ferdinand, at the time of her marriage to George, and that the marriage between George and Caroline was not truly consummated.

Shortly after the birth, George and Caroline were publicly estranged. They maintained separate households. George continued with his mistresses and greatly diminished the public trust in the royal family. Caroline hosted many male friends in her residence—she claimed innocently. Caroline enjoyed the support of her uncle, King George III, but he endured many bouts of depression and insanity that left him indisposed and unable to defend her against his vicious son and his wife, the Queen, who hated her daughter-in-law.

In the wake of the French Revolution and the Revolutionary Wars, Napoleon had come to power. A great general, he defeated various coalition forces, brought stability to France, and crowned himself its Emperor on December 2, 1804. Over the next eight years, he redrew the map of Europe, extended his empire by expanding France, creating dependent states in Spanish, Italian, German, and Polish lands, and fighting a continual war with the English.

Most immediately, he was enmeshed in a series of wars that would give him control of parts of Germany in the form of the Confederacy of the Rhineland. The Duchy of Brunswick was threatened. The Duke tried to secure some of his possessions and valuables, at times sending family members to England. The Duke and the

Brunswickers battled Napoleon's armies in 1805 and 1806, but with little success. In 1806, Napoleon ordered the Brunswick palace emptied of its artwork and other treasures, sending them to Paris. Princess Caroline's mother and her younger brother Frederick Wilhelm fled to England.

One of the things Napoleon was after were the remnants of the French Crown Jewels. He'd made their return and restoration a goal of his rule. For him, this was a matter of France's honor and standing.

Later that year, in October, the Duke was fatally wounded in a major battle at Auerstadt. He died the next month. Brunswick, as a Duchy, ceased to exist when months later, Napoleon created the Kingdom of Westphalia and enthroned his 23-year-old brother Jerome as its ruler.

Likely among the treasures removed by the Brunswicks and taken to England was a jewel necklace, visible in a lithograph in the Braunschweigishchen Landesmuseum. It depicts Caroline returning to London's Kensington Palace in 1806. She is wearing a gemstone necklace that hung down to her chest. According to Frau Strauss, an archivist for the Brunswick material, "Caroline is clearly wearing" the cut-down blue diamond.[3]

The quality of the lithograph is poor and does not allow for a precise measurement. Only the general shape can be discerned. It is oval. If it is the blue diamond, it is clearly not the triangular, heart-shaped French Blue, but rather a slightly asymmetric gem with a width to length proportion that comes close to matching the current Hope diamond. But the lack of detail does not allow for the best comparison.

Could the necklace contain the recut French Blue?

Napoleon might have thought so. The great general opined that he could not explain Dumouriez's victory at Valmy without recourse to the Brunswick bribe. More timely, in 1804 in the midst of an important counterfeiting trial, a man named Baba revealed that he had been one of the thieves of the Crown Jewels from the Garde Meuble. He declared: "Without me, Napoleon would not occupy the throne." Baba went on to describe how the jewels were vital in the military campaign to forestall Brunswick.[4] Napoleon must have heard about this new testimony.

Princess of Wales Caroline wearing the necklace in 1806.

When the Duke of Brunswick died his body was opened and embalmed. His heart was deposited in a silver box and his body dressed in full Brunswick regimental arms with boots and spurs and a large Prussian cocked hat, wearing the British Order of the Garter. He lay in state for a week. A request was sent to Napoleon asking that the remains be deposited in the family vault.

Napoleon replied:

> Tell the Duke of Brunswick that I would rather cede Belgium, I would rather renounce the crown of Italy, than allow him or any of his sons ever again to set foot within the Brunswick territory: let him take his money and jewels, and be gone to England.[5]

Knowing Napoleon wanted to defeat him and possess, or repossess, his jewels, the Duke of Brunswick—if he had the French Blue—may have ordered the 67⅛-carat diamond cut down sometime between 1804 and 1806. The cutting would have disguised the gem, making it difficult for Napoleon to claim that he was recovering state property. This could have been done easily enough as the Duke had many diamonds and did business with a cutter named de Lolme.

If the diamond in the necklace was the recut French Blue, we do not know the circumstances of how and why Caroline received it, but as the eldest surviving sibling and Princess of Wales, it would make sense for her to take possession—either when her family fled to England or prior to that, when it may have been sent to her for safekeeping.

Prince George meanwhile was proving to be incorrigible. He was generally disliked by his subjects. He had no fondness for administration and public service and performed no significant military duties, even though his country was in an almost continual state of war. Members of Parliament and Lords were challenged to treat him respectfully as he continued his overspending without regard for the public treasury. George was obsessed with expensive finery and high-cost architectural projects. He acquired treasures from the Continent and Asia, served as a patron of the arts, supported and lauded writers Byron and Jane Austen, painters Hoppner and Lawrence, composers Haydn and Rossini, fashion designer friend Beau Brummel, and architect John Nash. His projects—such as the creation of Regents Park, and improvements to Carlton House and later Windsor Castle, were high-quality, conspicuous, and much to the dismay of political leaders, expensive.

George spoke French and admired its regal styles in furnishing and decorative arts. He worked with Nash and others to fashion the marine pavilion at the seaside town of Brighton into an amazing, fanciful complex of towers and domes—Indo-Persian on the outside, and decorated with the most elaborate Chinese and French-style furnishings, carvings, wall art, and fine crafts on the inside.

George also loved gems, which he bought for himself and his mistresses, not Caroline. His purchases with the Royal Jewelers, Rundell and Bridge, typically ran up debts year after year. While indiscreet about his mistresses, George spent years hating Caroline and trying to prove her infidelity, oblivious of the double standard which so grated on English society and the somewhat amused public.

❊ ❊ ❊

In 1806, George IV engineered a government inquiry—a "delicate investigation" of Caroline's behavior. She was regarded as somewhat eccentric even among her own circle of friends. She'd sit on the floor, talk scandal, drink ale, eat raw onions, and playact a variety of vignettes. Among her activities was a rather strange one that would later inspire accusations of witchcraft. Following Napoleon's well-publicized and dramatic expeditions, the European elite was fascinated with ancient Egypt, imitating aesthetic styles and playing at "magical" practices. Reports her sometime companion Lady Charlotte Campbell:

> After dinner, her Royal Highness [*Caroline*] made a wax figure
> as usual and gave it an amiable addition of long horns; then
> took three pins out of her garment, and stuck them through
> and through and put the figure to roast and melt at the fire.
> If it was not too melancholy to have to do with this, I could
> have died laughing. Lady———says the Princess indulges in
> this amusement whenever there are no strangers at table;
> and she thinks her Royal Highness really has a superstitious
> belief that destroying this effigy of her husband will bring to
> pass the destruction of his royal person.[6]

Most of all, she was flirtatious with male visitors, sometimes disappearing for long periods of time with her guests. Many thought her to be having a variety of indiscriminate affairs. Her footman declared her to be "very fond of f___ing." It was even alleged that she had a child, William Austin, by one such liaison. This was no idle matter—adultery for Caroline, as the Princess of Wales, was legally regarded as an act of treason! It was a capital offense.

When asked if she had committed adultery, Caroline showed her mettle and cleverly responded, "Yes, with the husband of Mrs. Fitzherbert."[7] Caroline vigorously defended herself. As she wrote to a confidant, "tell Mr. Perceval [the Prime Minister] . . . that a Brunswick never has been conquered yet, and that my honour is more dear to me than all my jewels, that I am ready to pawn them all to defend my own honour."[8] The government inquiries of 1806 failed to prove her alleged adultery.

While conquering much of Europe, Napoleon also succeeded in restoring some of the French Crown Jewels. But by 1809 some of the most important gems still eluded him, most notably the French Blue and glorious Golden Fleece, the insignia of France's oldest knightly order. Napoleon, never one to be outdone, proposed a new *Ordre des Trois Toisons d'Or*—the Order of the Three Golden Fleeces. Napoleon planned to induct a group of knights into the Order, but never actually got around to doing it. The Order, thus, was aborted. But an insignia was designed. It consisted of a large crowned French imperial eagle, with a firestone at its claws, and three brass sheep suspended therefrom. One might say that Napoleon, in proposing the "triple" Golden Fleece, wanted to signal his superiority to his enemies. Given that the Austrians and Spanish fighting him both had their Order of the Golden Fleece, his French, third order, would encompass them.

The awful relationship between Prince George and Princess Caroline continued through into 1811. With King George III incapacitated, Prince George assumed the Regency and was able to increase the pain inflicted upon his wife. George deliberately plotted to tighten the social noose around Caroline, ostracizing and isolating her from society. He spread deleterious rumors, he discouraged people from seeing her, and he excluded her from various functions. He even tried to keep his daughter, Charlotte, from seeing her mother. Despite his efforts, and those of the Queen, Charlotte proved loyal. But her freedom of movement was largely restricted. Caroline became furious:

I was brought into this country to afford money to pay my
intended husband's enormous debts, and to give him
means to live in the greatest splendour with his numerous
mistresses! I am deprived of the society of my only child![9]

Caroline was at this point also running low on funds. She was not
alone. England was in an economic depression. Napoleon's exclu-
sion of English trade with the Continent and his 1810 Fontainebleau
Decree ordering the seizure and burning of British goods in Europe
was severely impeding business. Imports, exports, and profits were
way down. Problems with America (soon to lead to the War of 1812)
were also depressing income. England did not have the funds to
support an extravagant monarch nor be overly generous with its
royal family. With her father dead and the Duchy of Brunswick occupied by Napoleon, Caroline had few familial resources at her
disposal to support herself and her now exiled mother and siblings.
She was now forced to sell some of her gems. One of her confidants
writes:

The Princess sent for me to execute a commission, of selling
two enormous unset diamonds. I did not like the office, and
cannot understand what could induce her Royal Highness
to part with them, or why she should be in difficulty for any
sum of money which she can reasonably want.

I took the diamonds with which I had been intrusted
to several jewelers; one man offered only a hundred and
fifty pounds for them. I knew this was ridiculous, and so I
restored them to Her Royal Highness. What became of
them I know not, but this I do know, that one of the
jewelers, by referring to his books, declared that they were
jewels belonging to the Crown.[10]

Neither Caroline nor a close associate could walk into her husband's
Royal Jewelers, Rundell, Bridge, and Rundell, and place the Blue or

any other diamond on the counter to sell. More likely, her confidants sought out a more independent gem merchant, one less likely to go public with her actions. There is no record of who was approached, nor any receipts of documents for sales. But Caroline may have received help from two sources—her empathetic brother-in-law, Augustus Frederick, the Duke of Sussex, and her companion and confidant, Lady Hamilton. Both had been close friends with financier Abraham Goldsmid.

The Goldsmid family helped King George III finance his wars in America and on the Continent. The Goldsmids floated script for the East India Company. And they partnered with the Baring group to provide the funds for Prince George and the British Parliament to fight Napoleon. Abraham Goldsmid had known Lady Hamilton socially for years, and helped her out of a personal financial crisis. Frederick supported Abraham's causes—attending a Friday night service in London's Great Synagogue and serving as the Patron of the Jews' Hospital. Through Abraham, who committed suicide in 1810, both Lady Hamilton and Duke Frederick likely met Daniel Eliason. Eliason and the Goldsmids were business partners; Eliason was Abraham's brother-in-law twice over (they had married each other's sister), and also served on the boards of the hospital and synagogue. Daniel Eliason was also a prominent though independent diamond merchant. He had the familial discretion and the resources to buy Caroline's large diamonds, including the Blue.[11]

11

CONTRABAND

Eliason and the Blue Diamond stood between two owners, both at war with Napoleon and more dramatically, with each other.

Daniel Eliason was born in 1753. He formed Goldsmid & Eliason with financier Aaron Goldsmid, and married the boss's daughter. He became a pillar in the Jewish community, and is listed in London commercial guides of the period as a diamond and pearl merchant. Eliason bought and sold gems, and dealt in very large stones. In 1796 he sold a beautiful 34-carat diamond to Napoleon on the occasion of the latter's marriage to Josephine. He also supplied diamonds to the foremost jewelers of London.

Sometime before September 1812, Eliason acquired an unset, large, deep blue diamond—evidence of which appears in a drawing and memorandum authored by John Françillon.

Françillon, a French Huguenot immigrant to London, jeweler and naturalist, here traced its shape, showing the diamond in overhead and profile views, with facet lines. He colored and provided the top view blue, and a caption—"Weight 177 grains"—which is equivalent to 44¼ carats. Underneath the sketch, the jeweler wrote,

> The above drawing is the exact size and shape of a very
> curious superfine deep blue Diamond. Brilliant cut and
> equal to a fine deep blue Sapphire. It is beauty full and all

perfection without specks or flaws, and the Color even and perfect all over the Diamond. I traced it round the diamond with a Pencil by leave of Mr. Daniel Eliason and it is as finely cut as I have ever seen a Diamond. The color of the Drawing is as near the color of the Diamond as possible.

John Françillon
N^{er} 24 Norfolk Street
Strand London
19th Sept^{er} 1812[1]

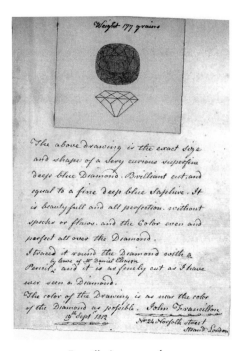

Françillon's memorandum.

Another document, a copy of which is in the Smithsonian's archives, seems to be a sales prospectus, likely of the period but of unknown origin, written in French in a style similar to Françillon's memorandum.[2] There are two drawings. The text describes the diamond and fixes its possession with Eliason. The statement begins,

"The subject of the attached drawing is a brilliant Oriental Diamond, unique and of very great value." The diamond is described as 44¼ carats and sapphire blue.

The diamond is soon described in *A Treatise on Diamonds and Precious Stones* by John Mawe, published in London. In the 1813 and 1815 editions of this book, Mawe mentions in a footnote "a superlatively fine blue diamond of above 44 carats, in the possession of an individual in London."[3] A later version makes clear the individual is Eliason.

None of these documents identify this new, mysterious blue diamond with the French Blue, heretofore the only widely known large blue diamond in all of Europe. The prospectus names it as an "Oriental Diamond," not a French one. The cut is certainly not in "Oriental" style. The mention of "Oriental" could have been important in amplifying its worth. Diamonds had been discovered in Brazil in the 1720s and had come onto the European market. But diamond merchants and patrons placed higher value on the Indian diamonds, so much so that for a time, the Portuguese would ship Brazilian diamonds to India and then reimport them into Europe so they could call them "Indian" or "Oriental."

The two-decade-long interval between the public disappearance of the French Blue and the appearance in London of a large blue diamond without provenance, but likely cut from it, has vexed historians.

If Brunswick had held it, cut it down when threatened by Napoleon, then sent it to Caroline, who sold it to Eliason because she needed cash in 1811 or 1812, there is not much to explain.

If however, the diamond was surreptitiously hidden or passed along through other channels, why didn't it surface earlier? The Smithsonian's Mary Winters and John White have advanced one scenario. When Napoleon came to power he instituted a new legal order, the Civil Code, often called the Code Napoléon. As part of that code, the French government passed a law on April 16, 1804, granting amnesty for all war crimes after twenty years. Hence, reasoned Winters and White, 1812 as the year of the reemergence of the blue diamond made sense, as Françillon's memo is dated September 19, almost twenty years to the date after the 1792 Royal Warehouse theft. If Eliason sold it after that date, it would not matter that the diamond had been improperly acquired. Given the amnesty, Eliason's ownership would be clearly established and he would be entitled to the proceeds of sale.

Though intriguing, this scenario seems quite unlikely. First of all, they would have to be particularly certain of the exact date of the theft of the blue diamond, which is doubtful given the circumstances of the robbery and the lack of public information, especially internationally. Second, it is not clear according to the Civil Code that amnesty would apply to the theft of the Crown Jewels. The provisions of the Code are complicated by countervailing measures concerning legal possession, particularly regarding state property. It would be hard to imagine Eliason relying upon the complex provisions of the Code to protect him and his claim from Napoleon. Besides, Napoleon had been Eliason's customer. Napoleon was hell-bent on restoring the grandeur of France and reconstituting the Crown Jewels as a symbol of that greatness. Napoleon was at this point the most powerful and aggressive leader in all of Europe. He would have strenuously pursued the French Blue diamond as he'd done with other Crown Jewels, and had his agents acquire the diamond, amnesty or no amnesty. He would not have been dissuaded by a legal code he himself established.

For the amnesty to mean anything Françillon and Eliason would have to know they had the cut-down French Blue. If they knew, why not advertise the diamond as such? It would bring a heftier price and given the amnesty, leave them in the clear. Neither Françillon nor Eliason knew they had the famed blue diamond. Nor did others—at least for some time. For several decades after 1792, books about diamonds and encyclopedia entries continued to refer to the French Blue as part of the collection of Crown Jewels of France, seemingly unaware of the theft. John Mawe described Eliason's blue diamond as a *"fine blue"* in the first, 1813 edition of his book. Elsewhere in the book, Mawe described several famous diamonds known in Europe, writing: "Perhaps one of the largest and most beautiful coloured Diamonds is a *rich sky-blue* brilliant; belonging to the crown-jewels of France: it weighs 67%16 carats, and is estimated at three million *livres*."[4] Mawe was unaware of any connection in 1813.

Then there is the matter of the recut diamond itself. Some think Françillon recut the diamond around the time of his memorandum. But why? If someone were worried about holding stolen property, he would either sell the diamond quickly, or recut it so that it would be unrecognizable, or store it away safely for future sale. After the 1804 amnesty law—if one had faith in it, it would make more sense to leave the diamond uncut and to wait out the twenty-year period.

More likely, when she sold the blue diamond, Caroline had some idea of its genealogy, and Eliason did not.

T hough there is no direct evidence, Eliason probably bought the diamond for a good price and sought to turn a nice profit by selling it quickly. This would help with his own family's finances. The Goldsmids were overextended. In 1810 his brother-in-law and partner, Abraham Goldsmid, committed suicide because he could not make good on an East India Company payment. The debts were being paid off slowly. But England's economy was weak, and money was tight.

Eliason no doubt thought about Prince George as a potential buyer. Françillon knew the Prince from decades before. In 1795, George had purchased a diamond necklace from jeweler Nathaniel Jefferys for the outrageous price of £35,000. Supposed to be a wedding present for Caroline, its real intended recipient seemed to be either George's illegal wife, Mrs. Fitzherbert, or his mistress, Lady Jersey. In any case, George failed to pay, and Jefferys had to sue. Parliament formed a commission to investigate. They asked three jewelers to assess and testify to the fairness of the pricing—Françillon was one of them, his partner Cripps another.

There was another link. Eliason sold large, unset stones to Philip

Rundell and John Bridge on Ludgate Hill. Rundell and Bridge had been designated the Royal Jewelers by George III in 1803. Among the royal family, aristocrats, and wealthy, their best customer was George—Prince of Wales, Regent, and later King.

The partners were nicknamed "Oil and Vinegar." Bridge, the philosophical, humble, quiet, and timid partner was the salesman; he took care of George, held his confidence, and would visit the Prince's Carlton House residence to offer him jewelry.

Rundell, the violent, cunning, sly, mean, and despotic partner, was responsible for buying diamonds and negotiating prices. As the contemporaneous memoir of employee George Fox notes: "he knew well how to drive a bargain with the Jew and other dealers who were in the habit of visiting his shop with parcels of diamonds and other precious stones for sale."[5] Reflecting the common anti-Semitism of the times, Fox declares that Rundell "completely Jewed his Jewish dealers."[6] The *Memoirs of the late Philip Rundell*, a rare copy of which I found in the library at the Victoria and Albert Museum, reveals the identity of the famed and bettered Jewish dealer:

> It may not be irrelevant to remark that the late Mr. Eliason, so famous, as a Jew diamond broker, candidly allowed Mr. Rundell's superiority in determining the precise value of any set of brilliants.[7]

This Rundell and Bridge connection may have put Eliason into direct contact with Prince George. As the *Chambers' Edinburgh Journal* retrospectively reported two decades later, "Eleason [sic] received his majesty's commands to visit the palace as often as he had any rare gem to dispose of."[8] The blue diamond would be such a rare gem. And it probably paid off for Eliason. When he died in 1824 at the age of 71 he left some £65,000—a sum of about $6 million in today's dollars to his wife, relatives, colleagues, and his beloved synagogue.[9]

12

GEORGE'S TROPHY

Napoleon's quest for the Blue Diamond and the Golden Fleece
fell short. His Russian campaign of 1812 was disastrous, and
British naval power proved too strong. Spain, ruled by Napoleon's
brother Joseph, fell to an English army commanded by Sir Arthur
Wellesley, then the Earl of Wellington. Wellesley received a knighthood in the Spanish Order of the Golden Fleece.

Prince Regent George fancied himself the triumphant leader,
the key military strategist working to defeat Napoleon, although he
performed no significant military duties. Caroline was once again
being investigated for her morals. She was accused of witchcraft, as-
sociating with Gypsies, and improper conduct. Caroline's mother,
the Duchess of Brunswick, and sister of the King died in March 1813.
Meanwhile, the Brunswicks were at George's mercy, living under
his protection in London. Caroline's brother Frederick Wilhelm
wrote repeatedly to his uncle, the infirm King George III, making
the case for English help in the retrieval of their Brunswick Duchy
once Napoleon was defeated.[1] Prince Regent George was named in
Frederick Wilhelm's will as the executor of the Brunswick estate.

In late 1813 Napoleon was being pressed by the allies on his eastern front, in Italy, and in Spain. Wellesley had defeated the French in
the Pyrenees; his army was marching into France. By April 1814,
Wellington had taken Toulouse; Prussian and Austrian armies were
marching into Paris. His empire dissolved, Napoleon abdicated the
throne and left for exile in Elba.

Louis XVIII, the descendant of the Bourbons, who had been living in exile, now became King of France. On April 20, Prince Regent George accompanied Louis XVIII on a triumphal visit to London. The next day George honored Louis by bestowing upon him the Order of the Garter. King Louis was moved to reciprocate and literally took the ribbon of the French Order of the Saint Esprit off his own shoulder and the star of the Order from his own breast and invested the Prince Regent with the regalia, exclaiming, "To you, Sir, I have owed my all!"[2]

This dramatic exchange of knightly honors initiated a spate of mutual self-congratulation among the monarchal leaders of Europe for their collective victory over Napoleon. The April events were a prelude to the massive June celebrations George planned for London.

George invited the allied heads—the Czar of Russia, the King of Prussia, the Emperor of Austria—to join him. The Czar and the King came; the Austrian Emperor sent his Foreign Minister Prince Metternich. British aristocrats were invested with knighthoods in the Orders of the Thistle, Bath, and St. Andrews. Wellington was made a Duke.

George loved the pomp and pageantry of the June 1814 celebrations. The delegations and leaders wore splendid uniforms. There were processions and fireworks, great banquets, concerts and special events, all celebrating the allied victory over Napoleon.

Prince Regent George was awarded his first Golden Fleece by Grand Master of the Austrian Order, the Hapsburg Emperor Franz I, on June 10, 1814. Metternich presented the investiture form of the jeweled insignia to the Prince Regent on the Emperor's behalf.[3]

The great Thomas Lawrence was commissioned to paint portraits of George and the visiting monarchs and generals. They visited his studio on Russell Square in Bloomsbury at the request of the Prince Regent, and posed for their portraits in all their finery. George didn't like Lawrence, believing him to be a friend, and according to gossip, sometimes lover of his estranged wife Caroline. But he must have been pleased with the work when it was completed the next year, for he awarded Lawrence a knighthood. Most of the portraits now grace the Waterloo Gallery at Windsor Castle. In his portrait, the Prince Regent George is featured in a heroic pose as a military commander in the dress of a field marshal; George, though actually 52 years old, is depicted as especially youthful. The *Champion,* a newspaper critical of the Regent noted, "Sir Thomas Lawrence has with the magic of his pencil recreated the Prince Regent as a well-fleshed Adonis of thirty-three . . . It goes far beyond all that wigs, powders and pomatums have been able to effect for the last twenty years."[4]

Lawrence was, as other painters of the time, quite accurate with regard to the representation of military honors.[5] On his chest, George wears his knightly insignia—the stars of the Garter, the Bath, and the Saint Esprit. Around his neck is a red ribbon, from which hangs the Austrian version of the Order of the Golden Fleece. At its top is a crown-shaped ornament designed to hold the Order's motto. Just below, red flames made of enamel or chrysolite shoot out horizontally. In the center, set in gold, is a rounded oblong blue gemstone—

certainly not a diamond, and hanging from it, the Golden Fleece. The insignia is a direct descendant of that first developed by the Duke of Burgundy and worn by a succession of Kings in France, Spain, and Austria.

The Golden Fleece was of special significance to Prince Regent George. For him, the knighthood signaled the accomplishments of Crown and country. George requisitioned information about various European Orders from the head of the Kings Arms at Windsor and had received a detailed account concerning the degradation of the Order of the Garter and of the Golden Fleece. When he became the first British leader ever to receive the Austrian Golden Fleece, the award, usually reserved for Catholics, required the Pope's

Prince Regent George in 1815.

permission. A few months later George received a Golden Fleece from Spanish King Fernando, becoming the first British ruler to receive the Order from both houses.

George also liked to express triumph through appropriation, particularly when it came to Napoleon. In 1810, George had commissioned a medallion depicting himself wearing a laurel wreath in the same style as Napoleon at the latter's 1804 coronation. George was keenly aware of Napoleon's efforts to restore the stolen French Crown Jewels and the Golden Fleece. Stories about the mysterious appearance of one or another of the gems over the years, particularly on the London market, and often through dealings with Royal Jewelers Rundell and Bridge, were widespread. George's ally French King Louis XVIII had even returned his own Golden Fleece to Spain following Napoleon's takeover, not wanting to be a member of the same knightly order as his enemy. The idea that George could enjoy his Golden Fleece knighthoods—indeed, more than one—while Napoleon could not, probably sat very well with the English leader.

F ollowing the 1814 celebration, Caroline's life in England became increasingly unbearable. George refused to take responsibility for her expenses. Charlotte was ready to marry. With the defeat of Napoleon, Caroline now had an option. She could return home to Brunswick where her brother, Frederick Wilhelm, had now resumed the position of the Duke of Brunswick. Traveling under the name of the "Countess of Wolfenbüttel," she quit England and returned to her native Duchy to the acclaim of its residents.

In 1815 Caroline, George, and everyone else in Europe held their collective breath as Napoleon returned from exile and marched on Paris. Napoleon was, however, quickly and decisively redefeated by Wellington and the Prussian and Austrian allies, this time at Waterloo.

Caroline traveled through Europe. She purchased a home in Bellagio, on the shores of Lake Como, calling it Villa d'Este (Villa of the East). She traveled through northern Africa, and to Jerusalem in 1816. Not to be outdone by George, she started a knightly order as a result of her trip to the Holy Land—the Order of Santa Carolina. Her companion and supposed lover, an Italian named Bartholomo Pergami, was named the Grand Master; William Austin, her "adopted" son, was made a knight.

Caroline continued her contacts with aristocrats and artists throughout Europe in the ensuing years. She openly lived with Pergami, yet continued to formally deny any impropriety. She was widely regarded as a spirited, freewheeling, unconventional eccentric. In one public outing she wore a pumpkin on her head, in another, she reportedly bared her midsection.

George was obsessed with ridding himself of the loathsome Caroline. Investigations by English authorities ensued to gather evidence of her affairs. Spies literally watched her and her home, and took reports of her sleeping arrangements on various trips. Reports came back to George. She'd shared a sleeper, shared a tent, and shared a bath with her lover. Evidence was collected by a committee of the House of Lords and put in a green bag—an item that became an icon for cartoonists and satirists.

Another obsession George could not quite fulfill was his love of fine things, including gemstones. John Mawe had dedicated the 1813 and 1815 editions of his book "by permission" to His Royal Highness the Prince Regent:

> It appeared that a Treatise on Gems and Precious Stones
> which not exclusively appropriated to the service of the
> great, should be with peculiar propriety, be inscribed to your
> Royal Highness, whose exalted Rank and acknowledged
> Taste, render you Sir, the natural Patron of the most rare and
> beautiful productions of the Mineral Kingdom.[6]

In 1816 Rundell and Bridge regained possession of the famed Pigot diamond. According to company accounts, they tried to sell it to the Prince Regent for £30,000 to no avail. George was in such debt and so short of cash at the time, he could not make the purchase. They eventually sold it to the Pasha of Egypt, who later presented it to the Sultan of Turkey. But if George could not afford the Pigot, neither could he afford Eliason's Blue.

George did have other sources for diamonds—his own relatives. When his daughter Charlotte died in childbirth in 1817, he reclaimed her jewels, including the famous Stuart Sapphire, from her husband, Prince Leopold of Belgium. He claimed the sapphire was a Crown Jewel, but then years later proceeded to let his mistress, Lady Conyngham, wear it at his coronation. He took his mother's gems, among them the famous Arcot diamonds, upon her death in 1818. This represented a serious commingling of family heirlooms and state gems, which George failed to acknowledge. The pattern continued for years until his father's death.

George wanted gems for his own ornamentation. As reported by one of Rundell and Bridge's key employees:

> the splendour of the Prince Regent was such that having received all the Principal orders from the various Sovereigns of Europe, he commissioned Rundell, Bridge, and Rundell to make the whole of the stars and badges of these orders in diamonds and jewels, and some of these orders he had duplicates and even triplicates and these were made as splendid as possible without reference to expense. His Royal Highness had the Golden Fleece of both Austria and Spain, the St. Esprit and St. Louis of France, St. Ferdinand of Spain, Tower and Sword and Christ of Portugal, St. Januarius Ferdinand of Naples, Elephant of Denmark, Tower and Sword of Sweden, William of the Netherlands, & c., & c.[7]

George was not satisfied with what were called "investiture" pieces of his knightly insignia. As was customary in some of the orders, like that of the Golden Fleece, each knight could elaborate the insignia according to his own personal taste. George, who, as a contemporary noted, "had an encyclopedic knowledge of uniforms and decorations," did this with a passion, particularly with the Golden Fleece. A satirical cartoon of the period captured George's vanity.

This is THE MAN—all shaven and shorn,
All cover'd with Orders—and all forlorn;

Among George's 7,000 or so jewelry bills in the Royal Archives, which I diligently searched at Windsor Castle, there are 21 transactions for repairs to, resettings of, and purchases of various Golden Fleeces. Most of these were with Rundell and Bridge, but some are not, as for example, when in 1817 George ordered a Spanish Golden Fleece to be made by another jeweler, T. Lauriere.

Lawrence painted another portrait of George in 1818, with George wearing the robes of the Order of the Garter. Several versions of this

George bedecked with medals and orders.

painting depict a Golden Fleece. Most do not. In several versions, there is a blue gem set in the insignia. It appears faceted as it reflects light, but the proportions are not consistent with Eliason's gemstone.[8]

O n January 20, 1820, the long infirm King George III died. The Prince Regent became King George IV, though his coronation would not take place for another year. George IV was now free to feed his own excesses, which meant ridding himself completely of Caroline and spending England's money on gems, architecture, and other extravagances.

He issued an order immediately forbidding mention of Caroline in the liturgy, contrary to a long tradition wherein every parish church in the country named the King and Queen in their prayers. George arranged for Parliament to offer Caroline a huge annual stipend of £50,000 to stay away on the Continent, renounce the crown and give him a divorce. Caroline refused and expressed her intention to return to England to claim her place as Queen. George threatened to have her tried for adultery.

He also started spending money on jewelry and gems. In one day at the Royal Jewelers, he bought a £8,216 diamond circlet for his cap of state, a £5,988 diamond encrusted "sword of state," and other items for a total of £15,906—equivalent to a $1.3 million shopping spree today. He started planning for his coronation, one of the crowns for which would alone cost tens of thousands of pounds. Now George had money, and Eliason still had a diamond worthy of purchase.

Exactly when George IV bought Eliason's blue diamond is not known—no bill or receipt or record of purchase has been found.

Mawe makes first mention of George's acquisition in the 1823 edition of his book, writing that the "superlatively fine blue diamond weighing 44 carats and valued at £30,000 formerly the property of Mr. Eliason, an eminent Diamond merchant is now said to be in the possession of our most gracious sovereign."[9] That sovereign would be King George IV. Mawe would not have made this claim lightly; he'd known George for at least a decade, maybe two, and viewed him as a patron. The acquisition was also reported by John Murray, a member of various scientific societies, who actually called the blue diamond the "George IV diamond"[10] in his *Memoir of a Diamond*, published in 1831. Murray also attributed the sale to Mr. Eliason, but at a price of £22,000. Murray indicated its weight at 29½ carats, but allowed that he may have gotten that wrong given the 44-carat blue cited by Mawe. An article in *Dumfries-Courier*, a newspaper of the Scottish borderland, also identified the blue diamond as the "George IV" diamond.

Mawe noted in flowery language that the blue diamond

> from its rarity and color, might have been estimated at a higher sum. It has found its most worthy destination in passing into the possession of a monarch, whose refined taste has ever been conspicuous in the highest degree.[11]

Mawe's description encoded two important details. The first provided a defense of George IV's spending habits. In this 1823 edition he notes that the 67-carat French Blue was valued at £100,000; George's new 44-carat Blue seems like a bargain at £30,000. Mawe's backhanded compliment makes George, with a reputation for extravagance, seem thrifty.

The second concerned the relationship of the two blue diamonds. Mawe goes out of his way to disconnect the diamonds—describing George's as a *deep sapphire blue* and the French gem as being a *fine light blue*—essentially "lightening up" the gem he'd described in his earlier editions.

Mawe never saw the French Blue and had no direct way to compare its color to George's new diamond, so he couldn't have been confused. More likely his effort to distinguish the diamonds was a purposeful way of not causing George IV any problems with the restored French King. Mawe knew how symbolically important the large blue diamond could be, writing:

> Diamonds of larger size are, and ever have been, rare; and
> of the most celebrated for magnitude and beauty, the
> whole number in Europe scarcely amounts to half a dozen,
> all of which are in the possession of sovereign Princes.
> Hence the acquisition of a moderately large diamond, is
> what mere money cannot always command; and many are
> the favors, both political and personal, that have been
> offered for a diamond of uncommon beauty, where its
> commercial price in hard cash, neither could be tendered
> nor would be received.[12]

If it were publicly established that the George IV diamond was cut from the French Blue, it could create a problem. King Louis XVIII might have asked for it to be returned, creating a personal and national crisis for the new English King.

Caroline returned to England on June 20, 1820, to claim the crown and face trial. Upon landing in Dover, she was greeted by a large crowd of common folk, a band, and a parade of tradesmen and fishermen carrying banners and shouting slogans. Her return to London was tumultuous and triumphant. A huge crowd of 200,000 people gathered to greet her, lining her march into the city. Her return and her persecution prompted an outpouring of popular poetry, cartoons, artwork, and song.

The House of Lords initiated a Pains and Penalties Bill on July 5 to try her for the treasonous crime of adultery, using evidence gathered during the various investigations. Her cause was taken up by the Whigs against the royalist Tories. England's lower and middle class saw her as the wronged underdog, a symbol of their own battles with the aristocracy and a wasteful, hypocritical King. During the months of her trial some 100,000 people turned out for Caroline in Piccadilly Circus. Hundreds of thousands lined the Thames as she sailed its course. She became a popular folk heroine, while the King went into virtual hiding. An antiroyal spirit gripped the country— some feared a "Jacobin Revolution more bloody than that of France," and Caroline became its symbol.

There was little question of Caroline's impropriety. Cartoons and newspapers amply satirized both the King and the Queen. As Caroline passed by the crowds, they yelled, "Long live King Austin," presuming him to be her illegitimate son. All sorts of jokes were told about her sexual behavior. But the sense was that the laws that applied such an obvious double standard to the acts of the King on one hand, and the Queen on the other, mirrored the situation between the aristocracy and the rest of the English populace.

The trial continued for months beginning in the third week of August and concluding the first week of November. Evidence in the "green bag" was sent over to the Lords, who filled the chamber each day to hear the testimony. Witnesses were called to report on the arrangement of bedrooms at Villa d'Este, and who was seen in what type of clothing coming out of whose bedroom. There was testimony about chamber pots and stains on bedclothes, about a bottle used by Pergami for urinating while sharing a carriage with Caroline, and about whether or not the Princess's hand was actually seen in Mr. Pergami's underwear. Several key witnesses against the

Queen disappeared en route to London from Italy. Other witnesses were intimidated from testifying. The Queen attended, and in a painting by George Hayter is dramatically immortalized—as she sits, a sole woman, the spirited but injured Queen, facing the full weight of the House of Lords.

A sad commentary on the political state of the Kingdom, the trial was a mockery, an amusement, and a diversion. In the end, the testimony was inconclusive. There was no direct eyewitness account of the Queen caught in the act of adultery. The Lords could not muster the votes needed to convict the Queen. Caroline and the people won. Bonfires, street parties, and celebrations followed.

Queen Caroline on trial.

P ublicly and in her correspondence, Queen Caroline was always quite respectful to her husband the King. She was the injured wife, the loyal subject, and the proper Queen. Her letters to the King and England's top officials are masterful, both in language and logic, ever demonstrating the impropriety and hypocrisy of George IV, while maintaining correct decorum. Privately, she confided that she could "blow George off the throne." Sir Walter Scott called Caroline a "Bedlam bitch of a Queen."[13]

As preparations for the official coronation proceeded in 1821, the question was would Caroline also be crowned? In May, less than two months before the coronation, an aide came to King George IV:

"Your bitterest enemy is dead," reported the royal attendant.

"Is *she,* by God?" responded the King.[14]

No, it was Napoleon, not Caroline.

George's coronation was set for July 19, 1821. This was a huge and expensive undertaking, with a cost of over £238,000—about $20 million today. Rundell and Bridge rented diamonds and gems for the coronation ceremony, charging them to a state account, rather than the personal account of the King. The Royal Jewelers found that the old crown was filled with largely worthless stones, paste, glass, and fake gems. George ordered two new crowns: a state crown bedecked with some five pounds of gems for the ceremony itself, and a lighter crown for the following festivities. A large blue sapphire one inch wide and one and a half inches long was set into the more elaborate crown. Various sources across the world would later report that instead of a sapphire, this was a large, deep blue diamond, the "George IV."[15] The reports were probably incorrect. King of Arms George Nayler offered detailed descriptions and drawings of the crown and the rented and purchased gems. And even though some of his drawings made before

King George IV in coronation robes.

the ceremony are themselves incorrect, the documentation on the crown is quite extensive.

For the coronation, George IV wore his knightly orders—the Bath, the Thistle, the Garter, and the Golden Fleece as depicted in Naylor's large-scale illustrations. Immediately after the coronation, the King sat for Lawrence so that he could paint a full-length portrait of him in his coronation robes. Lawrence used the 1818 pose as the basis for this, turning the Garter robes into the coronation regalia.

Lawrence himself, as well as his associates, executed several versions of this painting. In many of these, George is depicted with the Golden Fleece. Some, such as Lawrence's original, depict a more traditional Burgundian variety with a round blue stone at its center. Other variants represent a more elaborate Golden Fleece, one with a deep, sapphire blue, faceted gem, another with a light blue stone.

It is impossible to conclude that George IV wore the famed blue diamond at his coronation, either in his crown or in the Golden Fleece. But if he did, it could be no coincidence that he placed it in the same insignia as used by the French kings. If Mawe knew the diamond was derived from the French Blue, so too did George, his patron. George was doubtlessly familiar with the rumors of the Brunswick bribe, and may have suspected, if he did not outright know, that Caroline had possessed the diamond. Thus he would have enjoyed being crowned while wearing a trophy of his triumph over both Napoleon and Caroline.

While the English populace had supported Caroline against the injustice of her trial, they were not ready to rally around her formal installation as Queen. Caroline offered a compromise. She was willing to be crowned a few days after George.

But she still felt it important to attend the ceremony. Caroline went to Westminster Abbey the morning of the coronation. Guards blocked the doors. Crowds gathered. Some cheered "The Queen, The Queen, The Queen Forever" and encouraged her; others cried out "Shame, Shame," and "Off, Off." When Caroline came forward with her retinue, the guards asked her for her ticket of admission. They would not give way for the Queen. Caroline was humiliated; turned away, she retreated to her apartments.

The coronation dispirited Caroline. She died of a bowel obstruction and other complications on August 7. She faced death bravely, and admitted that she had hoodwinked the investigating committees by appointing William Austin her heir to all her possessions. She wished her body to be sent back to Brunswick and she desired to have written on her tomb, "Caroline, The Injured Queen of England." Upon her death, her coffin was sent back, along with a crown of England, and now rests in the church in Brunswick. Her father's coffin, contrary to the declaration of Napoleon, was also returned to Brunswick, and rests in a nearby nave.

King George IV in 1822.

In 1822 after Caroline's death, George sat for another Lawrence portrait. This painting depicts George in civilian clothes wearing his Order of the Golden Fleece. One of the gems depicted in the painted insignia is the blue diamond, argued the Smithsonian's Winters and White.

The portrait was commissioned specifically for the Marchioness Conyngham, George's latest and last mistress. The picture's setting is probably her home, Hertford House. The painting may have been a make-up gift from George to Lady Conyngham, following a series of spats between the two. The gift followed a familiar pattern, as just the previous November George had given Lady Conyngham a miniature portrait of

himself framed by real diamonds. In the painting, the
Fleece is incredibly elaborate, far
more so than any of the other
Fleeces depicted or mentioned
in George's collection of jewels.
The original painting hangs in
the Wallace Collection, a private
museum in London. There are
at least two full-length and several half-length versions of the
painting on record.

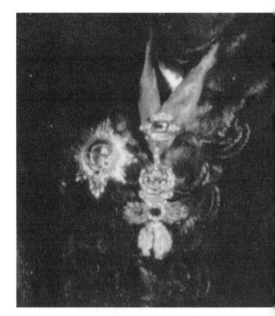

The blue gem depicted in
this painting is an exceptionally
good match with the George
IV diamond, as I was able to
discern during a visit to the

Detail of the Golden Fleece.

Wallace Collection. Visual inspection of the painting confirmed
the deep blue sapphire color. Holding a glass replica of the diamond up to the painted version—much to the amusement of the
gallery's guards, it was clear that the size and the shape seemed to
match exceedingly well. The actual diamond has a particular
asymmetry; it is straighter along one edge and more oval along its
opposite. In the painting, this slight asymmetry is apparent. When
I compared the diamond's actual measurements to the photographic reproductions of the painting, this was confirmed. The
width to length proportion of the diamond depicted in the painting is almost a precise match to the real gem.

There is no record of George doing anything further with the
blue diamond after this portrait. There are no other paintings or
engravings depicting its use. While George did have work done on
new versions of the Golden Fleece by the Royal Jewelers, none of the
bills indicate the resetting of the blue diamond.

※ ※ ※

George IV died on June 26, 1830. His written will, made in 1796, left all his worldly possessions to "my true and real Wife, to my Maria Fitzherbert, my Wife, the Wife of my heart and soul." The Duke of Wellington, who had become Tory Prime Minister in 1828, was appointed as the executor of the King's estate.

Complicating the situation was a verbal will made a few weeks before George's death leaving all his jewels to Lady Conyngham. Lady Conyngham at first disclaimed the bequest, earning the Duke's rare praise, as he generally regarded her as vain, petty, and self-interested. Then Conyngham reneged, claiming that she could not in good conscience refuse the King's request. Wellington confronted her. He reminded Conyngham of the terrible fate that had befallen the mistress of Louis XV, who had claimed his treasures. She had, Wellington pointedly noted, lost both her ill-gotten wealth and her head.

There was widespread concern that the greedy Lady Conyngham and her cuckold husband, Francis, the Lord Steward of the Household, would swipe George's gems. Cartoonists lambasted

The Conynghams loot George's treasures.

Lady Conyngham's avarice, depicting her making off with bags and wheelbarrows full of loot.

Apparently there was truth to the allegations. Bridge's man reports in his memoir that the "lady in question took possession of some diamonds after the demise of George IV."[16] She took the other gems she claimed were given to her as gifts by the King. The Duke of Wellington aggressively pursued their return, noting that some of the jewels might have been improperly taken and some may have been Crown property, improperly given.

On September 16, 1830, Bridge conducted an inventory of George's jewels. This was no easy task. Bridge did not have all the documentation, as George IV ordered various records destroyed before his death. The Conynghams had taken gems. Two reports resulted: *An Account of Sundry Crown Jewels received from His Majesty per Sir Henry Wheatley and showing . . . how the same were employed,* and *An Inventory taken of Sundry Crown Jewels etc. at Windsor Castle—16 Sept 1830—by Messrs. Bridge. . . .* But reconstructing that inventory to track the George IV diamond is problematic as only a copy of the former document survives.

According to Wellington's letters, published and unpublished, the Conynghams admitted to possessing hundreds of diamonds, jewelry that had belonged to Queen Charlotte, the Stuart Sapphire, hundreds of pearls, and a badge of the Order of the Bath. They provided a list to Wellington by the end of November, and duly returned the gems.

The status of many of George's gems was questionable, as Wellington, his successor William IV, and others had to distinguish which jewels might have been personal property or family heirlooms or state property—each of which had different consequences for inheritance. William IV held that the Stuart Sapphire, for one, was George's personal property, and thus was properly gifted by him to Lady Conyngham. Wellington was dismayed, but loyally followed his new King's orders, and returned the gem to the despised lady—though he, in ensuing years, persuaded Conyngham's son to return the gem; Queen Victoria wore it in her coronation crown in 1838.

The resolution of ownership of George's jewels was complicated. Since he had held the crowns of both Great Britain and of Hanover, the state property of each had to be separated. Both had to be distinguished from his personal property. Most of the gems passed into the possession of King William IV, who took a few of the gems for himself. George had at least four different versions of the Golden Fleece. The one pictured in Lawrence's 1822 painting was probably listed as the "Badge of the Golden Fleece, richly ornamented with jewels and precious stones." The gems from this and various other insignia were dissembled and in most cases turned over to Bridge for resale.

Lady Hamilton, a diarist close to Queen Caroline and often critical of the royal family, writes in her 1832 *Secret History of the Court of England,* that

> nothing satisfactory was said [*by the executors*] about the jewels of his Royal Highness, which were valued a very few days after his death, and were calculated as being worth £150,000 . . . These jewels, we are aware, were carried down to Windsor by desire of his majesty, but how they were disposed of remains to be explained.[17]

William IV and the Duke of Wellington, realizing the massive extent of George's debt, may have sought to alleviate it without provoking public scandal—much in the way the new King wanted a simple coronation to avoid the appearance of his brother's extravagance. Given that the trusted John Bridge was retiring, the quick and quiet disposal of expensive gems to insiders may have seemed best.

The Hope family could help. Members of this incredibly wealthy London family had known George IV for decades, were familiar within the royal household, and were friends with the Duke of Wellington. One of the Hopes had the preeminent diamond collection in all of Britain, and would surely want and be willing to discreetly pay for the rare blue George IV diamond.

13

HOPE'S COLLECTIBLE

I**t is by the name of Hope** that we today know the diamond derived from the "Tavernier Violet," and then cut from the "French Blue of the Crown," to form the "George IV diamond"—although when it was first formally recorded in Henry Philip Hope's *Collection of Pearls and Precious Stones,* it was modestly designated as "No 1."

Henry Philip Hope was born in 1774 into an originally French, then Scottish, family of wealthy merchant traders and bankers who'd been active in Amsterdam for generations and established their firm, Hope & Company, in London in 1762. They first traded tea, tobacco, textiles, and precious metals internationally. Later they provided major loans to national governments, including Russia, Sweden, Spain, and Portugal. Monarchs came to the Hopes and other merchant bankers for money to acquire lands, raise armies, and fight wars. In 1803, with war with England looming and needing cash, Napoleon decided to sell Louisiana for 80 million francs, having just acquired the territory a few years before through his conquest of Spain. Napoleon figured that he could not defend the territory given the need for thousands of troops to quell slave revolts in the French Caribbean colony of Haiti and the extension of England's superior sea power into the region. Hope & Company and Baring of London made the loan to the United States to finance the Louisiana Purchase. Napoleon used the money to fight against England, Russia, Prussia, and Austria. In return, those nations too sought loans from the banks to raise their armies and fight Napoleon.

The Hopes, like other merchant bankers, were in the vanguard of a newly evolving European society, more disciplined and rational, more engaged in trade, industry, and the generation of wealth than the monarchical order. That order, already successfully challenged in the American and French Revolutions, was dying. It was the ability to acquire raw materials, market finished goods, draw upon dependable sources of capital, and channel wealth to stable, productive investments that made for a healthy nation—not the preservation of aristocratic privilege. Merchant trade, industrialization, railroad building, urbanization, reform of the civil code, and educational and economic systems were under way throughout Europe. A series of uprisings across Europe in 1830 pointed to the increasing fragility and viability of kingship. Monarchy was an endangered institution. Just as the ability of Mughals and Oriental rulers to hold on to their power and wealth had been challenged by the British, Dutch, and French East India Companies, so too were European monarchies being challenged by mercantile capitalism. And just as with the loss of power Indian diamonds had previously made their way to European rulers, so too were the jewels in the possession of European royalty being dispersed, sold off to the newly rich and powerful merchant class.

Henry Philip Hope and his brothers, Thomas Hope and Adrian Elias Hope, were beneficiaries of mercantile success, rather than its producers. It was their grandfather, Thomas Hope, his brother Adrian and their cousin Henry who generated millions for Hope & Company, and ultimately for the family when the Hopes sold out to Baring by 1813.

Though a man of considerable means, Henry Philip Hope lived quite modestly, unlike his more famous and flamboyant elder brother Thomas. He never married, nor had any children. He was said to be "munificent in his charities." He was one of a number of wealthy collectors in Europe, following in a tradition at least conceptually traceable to the Medicis and other merchants of Venice who formed their cabinets—personal, private museums—for enjoyment and contemplation. Henry may have developed his interest as a result of the Hopes' trade in diamonds and their support of the diamond cutting industry in Amsterdam prior to his having fled the city as a youth in the wake of the French revolutionary wars.

Henry Philip Hope.

It was through Thomas that the blue diamond came to Henry Philip. Thomas Hope was an eminent author of the era, and an expert in decorative arts and design. In 1802, he designed a silver-gilt tea urn with Greco-Egyptian motifs that had been adapted by the Prince of Wales as the style for the royal grand service. Thomas shared with Prince George a fascination with Oriental design, and was drawn into a number of decorative projects at George's Brighton. The writer Lord George Byron called Thomas Hope the "house furnisher withal."[1] Hope served on the Prince Regent's committee for rebuilding the Royal Theatre and advised on Flemish and Dutch paintings. Both were collectors. George bought a Dutch masters collection from Baring, the Hope family's banking firm partners.

The relationship extended to other family members. Thomas's wife, Louisa, was a Lady of the Bedchamber for the King—a largely honorary role, providing status for the nontitled Hope family. Thomas's son, Henry Thomas Hope, was also one of the Lords of the Bedchamber for George IV.

The Hopes had also developed a close relationship with the Duke of Wellington, though it had not started out so well. Louisa aspired to aristocratic status, and in 1823 instigated a scheme with her husband

Thomas Hope.

to enlist an intermediary to approach the Duke of Wellington, offering him a huge £10,000 bribe if he would help them obtain a baronet—and thus a peerage—making them aristocrats. Wellington was outraged. He uncovered the fact that the Hopes were behind the bribery attempt but did not prosecute the matter further because he did not want to expose the famed, and Crown-friendly Thomas Hope. By 1828, Wellington was a family friend. He dined at the Hopes' home, and surely knew of Henry Philip's collection. Louisa was a close friend to Wellington's companion and confidant, Mrs. Arbuthnot.

Wellington, as George IV's executor, most likely sold the blue diamond, discreetly, to the Hopes in 1830. Later accounts report the bargain price as £18,000, though no records have been found.

Henry Philip's collection of hundreds of diamonds, emeralds, pearls, and other precious gems was kept in a mahogany cabinet with sixteen drawers—each drawer generally representing a particular category of gem. The collection was valued at the time at about £150,000, or the equivalent of about $15 million in today's currency. For Henry, gems were "specimens," admired for their intrinsic characteristics, not their historical associations or uses. The gems were labeled and numbered. The blue diamond was placed in drawer 16, along with other larger stones. It was an outstanding collectible, admired for its beauty and rarity, a most valuable acquisition.

Several years later, Henry Philip Hope hired gemologist Bram Hertz to compile a catalogue of his collection that was published in 1839. Hertz describes the blue diamond, which is designated "No. 1," as:

A most magnificent and rare brilliant, of deep sapphire blue, of the greatest purity, and most beautifully cut; it is of true proportions, not too thick, nor too spread. This matchless gem combines the beautiful colour of the sapphire with the prismatic fire and brilliancy of the diamond, and, on account of its extraordinary colour, great size, and other fine qualities, it certainly may be called unique.[2]

Hertz gives the weight of the diamond as 177 grains (equivalent to 44¼ carats) and provides a top-view, full-scale drawing with a mistaken caption of "176 Gr."

Hope's "No. 1," set in medallion.

The catalog entry stresses the unique nature of the diamond. No mention is made of it being the George IV diamond. Nor is anything said about a possible connection to the French Blue. Hertz writes, "In vain do we search for any record of a gem which can, in point of curiosity, beauty, and perfection, be compared with this blue brilliant."[3] As a gemologist, Hertz surely knew full well about the French Blue. Hertz, presumably with Henry Philip Hope's guidance, purposefully avoided any mention of the diamond's history, perhaps not wanting to unnecessarily complicate Hope's legitimate ownership of the gem.

Hertz notes that the diamond is mounted on a "medallion, with a border en arabesque of small rose diamonds, surrounded by 20 brilliants of equal size, shape and cutting, and of the finest water, and averaging four grains each."[4] Clearly the blue diamond had been removed from the Golden Fleece and reset.

Hertz writes—with a non-cited reference to Mawe, that the diamond was once priced at £30,000, but could have been bought at an even higher sum. He asserts, "We may presume that there exists no cabinet, nor any collection of crown jewels in the world, which can boast of the possession of so curious and fine a gem."[5]

Hertz's treatment of the blue diamond and the collection as a whole provides a commentary on how the attainments of the royal class were shifting to the wealthy class. Hertz describes the necessities for putting together Hope's collection.

> It is only as the result of the rare combination of the most
> refined taste, the highest and most ardent love for the
> beautiful productions of nature, and the abundant means
> of procuring them, that so rare and unique an assemblage
> of precious gems has been brought together; an assemblage
> which, from the number of magnificent and unique
> specimens is unrivalled. . . .[6]

The blue diamond, sold by the King's impoverished estate to Hope, signaled that the ability to realize refinement depended upon wealth. This epitomized the transformation of power that would characterize 19th century and early 20th century Europe.

Henry Philip Hope died in 1839. His *Gentleman's Magazine* obituary noted his charitable giving, his habits "of the most simple and unostentatious nature," and his collection—one of the most perfect collections of diamonds and precious stones that has, perhaps, ever been possessed by a private individual.[7]

His closest relatives and heirs were his nephews, Henry Thomas, Adrian, and Alexander Hope, the three sons of his celebrated brother Thomas. When Thomas died in 1831, he'd left £180,000 to his wife, Louisa, and his sons. Henry Thomas, the eldest, got the art collection and the family's London home on Duchess Street. Louisa got the mansion and estate at Deepdene in Surrey, which she left to Henry Thomas the following year when she married Lord William Beresford. In 1834, Henry Philip's other brother, Adrian Elias, had died without will or children. Some £500,000 worth of property came to

Henry Philip, and £193,000 to each of the three nephews. Henry Philip also gave Louisa £37,000. Thus, by the time Henry Philip Hope passed away, the nephews were already amazingly wealthy.

Henry Philip had written a letter to his three nephews, to be delivered posthumously, advising them "to cherish and cultivate a fraternal regard and affectionate feelings for each other, and not to dishonour or disparage the memory of your parents and uncles by unworthy differences among yourselves."[8] His will left them each £30,000 in cash and a division of his properties. But left out of the will was the disposition of the gem collection.

The collection became a subject of great dispute among the three brothers when deeds drafted by Henry Philip concerning the matter came to light. The first, from 1821, gave the collection to an unnamed nephew that Henry Thomas Hope argued meant him. The second and third deeds, respectively from 1832 and 1838, named Alexander Hope as the beneficiary. What ensued was years of fraternal argument, vitriol, and lawsuit for control of the immensely valuable collection. Given that Henry Thomas and Alexander were both Members of Parliament and that the Hopes were involved in high society, the dispute was well known—even by Queen Victoria, who had assumed the throne in 1838. Benjamin Disraeli, a Member of Parliament at the time, and later Prime Minister, knew the Hopes personally. He commented,

> The three brothers Hope, though the wealth of the whole family had become concentrated in them, were always at war. There were some famous jewels, which had belonged to their uncle Philip Hope, which were a fruitful subject of litigation. There was a blue diamond that all the brothers wanted. They hated each other.[9]

Looking back on the internecine battle, one author noted that, "Henry and Adrian were so intent on keeping the jewels out of Alexander's clutches that they even suggested selling the lot and using the money to found 'some institution for the benefit of mankind.' "[10]

Mother Louisa defended Alexander. In the end, after a decade of dispute, the brothers finally settled. Henry Thomas received the Hope diamond and seven other important gems, Adrian inherited property, and Alexander came into possession of the huge Hope pearl and some 700 other gems and precious stones; Louisa kept her money.

Louisa died in 1851. With his mother gone, Henry Thomas married his longtime French mistress Anne Adéle Bichat, who had, some 10 years before, given birth to an illegitimate daughter. They moved into the new London home he had built at 116 Piccadilly.

The issue of ownership settled, Alexander began to sell the diamonds he had inherited from his uncle. Bram Hertz, cataloger of the Hope collection, served as a middleman.

Henry Thomas was willing to show off his blue diamond and other gems. He became the deputy chairman of a group putting together the section on precious metals and jewelry to be mounted for London's Great Exhibition of 1851 to take place in the marvelous Crystal Palace. The Great Exhibition was a benchmark for the Victorian era, displaying all sorts of machinery, weapons, models, scientific equipment and processes, craftwork, and gems to 6 million British and foreign visitors. It defined the genre of 19th century World Expositions. Among the featured items was the Koh-i-Nur diamond, recently acquired by the British East India Company and presented to Queen Victoria.

Henry Thomas's brother Alexander must have cooperated in the display effort, for according to a catalog, "28 diamonds of the late Henry Philip Hope" were exhibited, including in section 7, number 73, a diamond of 177 grains "tinged . . . with blue as Mr. Hope's."[11]

But before the blue diamond went on public display, someone else expressed interest in seeing it. It was the same collector who had started buying Hope's gems through Hertz; someone whom Hertz thought would give them the same loving attention as had Henry Philip. That collector turned out to be none other than Charles, Duke of Brunswick, the nephew of the "injured" Queen Caroline and the grandson of Carl Wilhelm Ferdinand.

14

BRUNSWICK'S OBSESSION

*C*harles *of Brunswick thought he had* the missing piece of a historical puzzle.

With the publication of the Hope catalog, it was inevitable that someone would formally make the connection between the 44¼-carat blue Hope diamond and the 67³/₁₆-carat French Blue. On April 16, 1850, Charles of Brunswick contacted Henry Thomas Hope asking if he could see the notable blue diamond. Hope wrote back[1]

> Absence from London has prevented me from replying to your letter before this time. If his Royal Highness the Duke of Brunswick will name any morning except Saturday at which I will be [*unreadable*] to him to call at my house at about twelve o'clock. I will have the pleasure of showing to him the blue brilliant.
>
> I have the honor to be your obedient servant,
>
> Henry Th. Hope

They arranged a visit. Brunswick, who briefly noted his daily activities, records the visit at 5 p.m. on May 17, 1850.

Charles had to know a good bit about Hope's Blue, for he had been buying and selling diamonds since 1828 with Bram Hertz, the elder Hope's cataloger. In the 1840s, he saw Hertz regularly. By November 1849 Hertz was selling some of Hope's diamonds to Brunswick. Given the terms of the Hope inheritance settlement, most of these diamonds must have come from younger brother Alexander, but a few might be from Henry Thomas.

Brunswick was a major collector, who after his death was labeled the "Diamond Duke."[2] He amassed thousands of diamonds. He compiled the histories of famous diamonds and had models produced of them, which eventually ended up in Geneva's natural history museum. He had a very specific reason for visiting Hope and personally inspecting the blue diamond. A few years later, the suspicion that the Hope diamond was cut from the French Blue was published by a fellow Parisian and French gemologist Charles Barbot in *Traité Complet des Pierres Précieuses.*[3]

If the Hope brothers seemed contentious, litigious, and off-putting, they had nothing on Charles and his family. Charles was born Carl Frederick Augustus Wilhelm in Brauschweig in 1804, just as Napoleon was battling with Charles's grandfather, Duke of Brunswick Carl Wilhelm Ferdinand, for control of the region. The elder Duke was killed, the estate was pillaged, and the family, with valuables and jewels, fled to England. Wilhelm, son of the elder Duke and brother of Princess Caroline, succeeded to the title, and lived under the protection of English King George III who simultaneously served as the King of Hanover—the German state that encompassed the Duchy of Brunswick-Lüneburg.

Duke Charles of Brunswick.

In 1813 Wilhelm completed a codicil to his will. As the eldest son, Charles, or Carl II as he is often referred to, would inherit the Duchy. Other valuables would be split between Charles and his brother William, who was younger by two years. Given that Hanover and Brunswick had a formal agreement regarding the reciprocal guardianship for royalty that had not yet

The Brunswick - Hanover Genealogy

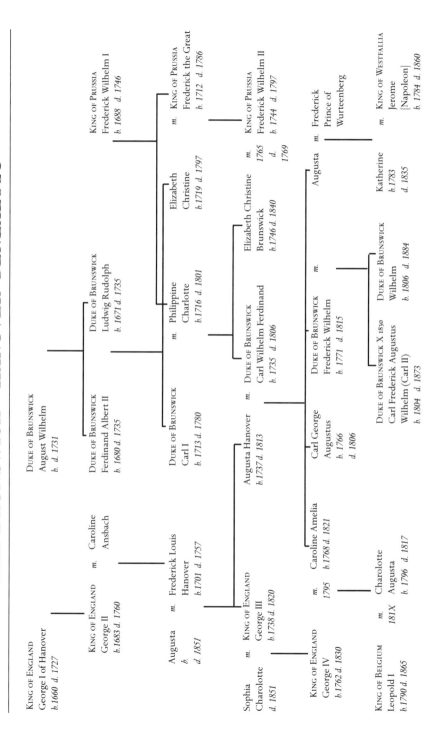

KING OF ENGLAND
George I of Hanover
b. 1660 d. 1727

DUKE OF BRUNSWICK
August Wilhelm
b. d. 1731

KING OF PRUSSIA
Frederick Wilhelm I
b. 1688 d. 1746

m. KING OF PRUSSIA
Frederick the Great
b. 1712 d. 1786

Caroline
Ansbach

DUKE OF BRUNSWICK
Ferdinand Albert II
b. 1680 d. 1735

DUKE OF BRUNSWICK
Ludwig Rudolph
b. 1671 d. 1735

Elizabeth
Christine
b. 1719 d. 1797

KING OF PRUSSIA
Frederick Wilhelm II
b. 1744 d. 1797

m. Frederick Louis
Hanover
b. 1701 d. 1757

m. Philippine
Charlotte
b. 1716 d. 1801

DUKE OF BRUNSWICK
Carl I
b. 1713 d. 1780

Elizabeth Christine
b. 1746 d. 1840

m. 1765
d.
1769

Frederick
Prince of
Wurteenberg

KING OF WESTFALLIA
Jerome
[Napoleon]
b. 1784 d. 1860

Augusta
b.
d. 1851

Augusta Hanover
b. 1737 d. 1813

Elizabeth Christine
Brunswick

m. DUKE OF BRUNSWICK
Carl Wilhelm Ferdinand
b. 1735 d. 1806

DUKE OF BRUNSWICK
Frederick Wilhelm
b. 1771 d. 1815

Augusta

m.

Katherine
b. 1783
d. 1835

m.

Sophia
Charolotte
d. 1851

m. KING OF ENGLAND
George III
b. 1738 d. 1820

Caroline Amelia
b. 1768 d. 1821

Carl George
Augustus
b. 1766
d. 1806

DUKE OF BRUNSWICK
Wilhelm
b. 1806 d. 1884

m. 1795

KING OF ENGLAND
George IV
b. 1762 d. 1830

DUKE OF BRUNSWICK X 1830
Carl Frederick Augustus
Wilhelm (Carl II)
b. 1804 d. 1873

Charolotte
Augusta
b. 1796 d. 1817

KING OF BELGIUM
Leopold I
b. 1790 d. 1865

m. 181X

reached the age of majority, the trustee and executor of the Brunswick estate would be the functioning sovereign of Hanover, which, because of George III's incapacity at the time, was none other than the uncle of the two young Brunswicks, Caroline's husband, Prince Regent George. When, in 1815, Wilhelm was mortally wounded fighting Napoleon's army near Waterloo, the title of the Duke of Brunswick fell to his son Charles. Given that he was only 11 years old, his guardian, Prince Regent George, took up management of the Brunswick property, estate, and possessions.

There is no record of what Prince Regent George IV did with those possessions over the next few years, though Charles was later to claim that his uncle had committed various "illegalities" that cast a "lasting disgrace on England." Charles, like his sister the embattled Caroline, alleged that the Prince Regent was usurping the Brunswick fortunes for his own venal purposes. In 1822, George IV, having become King, informed Charles and his brother that he intended to continue the guardianship indefinitely, even beyond Charles's 18th birthday. Charles wrote back, boldly asserting his hereditary right—to no avail.[4]

By 1823, Charles assumed the role of the Duke of Brunswick and returned to the Duchy, which he immediately proceeded to mismanage. George IV tried to get the ineffectual German Diet to declare Charles insane in order to strip him of his Duchy; others too recognized Charles's ineptitude; and finally in 1830, Charles was deposed. Charles went into exile with a fortune in cash, property titles, gold, and jewels valued at 8 million *thaler,* or probably over $100 million in today's dollars. He settled in Paris where he continued to call himself Duke Charles of Brunswick.

What followed over the course of decades were suits and countersuits, charges and countercharges. Charles sued his brother, his relatives, the Prussians, and the King of England and Hanover. His case in England went to the House of Commons and then the House of Lords, with the latter body deciding that the sovereign could not be sued. Brother William, who had taken over the Duchy and whom Charles called the "little usurper," counterclaimed that Charles had absconded with his inheritance, family heirlooms, and "diamonds and other precious stones, set and unset."[5]

From Paris, Charles launched his law suits and hatched various conspiracies to unseat his brother William. He loaned huge amounts of money to Napoleon Bonaparte's nephew, Louis Napoleon, who became President of France, and then Emperor Napoleon III in 1852. The Emperor apparently paid back the money well and on time. Charles hoped that Napoleon III would support the cause of his restoration of the Duchy of Brunswick by leading France to defeat Germany. Charles even had a written contract to that effect!

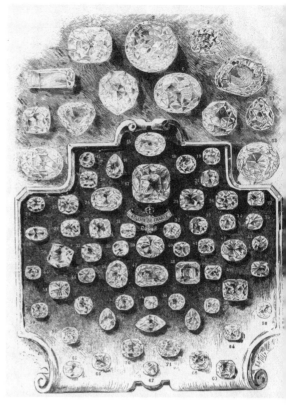

Napoleon III's model of the French Crown Jewels (with the blue diamond in the top row, right).

Charles began a diamond collection based upon those gems accumulated by his grandfather, great-grandparents, and diamond-loving great aunt. That collection grew over the decades to more than 2,000 cut stones, not counting numerous other gems, medallions, and jewelry. He annually bought scores of diamonds from the 1840s to the 1870s from major dealers, mainly in Paris and London. He recorded his sales in purchase books, noting the date, the price he paid, the number of carats, the shape and color of the diamond, the seller, and sometimes a comment. By 1860, urged by friends, he formally organized this information about his collection and published a *Catalogue de Brillants et Autres Pierres Précieuses.*

At the behest of Napoleon III, Charles followed the example of Henry Thomas Hope, and loaned several of his diamonds to the Paris International Exposition in 1855, the French follow-up to the Crystal Palace extravaganza. Charles's diamonds, and the models he had made of them, likely prompted Napoleon III and his diamond-loving Empress Eugenie to arrange for a similar set. Charles repeatedly said he would leave his fortune to Napoleon III and Eugenie, hoping they would make good on his contract—a hope unfulfilled with Napoleon III's loss of the Franco-Prussian War in 1870 and subsequent abdication.

As his diamond collection grew Charles became increasingly paranoid about its safety. More an armed fort than residence, his house was surrounded by a high wall topped with hundreds of iron spikes. He had belled alarms rigged throughout the property. His bedroom became, as one visitor commented, "a safe with wallpaper."[6] He kept his collection in a safe-cabinet connected to his bed, which was atop an iron chest. It was ingeniously equipped with spring-loaded pistols so that if someone tried to break in, four guns would fire at the thief. Charles also kept loaded guns next to his bed.

Charles accumulated all manner of weird people around him, some sycophants who supposedly, and foolishly, wanted him to be the Kaiser of all of Germany. As he grew older, he became increasingly eccentric. He wore a different wig each day. As an acquaintance commented, Charles "looks like a horoscope-reading charlatan, with a high hat and make-up on his eyes and eyebrows. He needed only a magic wand in the hand . . . to complete the picture."[7]

In 1870, with the defeat of France and the abdication of Napoleon III, Charles moved to Geneva. He lived in the Hotel Beau Rivage. According to visitors, he moved about his apartment in his underwear, wearing medals, heraldic orders, and diamonds. Outside, he "wandered about like a corpse dressed as a dandy."[8] He had a sultry mistress named Violetta.

Duke Charles of Brunswick died in 1873, having made a will leaving his possessions, valued at some 22 million *francs,* to the City of Geneva. About 4 million *francs* of this bequest went for a

Brunswick memorial sculpture in downtown Geneva. Visiting that memorial along the city's left bank, I could not help but be amused by Charles's gumption. The architecture copies that of the Duke of Scala of Verona—very elaborate and overstated. Charles is depicted in the most unlikely ways—heroically on horseback, and in his saint-adorned cathedral-like crypt the center of attention.

Among Charles's effects were some items, including jewelry, which the city returned to his brother William. While most of the inheritance was in stocks and bonds, his jewel collection was valued at an estimated two million *francs*. This the city auctioned off.

The auction of the Duke Charles of Brunswick collection was run by the Geneva firm of Rossel & Fils. It produced a detailed *Catalogue des Diamants, Saphirs, Emeraudes, Rubis, Bijoux, Argenterie*. The sale started on April 22, 1874, and was held in the Grande Salle de l'Institut, Palais Electoral in Geneva. Many important jewelry firms sent buyers from Paris, Vienna, London, Amsterdam, and Berlin; even the Shah of Persia and the Maharaja of Jaipur were represented according to the newspaper accounts.

The catalogue listed hundreds of diamonds, one of 80¾ carats, several of over 30 and 40 carats, and high quality colored brilliants. "*Un brillant bleu*," a blue diamond of 13¾ carats, is listed as lot number 37. The asking price listed was 14,700 *francs*, equivalent to $3,000 at the time, and $47,000 in today's dollars. The *Journal de Genève* reported that the 13-carat blue had been sold for 17,000 *francs*.[9] It was one of the more valuable items in the auction. Overall, sales of the auction amounted to over 990,000 *francs*, and included among other items the Duke's knightly orders and an enameled and jeweled insignia of the Order of the Golden Fleece that had been awarded to Charles by the King of Spain. A number of items were held over because they failed to meet the reserve price and in a few cases because their authenticity was questioned. It took the City some eight years to finally sell off all of Charles's collection.

*   *   *

A few years after Charles's death, in 1877, Edwin Streeter, a distinguished gemologist, member of the Royal Geographic Society, published his book *Precious Stones and Gems*. He argued, following Barbot as well as English gem historian C. W. King, that the Hope could have been cleaved and polished from the French Blue. In the six editions of his book as well as in his *The Great Diamonds of the World* published in subsequent years, Streeter went on to provide ever more elaborate accounts of the likely cleaving and of the smaller satellite or remnant stones created in the recrafting of the diamond. Streeter's view became the conventional one and acquired added legitimacy when he served as an expert authority for the English courts in deciding on the disposition of the Hope diamond in 1898.

Streeter noted the 23-carat difference in weight between the French Blue and the Hope and asked, "Was the weight lost simply in the cutter's hands, or were one or more pieces removed by simple cleavage, and preserved?"[10] He writes that the French Blue had a "drop form," which must have meant the existence of a cleavage plane just below its triangular end. Streeter hypothesized that "a triangular piece" could have been cleaved off of the French Blue. This would account for the Hope being straighter on one side than the other and for a satellite stone. The bottom edge of the remnant stone would correspond with the cleaved—that is, the straighter—edge of the Hope. It would also be identical in color to the Hope. Streeter initially supposed that such a stone would at first weigh about 10 or 11 carats before being finished off as a rose cut, and likely reduced to about 6 or 7 carats. He then goes on to say "such a stone did actually come into the market in the April of 1874" at the sale of the late Duke of Brunswick's jewels.[11]

In one edition, Streeter claims that competent judges examined the Brunswick Blue next to the Hope and found:

> in color and quality it bore a remarkable resem-
> blance . . . The conclusion that [*this diamond*] once formed the
> projecting side which appears to have characterized the
> original shape of the 'Hope brilliant' was inevitable.[12]

In his next edition, Streeter supposed the *finished* weight of the satellite stone to be "12 or 13 carats" and made a dramatic claim:

> The purchaser put the stone for a short time into my hands, and I examined it in juxtaposition with the Hope diamond. It is identical in colour and quality. I know not how to avoid the conclusion that the Duke of Brunswick's 'Blue Drop' diamond once formed the triangular salient gibbosity which formerly appears to have characterized the stone now known as the 'Hope' brilliant.[13]

In his 1877 *Precious Stones and Gems,* Streeter asserts that the French Blue was reduced into two fragments, the large one being the Hope and the smaller one being the Brunswick Blue. He later notes the purchase of the 13¾ carat Brunswick Blue by the Ochs Brothers of Paris, who obtained it for 17,000 *francs* or £680. Subsequently, Streeter offers that the French Blue was divided into three—the Hope, the Brunswick Blue, and a smaller, 1¼ carat fragment that he termed the "Pirie." Streeter asserts that this stone was purchased by Messrs. Hertz & Co. of Paris. Streeter then bought it from them in 1876 for £300, set it in a colored diamond butterfly and displayed it in his jewelry salon at 18 New Bond Street.

Streeter's account of the blue diamond is somewhat inconsistent. His very minimal financial interest—owning the small Pirie—can probably be discounted as the cause. Sloppy editing by his compilers is definitely a factor. But the changes in his account also seem to reflect increasing knowledge and familiarity with both the Hope and the Brunswick.

Streeter's model of the cutting of the blue diamond (from top to bottom the Tavernier Violet, the Pirie, the Brunswick Blue, and the Hope). The lower three together form the French Blue.

How likely is it that Streeter actually held the Hope, Brunswick, and Pirie in his temporary possession? One has reason to be skeptical, but then again, if anyone was in such a position to do so, it was Streeter. It could have happened sometime between his published accounts of 1879 and 1882. If he was temporarily given the Brunswick to inspect, he might have prevailed upon the Hope family to also inspect their gem. After all, there was precedent—Adele Hope might have remembered the May 1850 visit of the Duke of Brunswick to her home. In ensuing years Streeter is asked by the family to appraise the Hope diamond. The British courts rely upon his expert opinion that the French Blue was indeed cut into three pieces, the Hope, the Brunswick Blue, and the Pirie "of *precisely* the same colour and quality."[14]

Charles of Brunswick kept detailed and fastidious account books recording his thousands of diamond purchases in a horrid, idiosyncratic scrawl over a period of four decades. I spent days on end, scrutinizing and deciphering each transaction in those books at the Brunswick Collection housed at the University and City Library of Geneva. There is simply no record of Duke Charles ever having purchased a 13¾-carat blue diamond.

So, how did he get it? It is most likely that the diamond came from the Brunswick holdings—whether as part of his direct inheritance, or that plundered from his brother or the Duchy itself. There is no indication Charles's father Wilhelm acquired it. For most of the time the Brunswicks were exiled to London the family was living bereft of their income. They, like Caroline, would more likely have to sell diamonds than acquire them. Inheriting the Brunswick Blue doesn't necessarily mean that the elder Duke of Brunswick, Charles Wilhelm Ferdinand, was bribed at Valmy. He could have purchased the Brunswick Blue after 1792 and not even known its genealogy. Alternatively, he could have purchased the French Blue, known exactly what it was, had it cut—as Streeter suggested—and sent to London with son Wilhelm for Caroline.

When Charles visited Henry Thomas Hope in 1850 he was checking to see if his small blue diamond matched Hope's blue. If it did, it could mean that his 13¾-carat gem was cut off from the French Blue to form the Hope. If so, the remnant or satellite stone could be proof of the treachery of his grandfather at Valmy.

It is not likely that Charles would advertise that possibility. Unfortunately, there is no direct record in any of his papers and correspondence of what he concluded. Intriguingly, though, he placed a representation of the Order of the Golden Fleece in the center of the cover of his catalog of diamonds, perhaps as if to symbolically say to the detested George IV, "I too have a piece of the blue diamond."

So where are the Brunswick Blue and the Pirie? The latter disappears after Streeter's possession, sold perhaps to an unknown customer. An annotated version of the 1874 auction catalog supports Streeter's version that the 13¾ Brunswick Blue was sold to the Ochs Brothers of Paris.[15] An article about the auction in the *New York Times* suggested a different buyer—the London firm of Blogg & Martin.[16] Brunswick had been a big customer of the firm. It is possible that Ochs bought the diamond at the auction and immediately sold or traded it to Blogg & Martin. There was a report that the Brunswick Blue was part of an ensemble designed and fabricated by Tiffany at the U.S. Centennial Exhibition in Philadelphia in 1876, but that diamond turned out to be a 30-carat yellow brilliant. Hence, the trail of those two supposed pieces had gone cold.

For the Hope diamond, however, things were just heating up.

15

FROM HEIRLOOM TO VALUABLE

T he *Hope diamond, exhibited publicly* at the Crystal Palace and in Paris, and reconnected with its French history, stayed in the possession of the Hope family through the remainder of the 19th century. But its place in that family changed. The diamond, passed down to Henry Thomas's descendants as a family *heirloom*—in effect, "priceless"—exited the century as a *valuable,* an item over whose price tag family members and gem merchants bargained and haggled.

H enry Thomas Hope held on to the blue diamond until his death at the age of 54. He, unlike his uncle or father, was motivated less by study or the accumulation of beautiful treasures. He pursued wealth and status. His inheritances provided him the former, and the Hope diamond became its symbol. Owning such a diamond, as well as his fine London house, his inherited art collection, and a castle in Ireland, provided the pretensions of aristocracy. His position in Parliament provided some standing, but having married late in life to his former mistress, a Frenchwoman, and having fathered a child out of wedlock, the status-conscious Henry Thomas must have felt somewhat deficient in Victorian society. The legitimization he sought could only be realized by attaining aristocratic standing—something both his mother and his paternal grandfather strongly pursued.

To achieve that aim, in 1861 Henry Thomas Hope helped engineer the marriage of his daughter Henrietta to Henry Pelham Alexander, the Earl of Lincoln, and son of the Duke of Newcastle. Though the Pelham family had been a distinguished one, counting among immediate ancestors Prime Ministers of England, it was, like the Hope family, having problems. Henry Thomas basically had to bribe the prospective groom—"Linky," as he was known to friends—into the marriage. Though only 27 years old, Linky had accumulated a mountain of debts—some £230,000 (about $15 million in today's dollars) from horseracing alone. Linky was at times deceitful, a spendthrift, and a drunkard; Queen Victoria called him "worthless." He even extorted extra money from Henry Thomas just before the wedding. Linky's immediate family was, according to researcher Marian Fowler, also beset by disorder—his parents were divorced, his estranged father a dour character, his mother half-mad, his sister an opium addict, and his brother a transvestite. Given Linky's behavior, the Hope fortune could very well be squandered, and the diamond, so ardently contested, lost.

Henry Thomas Hope died in 1862. His widow, Anne Adéle Hope, inherited the estate at Deepdene, a collection of fine paintings (originally from Thomas Hope), the castle at Blayney in Ireland, the London house on Piccadilly (acquired by her husband), and the Hope diamond (inherited by her husband from the collection of his uncle Henry Philip). When in turn she finalized her will in 1876, she had two concerns: the Hope fortune and the family name. Normally, Adéle would have left the Hope family wealth to her daughter, Henrietta. But Henrietta's husband Linky, now the 6th Duke of Newcastle, was living at the edge of bankruptcy. Anne Adéle knew how hard her husband had fought for the family treasures and how little regard he had for Linky.

Adéle decided to skip a generation, and leave the Hope treasures to Henrietta's children, her grandchildren, thus providing for more able family members in the future. She also decided to make them heirs, not outright, but as "tenants for life." This was a particular legal status. It meant that the Hope estates and heirlooms, legally defined as such, could not be easily sold off. They would be available for the use of the heir during his or her lifetime, but then had to be passed on, either to the descendants, or back to a sibling and his or her descendants. This, she thought, would assure continuity of the Hope treasures.

Adéle had labored long and hard for the legitimacy of her daughter and acceptance into the Hope family. With no son there was no one to carry forth the Hope name. Henrietta had five children: two boys, the eldest, Henry Pelham Archibald Douglas, born in 1865 and Henry Francis, born the following year. Henrietta's three girls were Beatrice Adeline, born in 1862, Emily Augusta, and Florence Josephine. The eldest boy, Henry Pelham, would succeed his father as Duke of Newcastle. So Adéle chose Francis, then only 10 years old, as her primary heir—with the stipulation that he change his name upon reaching majority.

In 1879, Linky died. Henrietta remarried a reverend, Thomas Theobald Hohler, the next year. In 1882 Henrietta converted to Roman Catholicism and increasingly became caught up in ritual and service. Given these circumstances, Adéle was dissuaded from changing her will. In 1884, she passed away. Francis had to wait three years until he was twenty-one. On April 7, 1887 he became Lord Henry Francis Hope Pelham-Clinton Hope, and inherited the Hope home, castle, estate, art collection, and famous blue diamond. It did not take him long to lose most of this precious legacy.

As a young man Francis was tall, handsome, debonair, and possessed with a strong sense of aristocratic entitlement. He was a playboy of the Gay Nineties, traveling broadly, enjoying the best of food, clothes, and entertainment, gambling freely, keeping the company of beautiful showgirls, and staying a step ahead of creditors and moneylenders.

In November 1892 Francis was in New York City. He met a lively, intriguing showgirl named May Yohe at a Delmonico's dinner party. They hit it off. He escorted her to the Horse Show at Madison Square Garden. She knew he was British, but not that he was a lord. Francis was apparently smitten with May. She found him charming, enjoying the fact that he engaged her in polite, noncondescending

The Hope Family Genealogy

Archibald Hope
b. 1664 d. 1741

m. Anna Claus

Henry Hope
b. 1735 d. 1811

Adrian Hope
b. 1709 d. 1781

Thomas Hope
b. 1704 d. 1779

m. Margaret Marcelis

John Hope
b. 1737 d. 1784

m. 1763

Philippina van der Hoeven
d. 1789

Henry Philip Hope
b. 1774 d. 1839

Adrian Elias Hope
b. 1772 d. 1834

Thomas Hope
b. 1769 d. 1831

m. 1806

Henry Hope

Louisa Beresford
b. 1790 d. 1851

Lord William Carr Beresford
b. 1768 d. 1854

m. 1832

Henry Thomas Hope
b. 1808 d. 1862

Adrian Hope
b. 1811

Alexander Hope
b. 1820
d. 1854

Emilie Matilda Rapp
m. 1836
d. 1854

Lady Mildred Cecil
b. 1826 d. 1881

m. 1842

Anne Adéle Bichat
b. 1820 d. 1884

m. 1851

Henrietta Adele
m. 1880 b. 1843 d. 1913

DUKE OF NEWCASTLE 6th
Henry Alexander Pelham-Clinton, "Linky"
b. 1834 d. 1879

m. 1861

Thomas Hohler
d. 1892

DUKE OF NEWCASTLE 7th
Henry Pelham Archibald Douglas Pelham-Clinton
b. 1864 d. 1928

m. 1889

Kathleen Florence May Candy
b. 1872 d. 1955

May Yohe
b. 1866 d. 1938

m. 1894

DUKE OF NEWCASTLE 8th
Henry Francis Hope Pelham-Clinton Hope "Lord Francis"
b. 1866 d. 1941

Olive Muriel Thompson Owen
m. 1904 d. 1912

DUKE OF NEWCASTLE 9th
Henry Edward Hugh Pelham-Clinton
b. 1907 d. 1988

Beatrice Adeline
b. 1862 d. 1935

Sir Cecil Edmund Lister-Kaye
m. 1880 b. 1854 d. 1931

Emily Augusta
b. 1863 d. 1919

Alfonso Prince Doria
m. 1882 b. 1867 d. 1914

Florence Josephine
b. 1868 d. 1935

conversation. Over the next week he courted her. May announced that she and her mother would be going to London for the staging of a new production; Francis offered to host her.

May Yohe had been born in Bethlehem, Pennsylvania, in 1866, though she often fibbed about her age. According to May's autobiographical account, her father was "a soldier, a man of courage and of the spirit of adventure."[1] He did serve in the Civil War and went on to work in his family's hotel. Her mother was a seamstress. As May reported, after her father's death, they moved to Philadelphia. Apparently her mother was very talented and made costume dresses for some of the stars of the day such as: Mrs. John Drew, Georgia Drew Barrymore, Marie Van Zandt, and others. Contact with actresses fired in May "my childish imagination and fanned that desire for the footlights which later led me to the heights—and to depths."[2] Aided by German friends of her mother, she was sent to school in Dresden and later to finishing school in Paris. Another source suggests that May had so impressed Bethlehem's miners with her child-acting that they "took up a subscription to send her to Paris for operatic training."[3] As is often the case with May Yohe and her statements, fabrication and contradiction are the rule.

Upon her return from Europe, May says she sang for a church choir. Susanne Patch asserts she joined a Pittsburgh burlesque show as a chorus girl, thus shocking her sponsors. May, impetuous, lively, and romantic, took on roles in theatrical productions in Philadelphia and Chicago, enjoying success for her leading role in *The Crystal Slipper* at the Chicago Opera House in 1887. Apparently, to the dismay of the show's producers, she shuffled off to Buffalo with a member of the company in the midst of the run, only to return when she discovered her friend to be a married man. During the next few years she performed in New York to measured success. Yohe saw herself a star, an independent woman of the 1890s, vivacious and glamorous; but she also acquired a reputation as the impulsive, optimistic, good-time-seeking "Madcap May."

* * *

May had her London debut on January 19, 1893, at the Lyric Theatre in *The Magic Opal*, a play, coincidentally enough, about a stolen jewel that gave its wearer the power to attract one's desired lover. A fan of the theater, Lord Francis was also an investor in the Lyric. The play closed in April, but May Yohe went on to star in several other plays, including *Little Christopher Columbus*. Her singing and dancing and sheer energy wowed the crowds and the show continued for more than a year. Reviews of May's performance were mediocre, but Lord Francis was undeterred in his delight.

While May's career was on the upswing, Lord Francis was falling further into debt. His investments, lifestyle, and gambling were largely supported on credit, his annual income being about £16,000, or about $1.5 million in today's dollars, and his debt equal to about $40 million. The year before, Lord Francis had been offered £27,000 for six of the paintings of Dutch masters he'd inherited. By June 1893, Lord Francis was trying to sell 83 Dutch and Flemish paintings for £80,000, but he needed the courts to approve the sale given his status as tenant for life under the terms of his inheritance from Anne Adéle. His siblings opposed the sale. They would inherit the property if Lord Francis died without an heir, and since he had no children at the time, that seemed like a reasonable possibility. Lord Francis's elder sister, Lady Beatrice Lister-Kaye, would have precedence, followed by her son, and so on. The Chancery Court Lord Justice Chitty declined to allow the sale under the terms of the Settled Land Acts. He argued that Lord Francis's financial situation was one of his own making and that extravagant

May Yohe.

Lord Francis Hope.

spending was not cause enough to negate the family interest in the property.

By September 1893 Lord Francis's debts had swollen to over £405,277, and his creditors initiated bankruptcy proceedings. Lord Francis, desperate for funds, rented out Deepdene, the Hope estate.

Meanwhile, Lord Francis enjoyed the company of May, or "Maysie" as he called her, despite his mother's disapproval. Henrietta had increasingly become more religious and ascetic. Lord Francis and May began living together and married in secret at the Hampstead Registry Office on November 27, 1894.

The poorer May and Lord Francis got, the more it seems May apocryphally inflated their wealth and standing. In her 1921 autobiography, May claimed that Lord Francis had an annual income of about £120,000. She claimed he gave her all sorts of jewelry. No doubt he did, for such items were later pawned or stolen. But May likely overstated their value.

It was during this time that Lord Francis and May were invited to a London dinner party by Lord Alfred Rothschild. May later contended that she wore the Hope diamond that evening and was the hit of the party, particularly enjoying the conversation with and attention of His Royal Highness, Edward, Prince of Wales and son of sitting Queen Victoria. Yohe wrote, "I was as popular as Lady Francis Hope in society as I was as May Yohe on the stage. I was very happy when I went home that morning with the Hope diamond blazing about my neck."[4] In her examination of the Hopes, Marian Fowler raises doubts about the account, asserting that Yohe was purposefully ignored by the other distinguished guests that evening. Furthermore, Lord Francis, issuing a statement years later, in 1911, said, "I became the owner of the stone in 1887 and from that year until I sold it in 1901 it was never worn by any one."[5]

May continued to appear in theatrical productions, earning £125 a week for her role in *Dandy Dick Whittington* in 1895. She was a popular performer in London, and no less an authority than George Bernard Shaw commented that May had "personal charm and gay grace of movement, with the suggestion of suppressed wilderness beneath."[6]

Meanwhile, bankruptcy proceedings continued as Lord Francis's debt grew to an estimated £657,942. Declared bankrupt and by arrangement of the trustee, the life interest in Lord Francis's settled property was purchased by the Gresham Life Assurance Society (somewhat like a lien or mortgage operates today). Gresham would provide Lord Francis with a meager £2,000 per year. Lord Francis could redeem the interest in the property if he could settle the bankruptcy account.

The bankruptcy discharged, Lord Francis resumed his pattern of spending money he didn't have. May's career continued, but somewhat in the decline. Shaw, reviewing her 1896 self-produced *Mademoiselle Nitouche,* panned her performance, "I take it that Miss Yohe is not now living by her profession. She is, is she not, in an independent position, gained by an alliance with the British aristocracy." In a clear reference to the Hope jewels, Shaw suggested May would do better than acting by "plastering herself with diamonds and sitting in an opera-box like a wax figure in a jeweler's shop window."[7] He continued, "Miss Yohe's own extraordinary artificial *contralto* had so little tone on the first night that it was largely mistaken for an attack of hoarseness. Her sustaining power seems gone; she breathes after every little phrase and cannot handle a melody in her old, broad rich manner."[8] Chiding May's role as the show's producer, Shaw called her effort a waste of time and money.

The financial pressures did not abate. Lord Francis was officially bankrupt and could not afford to care for the paintings. Making an agreement with sister Beatrice, his siblings dropped their opposition to the sale. In 1898 the court allowed the sale of the 83 paintings for £121,550. Such funds did not accrue to Lord Francis; rather, they went into a "sinking fund" to pay the creditors. As part of the agreement, a sum of £600 per annum was to be appropriated out of the sale funds to help educate his nephew, son of Beatrice and Cecil Lister-Kaye. Lord Francis still held another 153 paintings.

Lord Francis continued to rack up debts, most of them generated by gambling, a particular vice of his father and the aristocracy in general. Gambling was both a cause as well as a hoped-for solution for those with declining fortunes. On one hand, many of Lord Francis's ilk believed that given their station in life, they were entitled to win. And if they didn't, losing was, in its own bizarre way, a status symbol of conspicuous waste—for they, unlike commoners, could afford to lose mammoth sums.

In December 1898, Lord Francis Hope entered into a provisional contract with L.M. Lowenstein & Co. for the sale of the Hope diamond. The proposed purchase price was about £18,000. The newspapers reported that the sum of £18,115 had been suggested by Edwin Streeter, whose opinion had been solicited by Hope. (Years later, Streeter wrote the London *Times* that his appraisal was actually for £17,600.) Other family members contested the sale in court.

Justice Byrne, hearing the case for the Chancery Division of the High Court of Justice, accepted Streeter's assessment of the history of the diamond. According to the court proceedings, the diamond, set in a brooch surrounded by 22 smaller diamonds, had been deposited in Parr's Bank since 1894, and had not been used for many years.

The case was a complicated one. At issue was whether Lord Francis was entitled to sell the diamond or had to maintain it as a family heirloom. Lord Francis argued that he was effectively broke. He could not maintain the family estate. He could not pay his bills. Since he had been allowed to sell the 83 paintings also inherited as heirlooms, there was precedent for his request and the acquiescence of the court. Additionally, though the Hope diamond was an heirloom, it had not resided in the family for all that long. It was not unique, as other large blue diamonds had become known. It was a "mere curio," argued lawyers Farwell and Martelli for Lord Francis.

The other members of the Hope family argued that Lord Francis had inherited the diamond essentially as a caretaker. The diamond was unique and bore the family name. It was an heirloom to be passed on, not sold off. Lady Beatrice declared her desire to possess and wear the diamond if Francis should die without issue. Besides, if the diamond were sold, proceeds would merely go to creditors rather than provide any allowance for Lord Francis's living expenses. Furthermore, the lawyers noted, the price Lord Francis had agreed to in the contract was too low. The *Encyclopaedia Britannica* had estimated its worth at £25,000, while the London firm of Collingwood and Co. submitted their opinion to the court that the Hope diamond might fetch £50,000 or even more at auction.

Streeter noted that he might have valued the diamond at a higher price only a few years earlier when the Hope was thought to be the only large blue diamond known. He had lowered his estimate "because recently a large blue diamond in the rough double the size of the Hope diamond had come into the market, which had been cut and divided into a fine lozenge-shaped diamond and a fine drop, the two diamonds weighing in the aggregate 34 carats."[9] Other jewelers gave estimates in line with Streeter's.

The court refused to approve the sale. Judge Byrne found Lord Francis's case for the sale of the diamond quite weak under the relevant statutes. Unlike the situation of the inherited paintings that required funds for their proper upkeep and maintenance, the Hope diamond was in no danger of deteriorating for lack of funds. Judge Bryne found that the Hope diamond was indeed unique given its historical connections, color, and size. He also agreed that there was good enough reason to suppose that the proposed purchase price of the Hope diamond was too low. A few months later, Lord Francis appealed the decision to Lord Justice Romer and the Master of the Rolls, and again lost.

The case provoked much commentary at the time in the British press because it raised larger issues affecting the society as a whole, particularly the transformation of a wealthy aristocracy given the "vicissitudes of fortune." There were two basic issues. The first concerned the interests of the state or the society as a whole in the property of the aristocratic class. Land reform legislation had recognized that recent agricultural depressions had left good land in the hands of poor estate owners. If they could not care for those estates, improve the land, or be allowed to sell it, the nation as a whole would suffer. Family estates could thus be sold upon certain conditions. Similarly, a London *Times* commentator wrote, "England has treasures in private collections that far surpass those of any other country."[10] Those treasures provide a healthy continuity with the past and should not so easily be dispersed or neglected. If such nationally important heirlooms or treasures could not be taken care of properly by the holder or family, it was still nonetheless important to preserve them. In the interest of the larger society the *Times* opined, it would be quite appropriate for such treasures to pass to people or curators who would do so. The Hope paintings fell into this category.

The other issue was framed as the struggle between the desire of the individual and family pride. One writer offered that Hope was selling "what did not belong to him." A May 18, 1899 *Times* commentary pointed out, "There have been families to which ornaments in dubious taste and of uncertain value were a sort of fetish. They would dread ill-luck if those articles were sold or lost."[11] That is, sentimental value within the family mattered. As a July 17 article pointed out, "A diamond identified with the family and known all over the world by its name is not exactly upon the same footing as the sum of money it might fetch in the market. Family pride in the procession of such a jewel is rightly taken into account."[12]

In 1900, Lord Francis and May headed for New York. On their trans-Atlantic voyage back to England, May met Captain Putnam Bradlee Strong, the son of William L. Strong, the former mayor of

New York City, who had supposedly been assigned by President McKinley to France to observe army maneuvers there. Yohe found Strong "a fascinating man, with a suave gallantry which charmed women."[13]

Upon arriving, the Duke of Newcastle, Lord Francis's brother, hosted them at a London dinner party. Captain Strong too was invited. The Duke's aristocratic wife showed off her diamonds originally worn by France's Empress Eugenie. May Yohe, in her memoir, claims, probably falsely, to have worn the Hope diamond on this occasion as well.

Lord Francis and May spent more time with Strong in England. May and Strong journeyed to France, and in Paris, showered by his gifts of candies and flowers, attention and wistful gazes, May fell in love with him.

Later in the year, May returned to New York, alone at first. Captain Strong sent her flowers and numerous cables, actively courting her. She was taken with the attention and affection. When she fell seriously ill with pneumonia, Captain Strong came back to New York with flowers in hand and attended to her. Meanwhile, according to Yohe's account, Lord Francis, who was in Florida fishing with his brother the Duke, received a cable from May's doctors—WIFE DANGEROUS CONDITION. RECOVERY NOT ASSURED. SHE ASKS YOU HURRY HERE. Lord Francis responded, SORRY CAN'T COME NOW. MIDST OF FISHING SEASON. DEPARTURE WOULD SERIOUSLY DISARRANGE TRIP. ADVISE OF DEVELOPMENTS—HOPE.[14] As May Yohe wrote so melodramatically, "I dropped the telegram to the floor. That instant I became the property, body, soul, and mind of Putnam Bradlee Strong."[15]

Lord Francis realized he'd lost May to Strong when the couple ran off together in April 1901, headed for San Francisco and then on to Japan. According to May, Strong was absent without leave, so they used an assumed name—Mr. and Mrs. M. L. Hastings. Presumably no one noticed the 18 trunks, five dogs, and two servants Madcap May says they took with them.

Later that year, Lord Francis, still desperate for money, again sought permission to sell the Hope diamond. This time, the family apparently did not oppose the sale. On November 13 the London *Times* carried the notice that Hope had sold "the famous Hope blue diamond."[16] By March 1902, Lord Francis and May Yohe were divorced. Hope was now freed of "two treasures." May was off to find romance in marriage, and the Hope diamond to find a price in the marketplace and a place in society's imagination.

16

ORNAMENT OF THE EAST

T*here was no contemporaneous suspicion about* the Hope diamond somehow being unlucky or cursed during the period it was owned by Lord Francis. While the blue diamond was referred to as his *damnosa hereditas*—a burdensome inheritance because he couldn't dispose of it, there is no indication that the Hope was itself regarded as tainted or served as the vehicle of a vengeful Indian god.

There were, however, stories about ill-gotten diamonds that did raise the issue about the morality of possessing such gemstones. The most famous story of the mid-19th century was that attached to the extraordinary Koh-i-Nur, or "mountain of light." The 186-carat Koh-i-Nur had passed in succession to Persian, Afghan, and Sikh rulers as a result of war and conflict. Stories circulated that misfortune and defeat would follow those who possessed the diamond, although one of those rulers who lost the diamond is supposed to have said, "Its value is good fortune, for whoever holds it is victorious over his enemies."[1] Upon the British conquest of the Punjabi Sikh kingdom in 1849, the Koh-i-Nur was turned over to colonial officials for conveyance to Queen Victoria the following year. It went on prominent display at the 1851 Crystal Palace Exposition, placed close to the Hope diamond. The next year it was refaceted and reduced to 106$\frac{1}{16}$ carats. It was then worn by Queen Victoria variously in a brooch, bracelet, and hair circlet. The Koh-i-Nur came quickly to represent India as a prized possession of the Crown—literally the "jewel in the crown," particularly after 1857, when, following the suppression of the Sepoy

Rebellion, India was declared to be part of the British Empire; Queen Victoria later became its Empress. The Koh-i-Nur represented a secular theft of sorts, as the British military and political forces had defeated those of India. The possession of the diamond signified superior accomplishment for the British; for the Indians, it represented defeat and colonial subservience, something that could be symbolically reversed by its repatriation.

The story of another diamond, the Orloff, suggested a more morally disturbing transaction. John Mawe, in his *Treatise,* wrote that Catherine the Great's famous Orloff diamond "is said to have represented the eye of an idol [in India], and to have been stolen from its position by a French soldier."[2] The Orloff was supposedly acquired not through official surrender and public rite, but through secret theft by a renegade soldier as an expression of individual greed. Taking an idol's eye was a transgression of the sacred, albeit from a European's point of view, "someone else's" sacred. Nonetheless Russian ruler Catherine the Great enshrined the diamond in her royal scepter, crowned with a two-headed eagle. She also rewarded its donor with money and title. No one in Europe suggested that the Empress return the diamond to India.

Wilkie Collins.

Author Wilkie Collins, a contemporary of and collaborator with Charles Dickens, took the tales of the Koh-i-Nur and the Orloff and in 1868 spun them into *The Moonstone*—the first of the new genre of detective story. It was very popular at the time and remains a classic today.

In the story, a large yellow diamond was originally set in the forehead, as a "third eye" of the Hindu god Vishnu, and had the special power of waxing and waning with the moon, hence the name of the gem. The idol was ensconced in a sacred

Hindu temple. It was saved from the looting of a Muslim invader by three Brahmin priestly attendants to the god. According to the dream of the Brahmins

> The deity breathed the breath of his divinity on the diamond in the forehead of the god . . . The deity commanded that the Moonstone should be watched, from that time forth, by three priests in turn, night and day, to the end of the generations of men. And the Brahmins heard, and bowed before his will. The deity predicted certain disaster to the presumptuous mortal who laid hands on the sacred gem, and to all of his house and name who received it after him.[3]

The three Brahmins and their successors watched over the Moonstone for centuries, until this temple was looted and destroyed by the army of Mughal Emperor Aurangzeb. Then

> the Moonstone passed (carrying its curse with it) from one lawless Mohammedan hand to another, . . . the successors of the three guardian priests kept their watch, waiting the day when the will of Vishnu the Preserver should restore to them their sacred gem.[4]

It was in the hands of Muslim rebel leader Tipu Sultan in 1799 when he was defeated by the British army. Collins has a fictional soldier—Herncastle—stealing the diamond and murdering the three Brahmins, the last of whom shouts with his dying breath, "The Moonstone will have its vengeance yet on you and yours!"[5] The soldier's cousin, the narrator, declares

> although I attach no sort of credit to the fantastic Indian legend of the gem, I must acknowledge, before I conclude, that I am influenced by a certain superstition of my own in this matter. It is my conviction, or my delusion, no matter

which, that crime brings its own fatality with it. I am not only persuaded of Herncastle's guilt; I am even fanciful enough to believe that he will live to regret it, if he keeps the Diamond; and that others will live to regret taking it from him, if he gives the Diamond away.[6]

The Moonstone is taken by Herncastle to the English countryside and years later inherited by his niece. A successor set of Brahmins arrive on the scene. A series of deaths and deceptions ensue, to the detriment of Herncastle's heirs and household. The curse is thus fulfilled—Herncastle's family bears the vengeance of the god; and the diamond is in the end returned to its rightful place in India, adorning the deity.

Prior to *The Moonstone,* European "stories" of Indian diamonds were very thin, mere tidbits, with occasional notions of cursed gems with no real narrative construction. It was Collins who put flesh on these notions and developed a logical structure for the tale of the cursed diamond. Like any good writer of historical fiction, Collins had done his research. He read about the history of diamonds and about India. Collins used Tavernier's information about the Koh-i-Nur. He made Mir Jumla, Tavernier's trading partner and diamond loving prime minister, a character in his prologue. Most of all, Collins mined Tavernier's retold anecdote about the mysterious death of the diamond thief in an Indian temple.

The Moonstone is an anticolonial, anti-imperialistic tale. In sending the diamond back to India, Collins was providing a critique of the ill-gotten and unjust gains of British colonialism. For Collins, the idea of a cursed diamond was a cautionary tale. Possession of the moonstone brought havoc—not to mention Indians to the English heartland. An English family had to confront its own injustice wreaked upon a conquered India. The curse of the moonstone is the curse of colonialism gone awry.

The Moonstone established a whole genre of stolen and cursed diamond stories. The serial version, and its later full compilation, was widely read in England, translated into French, and performed on the stage at the Olympic Theatre in London. It had several imitators, and its influence was boosted by the subsequent popularity of Arthur Conan Doyle's 1890 publication of *The Sign of the Four,* wherein Sherlock Holmes finds a ruthless brotherhood seeking the Great Agra Treasure.

Collins's story likely influenced Edwin Streeter who, in his 1882 edition of *The Great Gems of the World,* wrote:

A symbol of power, the diamond has been a talisman of not less influence in the East than the very gods whose temples it has adorned. It has been a factor in tragedies innumerable, supplying the motives of war and rapine, setting father against son, blurring the fair image of virtue, making life a curse where it had been a blessing, and adding new terrors to death.[7]

Streeter erroneously presented the ill-luck that befell Tavernier:

Alas! The ill-luck which was said to pursue the merchants in these gems from India seems to have attached itself to this famous traveler. The son involved his aged father in such unfortunate speculations, that he was compelled to sell his estate to pay his debts, and at the age of eighty-four to venture out once more to the East. On his journey he was attacked by fever and perished. It is very noteworthy that Emir Jemla [*Mir Jumla*] died, after the miscarriage of his son, in a similar manner.[8]

If the stories of cursed Indian diamonds said "give them back," the Orientalism that emerged in the Victorian era, in the mid-19th and early 20th century in England, as well as in France, and to some extent the United States, said about things Indian, "make them your own."

Among Europeans and Americans, Orientalism was a stylish

mode of appropriating elements of "Eastern" beliefs and material culture, and representing them in Western contexts, for Western audiences. The Orientalism of the Victorian era had its precedents. The Portuguese imitated Golcondan fashions in Goa including the use of turbans and the *sarpanch,* or diamond head jewel associated with authority and standing. Tavernier wore his "Oriental robes," and French King Louis XIV encouraged Tavernier to decorate one of his rooms in Oriental style. Napoleon's expedition to Egypt resulted in the incorporation of Egyptian motifs into French culture as a matter of contemporary style. England too was affected. George, as Prince and as Regent, "orientalized" the Brighton Marine Pavilion, a royal getaway in the English coastal town—at a huge expense to the nation, redoing the architecture in the style of an Indo-Persian palace.

The resurgence of Orientalism under Queen Victoria followed England's engagement of India as a colony and part of its empire. British troops and civil servants spent lifetimes, even generations in India. Indian words, peoples, ideas, and things were flowing back to England. India had to be appropriated into popular consciousness. Authors like Rudyard Kipling, among others, helped fashion

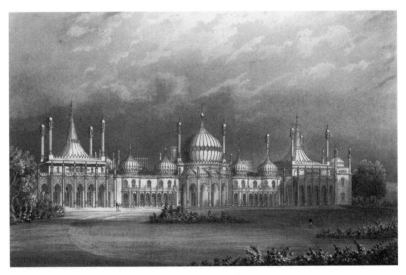

Brighton, George's Orientalist Fantasy.

a vision of India as a mysterious, fascinating place, with strange religious practices, rich maharajahs, and varied, interesting peoples.

A good number of Indians, generally of higher caste and standing, came to England for education, business, and the task of colonial rule. To what extent could the British trust having Indians within their midst? The question came to the fore most dramatically from 1887 onward when Queen Victoria, over the objections of her household and national leaders, hired several Indian domestic servants as well as a clerk, Hafiz Abdul Karim. Wrote one court onlooker,

> The Queen was the victim of her good heart and her naiveté, which got the better of her native shrewdness . . . She felt that England owed atonement for many things to India, and in a small way she wished to show that her Indian subjects were as precious in her sight as her British.[9]

Karim was particularly gifted and became Victoria's Hindustani language tutor, and later Indian Secretary and personal emissary.

*The Queen's family and servants in a Victorian
Orientalist tableau vivant.*

He and the other Indians were continually distrusted by British aristocrats and civil servants who scrutinized their behavior for acts that could be interpreted as evidence of disloyalty. Although Queen Victoria repeatedly defended them, for many they became a symbol of India in disguise—Indians close to the center of power masquerading as loyal subjects but harboring vengeful motives, just waiting for the right moment to strike.

Karim and the attendants wore turbans and "Oriental clothing." In an effort to show solidarity and appreciation of things Indian, the Queen's family occasionally donned Indian dress and posed in *"tableaux vivant,"* or living portraits.

Such displays showed that India and Indians were no threat at all. Royals in Indian dress illustrated how elements of India could be acquired and controlled. It did not take long for other Victorians to begin imitating in appearance the very Indians they ruled and mistrusted.

Dressing in Indian clothing was laden with whimsy and humor—an amusement. On a large scale, this extended to state ritual. In the decades following its incorporation into the empire, India offered no military threat to British control. British and Indian colonial officials increasingly appropriated Indian rajahs, their uniformed and decorated troops, elephants, swords, and displays of military prowess into orchestrated celebratory exhibitions of the empire's grandeur. Historically serious elements of Indian culture became public spectacles, with marching troops, decorated elephants, and staged durbars or Indian courtly gatherings for the jubilees of Queen Victoria in 1888 and 1898—a practice that continued with the coronations of Edward VII in 1902 and George V in 1910. Indian culture was turned into an ornamental decoration for the British Empire and its ruling class.

Wealthy Europeans and Americans followed the royals, and in fact, used the occasions of donning fabulous, ostentatious, jewel-laden Indian and Asiatic dress to become sultans and maharajas for a day. They could, in this play, acquire royal positions not available to them in their own society, albeit temporarily. English royals, aristocrats, and the wealthy, as well as their French and American counterparts, adopted a decorative Orientalism. They staged "Oriental" balls, where Indian aesthetics provided the themes, fashions, and décor.

The socioaesthetic form of Orientalism was accompanied by adaptation of Middle Eastern, Indian, and Chinese jewelry styles, architecture and interior decoration, literature, plays, themes in early silent movies, and spiritual and theosophical movements.

India's diamonds and other gems were regarded in Collins-inspired stories in much the same way as Victoria's Indian subjects. They appeared to be valuable and attractive gemstones domesticated and controlled by English society through their purchase, incorporation into jewelry, and even recutting. But what if that were a mere disguise? What if they had a secret identity, one that could harm those who wrongfully possessed them?

European and American ideas about gemstones were reinvigorated in the Victorian era as the translations of Indian texts became available. Works such as Dr. H. Kern's *The Brhatsanhita or Complete System of Natural Astrology* (1865), Sourindro Mohun Tagore's *Mani-Mala, or A Treatise on Gems* (1881), Ram Das Sen's *Ratnarahasya: A Treatise on Diamonds and Precious Stones* (1884), and Frenchman Louis Finot's *Les Lapidaires Indiens* (1896) brought India's ancient *nau ratna* theories about gems to Western audiences.

These translations and the schema they embodied were refracted in popular thought. The Indian multiplicity of gods, the mythical stories, and the idea of casted gems made little sense to most Europeans and Americans. It all seemed too serious or supernatural or silly.

But other ideas resonated with those already long resident in the West. That gems were connected to astrological influence was well known through various notions of birthstones and lucky stars—a sentiment often captured by Shakespeare, as for example in *King Lear*—"We make guilty of our disasters, the sun, the moon, and the stars."[10] Some people both worried about and applauded the notion that gemstones had, in their very constitution, a power that could influence their lives. The coming to Europe of Oriental gems and styles, with their ideas, stimulated jewelers to standardize "birth-stones," and transform Indian cosmology into simple entertainment. Signs of the zodiac associated with particular gems were somewhat problematic, as they were organized from midmonth to midmonth, as are contemporary horoscopes. Jewelers needed a simpler method for popularization. And indeed, by 1912 birthstones were formalized by the American National Retail Jewelers Association, and gems, organized by the month, were mass-marketed for birthday celebrations and anniversaries. Ideas drawn from Indian *nau ratna* cosmo-gemology were reduced to a set of "lucky charms."

A similar transformation occurred in jewelry styles. Items of male honor and prestige in India—turbans and *sarpanches*, became headwear for Western women in the form of turbans with tiaras, aigrettes, and the like. Jewelers, especially Tiffany and Cartier, began crafting their pieces in Indian styles, turning once meaningful amulets and talismans into ornaments bereft of their original cultural significance.

This playful, ornamental Orientalism developed at the time that the ownership of diamonds was being transformed. Indian rulers were selling their jewels to Europeans to maintain their life styles in the midst of a colonial order that had reduced their sinecure. At the same time European aristocrats and the idle rich, like Lord Francis Hope, were strapped for cash and were routinely selling their diamonds and other jewels to maintain their standing and lifestyle. Wealth was shifting to a new continent—America—as a result of the post–Civil War industrial expansion of the U.S. economy. With that wealth came the demand for diamonds. This transformation was sealed in France. Napoleon III and Empress Eugenie abdicated the throne in 1871, following defeat in the Franco-Prussian War. By 1887, the remaining French Crown Jewels were sold at auction. The largest buyer, by far, was Tiffany—an American firm. The auction signaled the movement of diamonds away from the old royalty and toward the new kings of commerce and industry.

17

LOVE COMMODITY

Though Americans had money they had very few diamonds in 1867. That year, the United States imported just over $1 million in cut diamonds—amounting to a paltry 400 carats and virtually nothing compared to what was going to Europe. Most raw diamonds came from Brazil—the Indian supply having virtually dried up by the early 18th century. In the 1860s, Brazil was annually exporting about 200,000 carats a year—mostly to Europe. The diamond deposits in Brazil were, as in India, found in small concentrations in alluvial fields. Mining operations were difficult, tedious, labor-intensive, and expensive. By the late 1860s however, there was far more demand for diamonds than the Brazilian supply would allow; cutters in Amsterdam, Antwerp, and London faced shortages of rough gemstones.

This changed with the discovery of diamonds in South Africa. A 15-year-old farm boy named Erasmus Stephanus Jacobs found an intriguing, yellow-tinted gemstone in a field in Hopetown, at the intersection of the Vaal and Orange Rivers. This turned out to be a 21-carat yellow diamond. Shown at the Universal Exposition in Paris in 1867, it was later named Eureka, Greek for "I found it!" and cut into a 10¾-carat brilliant. The discovery led to the exploration of the alluvial fields in the area, and the mining of about 100,000 carats in 1870. More important, the pipes or vents that served as the conduits for the diamonds reaching the surface were discovered 12 miles away. The town of Kimberley, the Kimberley mines, and the term kimberlite for the diamond-encrusted rock were born. Mines were dug deep into the pipes and by 1871 were annually yielding more than 1 million carats—five times the Brazilian output. Over the years, the Kimberley pit yielded more than 14 million carats—equivalent to some three tons of diamonds! By 1888, an enterprising Englishman, Cecil Rhodes, had formed the De Beers Mining Company, Limited, bought out other miners, and exerted virtual control over the diamond mining industry.

With an increased, almost inexhaustible supply from South Africa, the price of diamonds in Europe, and in the United States, dropped dramatically. A one-carat diamond cost £529 in 1867, but only £110 pounds in 1878; in subsequent years, it fell considerably lower. Larger diamonds also saw their prices fall to one-fifth or one-sixth their former value.

There was now an opportunity to sell this new and cheap supply of diamonds to Americans, not only to those great entrepreneurs, traders, speculators, and treasure-seekers who had become fabulously wealthy in the industrial revolution, but also to the millions of others who had benefited from the expanding economy. New types of products were needed if diamonds were to be marketed to the masses.

American jewelers and retailers invented a successful product—the diamond ring. The diamond ring and other related jewelry, particularly earrings, equated in the public mind the association of diamonds with romantic love—at an affordable price.

This innovation was only loosely based on historical practice. Wedding rings were known in Roman times, and were thereafter Christianized. According to jewelry historian Diana Scarisbrick, Saint Augustine asked priests to permit weddings without an exchange of rings for those who could not afford them. Byzantine wedding rings were thick gold bands.

During medieval times, the wedding rings of the very wealthy bore gems of various sorts; by the fifteenth century, these rarely included a diamond. Miniatures in the Vatican library depict the wedding pageantry of Constanzo d'Aragona and Camilla d'Aragona in 1475. Diamond rings and flames are painted on the tunic of Hymen, god of marriage. He is depicted as standing beside an altar on which a huge diamond ring binds together a pair of flaming golden torches as a symbol of fidelity. In 1476, Maximilian von Hapsburg gave a diamond wedding ring to Marie of Burgundy—a practice only occasionally followed by other European royalty.

With the brilliant cutting of diamonds in the 17th century, rings appeared with sets of diamonds arranged in decorative clusters. By the 18th century, diamonds formed lovers' knots, flowers, crowned hearts. Single, larger diamonds cut in complex ways, such as the marquise—named for the paramour of King Louis XV—were in fashion. Still, this use of diamonds was rare and restricted largely to royalty, aristocrats, and wealthy mercantilists. In the period 1725–30, annual Indian diamond importation to Europe was only in the 2,000- to 5,000-carat range. The discovery of diamonds in Brazil and their subsequent exploitation brought a dramatic increase in the importation of rough diamonds after 1730, leading to somewhat more elaborate uses.

In 19th-century England, it was customary to give a wedding band made of the traditional gold. Those who could afford it studded their rings with various jewels, diamonds included. Among the elite, romantic motifs grew in popularity. In 1839 Prince Albert gave Queen Victoria a diamond ring of the heart-in-hand motif, a large central brilliant shaped like a heart, surrounded by smaller brilliants forming two hands, and topped with several brilliants forming a crown, completely obscuring the setting. Albert also gave Victoria an emerald-studded ring as a symbol of eternity.

But even by the mid-19th century, there still was no tradition or social practice of presenting a diamond ring upon engagement, marriage, or anniversaries anywhere in the world.

❊ ❊ ❊

With the influx of South Africa's stones to the United States, diamonds went retail; their use was democratized, and imports soared. In 1887 the Tiffany solitaire setting was invented—a ring with a single diamond in a claw setting. The next year, Sears Watch Company was selling diamond rings in the A. C. Roebuck catalog. The diamond ring was marketed as a prudent investment and as an expression of love. Americans could buy diamond rings by mail order for $30 or $140 or $320 or anywhere in between. In 1892, the price dropped even further. The A. C. Roebuck catalog asked: Who buys diamonds? and answered, "Nearly every class of people."[1] Trades people, mechanics, clerks, as well as bankers, capitalists, and merchants, said Roebuck. Through the Roebuck catalog, customers could pay C.O.D. after inspecting their mail order product. One-carat diamond rings with 14-carat gold settings were sold for $74 each. A one-quarter-carat diamond ring cost $15.95— the equivalent of about $330 in today's dollars. Americans could even get smaller diamond rings for as low as $5.75 each.

Predictably, the wide scale commercialization of diamonds prompted systems of standardization. The actual weight of the traditional carat had historically varied from place to place. The English measure was on the average 205.5 milligrams per carat. The French used two measures close to the English one. The Florentine carat was considerably less. Others measured carats between 1.86 and 2.25 grains troy. This is one of the reasons why a diamond—including the Hope—might seem to have slightly different weights during its history; it depends upon who is doing the measuring, where, and when.

In 1871, Parisian jewelers proposed to standardize the carat at 205 milligrams to facilitate trade and pricing. The proposal did not gain wide acceptance. In 1878, there was broader agreement to use 200 milligrams as the standard measure of a carat. In 1907, the International Committee for Weights and Measures endorsed this standard. Over the next few years it was accepted by France, the United States, Great Britain, and others in subsequent years. Further standardization was achieved at the time with the grading of diamonds, based largely on Tavernier's system.

D espite the widespread availability in the United States in the 1880s and 1890s of inexpensive diamond rings, earrings, pins, and other jewelry, there was ample room for the purchase and display of much more ostentatious jewelry for the elite. It was this conspicuous display of wealth that inspired Mark Twain to term the period, the "Gilded Age." Twain's sarcastic comparison with the Golden Age of Greece captured the vapid materialism and exhibitionism of a new elite class.

Conspicuous display is a common form of competition without violence. Males of wealth and means decorated their women in diamond jewelry in order to show off their success. The diamonds were set in rings, necklaces, pins, brooches, bracelets, earrings, tiaras, aigrettes, stars, and any other appurtenance invented for the purpose. Women's bodies, otherwise constrained, contained, and hidden amid bodices, full body dresses, capes, scarves, head coverings, and the like were used as part of the backdrop for a conspicuous decorative motif that sparkles in candlelight, gaslight, and newly invented electrical light.

In New York, this display was evident in the first tier of boxes at the Metropolitan Opera. Women were draped in sparkling jewelry, so much so that the seats were dubbed the "Diamond Circle." In Washington, a newspaper columnist, Frank Carpenter, described the social scene in 1885,

> There is enough silk worn here every winter to carpet a whole state. There are pearls by the bushel and diamonds by the peck. . . . At the White House the other night there were at least 500 women wearing diamonds of various sizes. I counted 50 pairs of solitaire earrings whose stones were as big as the end of my thumb, and 30 diamond stars and pendants, any one of which would buy a large farm.[2]

* * *

For American women, the size and quality of their diamond jewelry came to stand for their value as seen in the eyes of their husbands or lovers. May Yohe tried to use the Hope diamond in this manner. Europeans were put off by this kind of display. They saw Americans flaunting diamonds and other symbols of wealth in uncouth and unsophisticated ways. Good breeding and civilized manners could not be bought, no matter how many diamonds one could afford. French Prime Minister Georges Clemenceau, a former reporter who lived in the United States during the period, captured this sentiment, opining that America seemed to have gone from "barbarism to decadence without having achieved civilization."[3]

Among the poor, the ostentatious display of wealth fostered envy, and even more so, resentment. Many new immigrants to New York and other big American cities lived in terrible poverty. They saw or heard of extravagant social events. Not only did Gilded Age hostesses deck themselves in diamonds, they committed other excesses, like placing collars studded with diamonds around the necks of their dogs. Social reformers pointed out that the rich had more love for their pets than they did for their fellow human beings. Diamonds became a symbol of love and an index of wealth, with their differential use illustrating the large class inequality of the time.

18

UNLUCKY INVENTORY

T*he destination of the stone is America,* read an announcement in the November 13, 1902, London *Times.* Messrs. Maddisons, solicitors for the aristocratic but cash-strapped Lord Francis Hope, sold his family's famous diamond to one of the big New York Fifth Avenue jewelry firms—Joseph Frankel's Sons & Co. Adolph Weil, a London diamond merchant, conducted the negotiations on their behalf. Joseph's son Simon Frankel sailed to London to consummate the deal. One source reported the sale for $168,000, another for $250,000.

Frankel boarded the *Kronprinz Wilhelm* for the trans-Atlantic passage back to New York. The Hope diamond was locked in the strongbox of the ship. The ship arrived in New York on November 26, 1901, stopping in Quarantine before docking. Another enterprising Fifth Avenue jeweler, Emanuel Gattle, took a cutter out to the ship and met onboard with Frankel, supposedly offering $350,000 for the Hope. Frankel turned him down. Two days later, the ship docked and items were put through customs. Deputy Collector Quackenbush refused to allow any special arrangements for the diamond, so it was processed just like everything else. Frankel removed the diamond from its setting, and paid 10 percent of the $141,032 declared value of the diamond—the equivalent of about $2.9 million in 2004. Had he not removed the gem from the setting, the duty would have been much higher.

Despite persistent rumors that a wealthy New Yorker would

buy the Hope, no one did. According to the *New York Times,* Frankel's was unable to get a good price for the Hope diamond. Over the years J. P. Morgan, Lord Francis Hope's older brother the Duke of Newcastle, Charles Schwab, J. J. Hill, and former Senator William A. Clark were all rumored to have considered its purchase. But the Hope diamond continued to sit in a New York safe deposit vault.

The 1907 Christmas holiday season was particularly bad. The market for diamonds, especially large ones, declined due to a very sluggish economy. The Hope failed to sell despite the latest London fad for colored diamonds. As a 1907 *New York Times* gossip column reported, ladies were taken to decorate themselves with colored gemstones. "Diamonds in black, yellow, blue, topaz, green, and gray are highly prized."[1] The column noted the Hope diamond as the world's most famous blue diamond and the special attention it had received in London as a result of May Yohe's marriage into the Hope family.

By New Years 1908, Frankel's as well as several other jewelers faced severe financial challenges. They could not pay off loans used to build up their inventories. Frankel's debt amounted to about $4.5 million, and even though it claimed assets of over $6 million it was faced with potential liquidation as creditors began to call in their debts.

Frankel's problems made the *New York Times* on January 7. Two days later the *Washington Post* published an item in its "Gossip of Society" column.

> Buy the famous Hope diamond and besides getting
> one of the world's greatest jewels you will help the
> multimillionaire firm of Frankel's Sons out of its financial
> difficulties . . . It is said that this jewel, valued at about
> $250,000, was partly responsible for the troubles of Joseph
> Frankel's Sons, whose inability to pay pressing bills
> resulted in the appointment of trustees for it and three
> correlated concerns.[2]

This was followed by a fanciful article, REMARKABLE JEWEL A HOODOO—
HOPE DIAMOND HAS BROUGHT TROUBLE TO ALL WHO HAVE OWNED IT, in the
January 19, 1908 *Washington Post*.

The story began,

> Deep behind the double locked doors hides the Hope
> diamond. Snug and secure behind time lock and bolt, it
> rests in its cotton wool nest under many wrappings, in the
> great vault of the great house of Frankel. Yet not all the
> locks and bolts and doors ever made by man can ward off
> its baleful power or screen from its venom those against
> whom its malign force may be directed.

According to the author,

> Every gem has its own power for good or evil and that this
> power never dies, though it may wax or wane under the
> circumstances, may lie dormant for centuries only to
> reappear with redoubled energy when terrestrial and
> celestial conditions combine to bring into play the
> mysterious forces hid beneath its glittering surface.[3]

The article presented a fractured history of the diamond, beginning
with Tavernier. Clearly influenced by the popular turn-of-the-cen-
tury, Orientalized Indian cosmo-gemology, it asked whether the
diamond, sold by Lord Francis Hope only months after his divorce
from May Yohe, was blamed for both his "marital and financial difficulties." The author finally recognized the recent troubles of the
jeweler, Simon Frankel. "There are those who say they will never
regain their old position of supremacy in their trade so long as the
Hope diamond remains in their ownership."[4]

This article, ominous as it might be, did not catch the imagination of a large public. Nor did it immediately redefine the way the
Hope was written about and discussed in the press. A feature article
in the *New York Times* on April 5, 1908, for example, specifically

addressed the stories of famous gems and superstitions. "The Hope Blue is celebrated in every country," writes the reporter.[5] Nothing is mentioned about any superstitions or mysterious influences connected to it.

F rankel's sold the Hope diamond to Sergeant (or alternatively Selim or Saloman) Habib in 1908. According to the London *Times* Habib made the purchase on behalf of the Sultan of Turkey. He was said to have paid $400,000 for the gem though the article indicates skepticism over the price, saying Frankel's firm considered $200,000 "a fair bidding price."[6]

According to the *New York Times,* Habib soon ran into financial difficulty, too. In 1909, the London *Times* reported the June 24 sale of the Habib jewel collection in an auction at the Hotel Drouot in Paris. The price supposedly paid for the Hope diamond was £16,000, even though £25,000 had been asked. The *New York Times* reported that it was bought for the equivalent of $80,000 by Louis Aucoc as agent for an unnamed customer.

A small but elegant hand-annotated catalog, *Joyaux Provenant de la Collection Habib* was produced for the auction. A rare copy still exists in the collections of the Bibliothèque d'Art et Archéologie–Jacques Doucet, which I was able to visit in Paris. The eight diamonds for sale, it explains, are historic and fantastic ones, including a 70$\frac{1}{16}$-carat aquamarine diamond, a 31½-carat rose diamond—supposedly one of the famous French Mazarins, a 16-carat diamond owned by the Princess Mathilde Bonaparte, a 58-carat diamond designated Le Mi Regent, and of course, the Hope. Louis Aucoc is listed as the expert overseeing the sale. Aucoc was a jeweler and distinguished gemological authority, having served as a member of the jury for the jewelry competition at the 1889 and 1906 Paris Expositions. He later clarified that he had not bought the blue diamond; rather, it was withdrawn from sale and later purchased by a jeweler named Simon Rosenau. Aucoc knew Rosenau at least from the time of the 1906 Exposition, as he'd judged the latter's antique jewelry reproductions.

In the sales catalog, there is a handwritten inscription, indicating that the Hope diamond was sold to Rosenau for 400,000 francs.

The entry for the Hope diamond indicated that it had indeed been sold by an American to Habib in 1908. Quite importantly, the sales catalog directly and explicitly states that all the diamonds had been in Constantinople, quite possibly in possession of the Sultan of Turkey, *except* for two—the blue Hope and the Princess Mathilde.

The Hope diamond had left Frankel's in New York and gone back across the Atlantic, most likely staying with Habib in France during the year. All seemed quite straightforward. At least until the next day when the modern legend of the Hope diamond received a huge boost.

The article in the London *Times* on Friday, June 25, 1909, was by-lined "from our own correspondent," dateline Paris.

The reporter writes, "Like most other famous stones, its [the Hope's] story is largely blended with tragedy . . . Its possession is the story of a long series of tragedies—murder, suicide, madness, and various other misfortunes."[7] The article repeats Streeter's assertion about Tavernier's bad luck and continued making all sorts of new claims:

> When it became part of the Crown Jewels, Madame de
> Montespan was in monopoly of the King's affections,
> and he yielded to her request to wear the famous blue
> diamond. But by a curious coincidence her influence over
> the King declined from about this time and Madame de
> Maintenon took her place. Nicolas Fouquet, Surintendant
> General des Finances . . . borrowed the diamond from
> Louis XIV for one of those costly fetes which he gave,
> and which appear to have roused the jealousy of the
> King. He kept it for some time; he fell into disgrace, was
> imprisoned . . . Marie Antoinette heard of its extraordinary
> beauty, and by the command of Louis XVI it was given to
> her. She wore it, we are told, about her throat at a great ball

at the Tuileries; the Princesse de Lamballe, her bosom friend . . . occasionally borrowed and wore the blue diamond. Marie Antoinette was beheaded, and the Princesse de Lamballe was done to death by a Paris mob.

For nearly 40 years the diamond remained perdu . . . Wilhelm Fals, an Amsterdam diamond cutter, had been commissioned to cut it, . . . it was stolen from him by his son—the former was ruined and the latter committed suicide. The younger Fals is further said to have given it to a Frenchman Francis Beaulieu, a native of Marseilles, who came to London and, when in the last stages of destitution and ill-health, sent for Daniel Eliason . . . the next day Beaulieu died of starvation.[8]

The article states that Eliason sold the diamond to Henry Thomas Hope in 1830 for £18,000, but admits that it did "not appear to have exercised any evil influence on Mr. Hope."[9]

The article continues,

It was purchased by Mr. Weil . . . and by him sold almost at once to Simon Frankel . . . and here the influence continued; for Frankel could not find a purchaser, and he fell into financial difficulties. Last year, it was sold to M. Jacques Colot, a French broker, for, it is said, $300,000. Colot sold it to a Russian, Prince Kanitovski, who lent it to Lorens Ladue, a beautiful actress at the Folies Bergere, and shot her from a box the first night she wore it. The Prince proved the diamond to be his property, took possession of it, and was stabbed two days afterwards by revolutionists. Colot, the broker, went insane and killed himself within a few days of these tragic events. The next owner of the stone is stated to have been Simon Montharides, a Greek jeweler, who is said to have been thrown over a precipice and killed, with his wife and two children. Montharides is stated to have sold the diamond to the ex-Sultan Abdul Hamid, whose passion for precious stones was well known. Whether the ex-Sultan ever owned the Hope diamond is a point upon which it will perhaps be wise not to insist too strongly; but there is no possible doubt about the fact that it was in Constantinople until comparatively recently, and very little that it was in the Sultan's possession. Its alleged adventures for the brief space while there seem to beggar the wildest fiction, and we give it with all reserve. Briefly it is this . . . the Sultan's favorite, Salma Zubayba, was wearing it on her breast when the Young Turks broke into the Palace, and was shot dead by her master, the bullet striking close to the diamond.[10]

This was quite a tale; the Hope was implicated in at least three major revolutions—the French, early Russian, and Turkish. The story was chock-full of clearly erroneous and fictional material, most easily dispelled. The long-lived Tavernier proclaimed himself blessed. There is no evidence Madame de Montespan ever wore the blue diamond. Her influence did not wane with the acquisition of the diamond in 1668, as she was Louis XIV's mistress until he secretly married Madame de Maintenon in 1683. Fouquet did give a famous fête at Vaux that made Louis XIV furious. He was arrested and relieved of his responsibilities. But all that took place in 1661, seven years *before* the blue diamond even arrived in France.

The errors go on. While Princess Lamballe was killed by a mob in Paris, she could not have worn the diamond because at that time the revolutionary guard had confiscated it. The story about Wilhelm Fals and Francis Beaulieu is totally without any evidence, and the idea that the latter would have the diamond, sell it to Eliason for cash, and die the next day from starvation is beyond credulity. Of course Eliason couldn't have sold it in 1830, having inconveniently (for the story) died on November 17, 1824. While correctly citing the financial troubles befallen the Frankel's, the firm was well out of such trouble by the time of the article. Jacques Colot was indeed a French diamond dealer, but never purchased the diamond. Neither Russian Prince Kanitovski nor Folies Bergère actress Lorens Ladue nor Greek jeweler Simon Montharides has been found to exist. The article's assertion that the latter sold the diamond to the Turkish Sultan Abdul Hamid and was part of the tumultuous revolt in Constantinople is directly discounted by the history of the diamond given in Habib's auction catalog and contemporaneous newspaper reports of the Frankels' sale in 1908.

The article is quite correct in concluding that the diamond's alleged adventures "beggar the wildest fiction."[11] The fiction was that created or elaborated by the reporter in the guise of news—precisely what legend making is about. The London *Times* story was quite simply a fantasy spun around a few facts from the diamond's history. It built upon the misfortune attributed to the Hope diamond in the 1908 *Washington Post* article, but added to it considerably.

The London *Times* article was the seminal one. Whether it was created by the unnamed journalist or was based upon the narrative of some imaginative other, we may never know. The article exhibits enough tongue in cheek to suggest the author knew he or she was spinning a fable, yet it is hard to be sure.

It wasn't until some eighteen months later, in 1911, that T. Edgar Wilson, the editor of the *Jewelers' Circular Weekly*, wrote a general rebuttal published in the *New York Times*. By that time it was too late. The story stood, and took on a life of its own. It served as a basis of most every later sensationalist account of the Hope diamond.

And the story grew. A series of misreports in the *New York Times* about Habib and the Hope diamond later in 1909 both confused and clarified previous stories. On November 17, a front-page story reported that:

Selim Habib, a wealthy Turkish diamond collector and merchant, who formerly owned the famous blue Hope diamond, was among the passengers drowned in the wreck of the French mail steamer Seyne at Singapore.[12]

Quite inexplicably, it also reported that Habib "had the diamond with him," adding another item to the "list of misfortunes associated with the ownership of the famous gem."[13] How Habib could possibly be traveling with the gem he had formerly owned was a mystery.

The *New York Times* followed the report with another puzzling item the next day. The Hope diamond, it said, was not likely to have gone down with the ship because it had been reported to have been "bought by Habib for the Turkish Sultan in Constantinople."[14]

Nonetheless, a salvage operation was mounted out of Singapore, and a Scottish expatriate diver located the sunken ship's safe. Brought to the surface and opened, there was, of course, no blue diamond.

By November 20, someone with a bit of sense caught up to the inconsistencies in the reporting and began to clarify the story. A front page *New York Times* report declared that the Hope diamond was, after all, not at the bottom of the sea off Singapore, but rather in Paris, in the possession of a jeweler named Rosenau of 9 Rue Chauchat.

By March 1910 there was more clarification, at least in the newspapers. Louis Aucoc, the Habib auction expert, was interviewed. He explained that the diamond had been held over for sale and later bought by Rosenau. He also commented on the erroneous reports about Habib's shipwreck and the diamond. Aucoc is quoted: "the story of the shipwreck of Habib with his blue diamond is a legend which must not be allowed credence any longer."[15] Finally, the *New York Times* gets to the "bottom" of the story. It turns out that it wasn't even the same Habib who sank with the ship—it was a different man entirely—just someone with the same name. Oops!

As fantastic and historically erroneous as it was, this story of the Hope diamond was about misfortune, "ill luck," as people termed it—not a *curse*. That touch was still to come courtesy of Pierre Cartier. But ill luck did not keep the Cartier brothers from buying the Hope diamond from Rosenau. They paid the equivalent of about $110,000, which would make the diamond worth about $2.1 million at today's prices. The Cartier brothers clearly thought they could sell the diamond—and its story.

19

CARTIER'S STORY

I*t was up to Pierre Cartier to sell* not only the diamond, but also its legend as a cursed stone.

Pierre was the showman and salesman of the Cartier brothers trio that included Louis and Jacques. Pierre was suave and sophisticated, good with rich American customers, having worked in the firm's New York branch office—and being himself married to a rich American. He and his brothers were in the process of building the family jewelry business begun in Paris by their grandfather, Louis-François Cartier in 1847.

Cartier's joined three traditionally separate artisan traditions—that of the goldsmith, the *bijoutier* or maker of gold and enamel jewelry, and the *joaillier,* or gemstone fashioner—into one unified and successful enterprise. After 1898, the business took off when eldest brother Louis, an aesthete, collector, intellectual, and master tactician joined his father, Alfred, in the business, and the firm moved to its present location on the Rue de la Paix. Sales increased, and customers became even more prestigious—Queen Victoria and Queen Alexandra among them. A London branch opened in 1902. In the early 1900s diamonds were sold in necklaces, pendants, brooches, pins, rings, and tiaras. The firm started to deal with large, historic diamonds and emeralds. Cartier's received official warrants to service King Edward VII of Great Britain, King Alfonso XIII of Spain, King Carlos of Portugal, the King of Siam, and Czar Nicholas II of Russia. Among their customers were the Aga Khan, Baron de Rothschild,

Princess Radziwell, and a growing group of wealthy Americans including Cornelius Vanderbilt and J. P. Morgan. This led to the opening of the New York branch office in 1909.

The Cartiers pioneered new designs in jewelry, combining those of the Orient with Art Deco. Louis, the scholar among the trio, studied Islamic, Indian, and Chinese styles. He had been inspired by the Orientalist design work of Diaghilev, who had organized an exhibition at the Grand Palais in 1906, produced *Boris Godunov* in 1908, and influenced the set and costume designs of the Ballets Russes in 1910. Louis traveled to the Middle East and India in 1910 and again the next year, learning about the culture, making arrangements for pearl and gem deals, and even studying Hindustani.

Cartier's made ample use of Indian designs in all sorts of jewelry, but particularly in tiaras, aigrettes, and *sarpanches*. Over time, the brothers developed strong relationships among Indian and

Alfred Cartier (second from right) is joined by his three sons, Jacques, Louis, and Pierre in 1910.

Arab aristocrats, turning them into clients by resetting their gems in "modern" European forms. The Cartiers attended Oriental balls and participated in events with the elite of European society.

It was in this context that the Cartiers developed the story of the cursed Hope diamond. The brothers were quite familiar with the writings of Tavernier and Streeter. Closely involved with Indian gems and aristocrats, they surely knew Collins's *The Moonstone.* Louis is likely to have read fellow Parisian Louis Finot's French translations of Indian gemological texts. Pierre certainly read or heard about the 1909 London *Times* article.

The Cartiers also knew about superstitions connected to gems. While they did make an opal heart pendant for soprano Nellie Melba in 1903, they generally declined to work with opals. Louis felt that customers, particularly the French, would be reluctant to purchase opals because of a widespread belief that they were cursed—even though he knew this belief was based upon a fictional account, *Anne of Geierstein,* written by Sir Walter Scott in 1829. The novel was in turn based upon a superstition invented about opals by Hungarian and Slovak mine owners in an effort to discourage use of competing Australian opals.

By the early 1900s, the idea of developing narratives for famous gems was well established. This had become more important to retailers after the discovery of South African diamonds. South African diamonds were found in nature. They had no history, no colorful biography. The Indian diamonds did. Where they didn't, such narratives could be invented. The creation of gemstone narratives in the early 1900s paralleled the creation of new visual designs for jewelry. Both were based upon Orientalist motifs, terms, and elements, but recast into consumable form for Europeans. The purpose of both was to delight, to stimulate visual interest for the body, and amusement for the mind.

Just down the street from Cartier, on New York's Fifth Avenue, where Pierre had worked, Marcus & Co. Jewelers published little booklets by Carlo De Fornaro, one for each month of the year.

The booklets were titled *The Legend of the Diamond, The Legend of the Ruby, The Legend of the Moonstone,* and so on, including tales about the pearl, sapphire, emerald, cat's eye, jade, coral, topaz, turquoise, and opal. Each had a simple text with illustrations. Most had the names of Hindu gods above the title, for example, "Krishna's Gift" and "Shiva the Destroyer." The booklets used elements from Indian texts, but were much simplified, turning complex myths and stories into children's "fairy tales." India was sanitized, romanticized, and Europeanized. "In days of old in Hindoustan, in the land of Maghada there lived a mighty Rajah named Neemee," began one.[1] "At each thought of charity, unselfishness and sacrifice, Krishna had dropped a diamond into the bowl," offered another.[2] In the *Legend of the Ruby,* the gem is originally a diamond. Its owner queen is murdered, her blood stains the diamond; the stain grows and grows until it recolors the whole gem—and then it is restored to the eye of the Shiva idol.

These stories engendered various emotions—love, loyalty, respect, and risk—associated with gems and provided something for jewelry salesmen to tell their clients. In turn, those clients would have something interesting to say when presenting gems for various occasions. Exotic Indian elements helped, though their religious, philosophical, and cultural complexities had to be stripped out for simplicity's sake.

Pierre Cartier understood the importance of intriguing and amusing clients.[3] He'd watched other jewelers create instant legends for gemstones. And so he joined Collins's basic premise about a diamond stolen from a vengeful Hindu god with the reported history of misfortune following the blue diamond to create the legend of the cursed Hope diamond.

Just as important as the story was Pierre Cartier's audience for the telling. He had to choose his mark well and wisely.

20

McLEAN'S TEMPTATION

Unconventional, young, rich, and spoiled, the McLeans were prime customers for the Cartier brothers. Ned and Evalyn were true children of America's "Gilded Age," an era now reaching its crescendo.

Evalyn, aged 24 in 1910, was the daughter of Thomas F. Walsh, an Irish immigrant gold miner from Tipperary who'd come to America penniless in 1869 at the age of 19, and Carrie Bell Reed, the beautiful daughter of a schoolteacher originally from Wisconsin. Evalyn was born in Colorado where her father was caught up with "mining fever," as they called it. Walsh moved around Colorado and South Dakota, went through periods of relative booms and busts, making do with small claims and finds, and living off borrowed money. Evalyn grew up living in miner's shacks and hotels, including one owned by her parents. She experienced the instability and uncertainties of a prospector's life. Her cohort, she claimed, in somewhat exaggerated fashion, consisted of "homicidal maniacs, nice women and prostitutes, Chinese and some Indians."[1]

In 1896, when Evalyn was ten, Tom Walsh whispered in her ear, "Daughter, I've struck it rich."[2] He'd found gold. His Camp Bird mine in Ouary, Colorado, turned out about $5,000 in ore per day. The family became wealthy, and the next year moved to Washington, D.C. Walsh was hailed as the "Colorado Monte Cristo," bought land in the city, and donated funds to the campaign of the successful Republican candidate for president, William McKinley. Walsh was named a U.S. commissioner to the Paris Exposition of 1900 along with Mrs. Potter Palmer (of the Chicago Palmer House hotel) and Michael de Young (owner of the *San Francisco Chronicle*). The Walshes lived in Paris for a year, entertained lavishly, and in their travels befriended, among others, King Leopold of Belgium.

Returning home, Walsh decided to sell his mine for $5.2 million plus a share in future profits. He commissioned the building of a magnificent Beaux Arts mansion at 2020 Massachusetts Avenue, where it still stands today. The mansion cost $835,000—the most expensive residence in the nation's capital. A large mass of gold ore was embedded in the arch of the main entrance. The mansion had 60 rooms, a theater, ballroom, a Louis XIV style salon, a beautiful main staircase in the style of luxury ocean liners, and about $2 million in furnishings. A staff of 23 servants cared for the premises.

The family, though wealthy and connected to Republican luminaries, was quite idiosyncratic. Politically, Tom Walsh had been accused of advocating "modified socialism" for the masses. He was a Freemason, but still "tethered to the [Catholic] Church." Carrie Bell Walsh was a Christian Scientist. Coming from this background it was no surprise that Evalyn candidly declared herself "just a heathen."

At age 18, Evalyn went to live in Paris without her parents. She went wild, by her own account, dressing like a prostitute, drinking, and dying her hair, blond, red, and then pink. Walsh ordered her home. The next year the family was again in Europe and acquired a red Mercedes, later exported to the States.

In 1906, Evalyn and her younger brother Vinson were in Newport, Rhode Island, driving the Mercedes back from lunch when a tragic accident occurred. Whether caused by speeding down Honeymoon Hill or a blowout, the car overturned. Vinson was killed. Evalyn was hospitalized with serious injuries—one of her legs shattered. This kept her in bed for months; morphine treatment for her pain led to a lifelong addiction to laudanum; the accident also left her with a leg-length discrepancy and a limp.

Evalyn became engaged to Edward "Ned" Beale McLean, broke

it off, and was reengaged and finally eloped. She had first met Ned in 1897, when she was eleven years old. Evalyn was taking dance lessons from Ned's mother and was invited to dine with the family. She found the lanky "Neddie" a spoiled, awkward, and shy teenager. "Gawky," she called him.[3]

The McLeans were originally from Ohio. Ned's grandfather, Washington McLean, had been a boilermaker and steamboat builder in Cincinnati. He made a fortune, and in 1857 became a partner in the *Cincinnati Examiner.* He turned the newspaper into one of national repute as a voice of the Democratic Party. In 1880, "Wash" retired, leaving control of the paper to his son, John R. John had been expelled from Harvard and played baseball briefly for the Red Stockings. He forged an unholy alliance with Republican Tom Campbell and the two proceeded to "milk the city dry through their complete mastery of political plunder."[4] The shakedowns and kickbacks ended in 1884 with riots in the city. John R. moved to Washington, D.C. Inheriting his father's fortune, he became the president of Washington Gas Light Company and a major director of the Riggs National Bank. In 1905 he bought the *Washington Post,* giving it a nationalistic bent following the lead of his friend, William Randolph Hearst. In 1911 he cofounded the Washington and Old Dominion Railway, naming one of its stops McLean, Virginia.

Ned and Evalyn were part of the same elite social circle that included Alice Roosevelt, the daughter of Teddy Roosevelt, who, two years Evalyn's elder, was also a bit wild and scandalous as a teenager. Evalyn found Ned a pampered, weak, bumbling youth, spoiled by his parents. As she wrote of him, "This fiancé of mine was not an editor nor was he a cub reporter. He was a rich man's son, twenty-two years old. He never had been other than rich."[5] Ned was already a serious alcoholic as well, and Evalyn saw from the outset that she would have to "control him completely."

Ned and Evalyn were married in 1908, forming one of the wealthiest unions in America. Their honeymoon brought them to Turkey, the Middle East, Paris and Cartier's. It was at Cartier's that on December 15 they'd purchased the beautiful 94¾-carat diamond—the Star of the East as a honeymoon present—for $120,000, overspending the $200,000 given to them by their parents for expenses. A year later, their son Vinson, dubbed by the press the "hundred-million-dollar baby," was born.

In 1910 they returned to Europe and heard Cartier's story about the blue diamond. Pierre must have counted upon Evalyn's ornery, flamboyant, spirited attitude in pitching the diamond to her. Ned, for his part, was in ill sorts with a hangover, and reportedly responded, "How much?"[6]

But Evalyn did not like the setting. It struck her as old-fashioned and matronly; quite unlike Cartier's new designs that featured interesting filigree patterns and a playful lightness of form. Those designs matched the new, sleeker woman of society coinciding with Evalyn's own self-image.

No deal was made at the Hotel Bristol. But Cartier persisted, convinced he could sell the diamond to the McLeans, and in effect turn over a quick profit to his company. To do so, he would come to America and meet the McLeans on their home turf.

Pierre Cartier arrived in New York on November 23, 1910. He declared the value of the Hope diamond as $110,000 for U.S. Customs and paid a 10 percent duty. Had the diamond been imported in a finished jewel setting, he would have paid 30 percent. Presumably Cartier brought the new setting with him and then at his New York store either reset the diamond or had one of his employees do it.

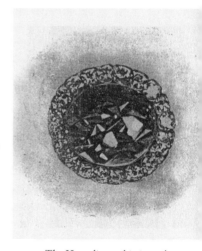

The Hope diamond in its early 20th-century setting.

In this new platinum setting, the Hope was surrounded quite simply with 16 small, clear diamonds in an oval arrangement, alternating between square and heart-shaped brilliants. It was most likely designed by Charles Jacqueau. Jacqueau elaborated Orientalist designs for Cartier, inspired by Les Ballets Russes the previous season. The new jewel was to be worn as a *bandeau*—head ornament—a European Orientalist adaptation of the Indian *sarpanch,* quite popular at the time. The jewel could also be attached to a necklace. This setting has remained essentially the same to the present day.

Upon his arrival in New York, Cartier's staff sent Ned McLean a cable asking for a meeting. Pierre wanted to leave the diamond with Evalyn for her inspection, hoping that if she kept it for some time she would agree to a purchase.

Pierre brought the Hope down to Washington. He left it and an accompanying necklace with the McLeans over a weekend—probably December 3–4. Ned put the gem on Evalyn's dresser. As Evalyn later narrated in her autobiography,

> For hours that jewel stared at me. The setting had been changed completely to a frame of diamonds, and there was a splendid chain of diamonds to go around my neck. At some time during that night I began to want the thing.[7]

Just about two months later the deal was sealed. Ned signed a note with Cartier:

> In consideration of the payment of $40,000, the delivery of an emerald and pearl pendant and the payment of $114,000 in three annual installments without interest, payable bi-monthly, I hereby agree to sell to Edward B. McLean what is known as the "Hope Diamond" and necklace, delivery to be made forthwith, and if desired by the purchaser, a necklace in the shape of a bowknot and diamonds to be taken at cost and deducted from the sum of $114,000 deferred payment. Should any fatality occur to the family of Edward B. McLean within six months, the

said Hope Diamond is agreed to be exchanged for jewelry
of equal value at the selection of Wilton J. Lambert [*the
McLeans' attorney*]. It is further agreed that the contract for
said deferred payment is not to be negotiated.[8]

Cartier valued the deal at $180,000, the $40,000 in cash, $114,000 paid
over three years, and a $26,000 credit for Evalyn's emerald and pearl
pendant with a diamond necklace. That would be equivalent to a
diamond purchase of $3.9 million today. As Evalyn dramatically
recounted years later, in putting on the Hope diamond, "I put the
chain around my neck and thereby seemed to hook my life to its
destiny of good or evil."[9]

Evalyn told biographer Boyden Sparkes that she called her
mother-in-law over the telephone after closing the deal with Cartier. "Mummie, I have bought the Hope diamond," she recounted.[10]

Her mother-in-law almost fainted and told Evalyn,

It is a cursed stone and you must send it back. Worse than
its being freighted with bad luck is your buying of it—a
piece of recklessness. Money is a trust for better things
than jewel-buying.[11]

Apparently Mrs. McLean and her companion, Mrs. Robert Goelet,
drove out to see Evalyn to urge her to change her mind, even as
"they handled and admired the gem."[12] Evalyn, feeling the obligation of a good daughter-in-law returned it to Cartier, who apparently sent it right back to her.

What happened after that depends upon whom you believe.
The *New York Times* reported the sale on its front page on January 29,
1911. According to the newspaper account, the diamond was sold for
$300,000 in a deal negotiated the night before by Pierre Cartier and
the McLeans at the residence on 2020 Massachusetts Avenue. Elaborate security arrangements were reportedly in place. The diamond
would be guarded by a former Secret Service agent who in turn
would be watched by two hired detectives. A special automobile

would transport the diamond nightly to a bank vault. But the price was certainly wrong, and much of the story hubris deliberately crafted by Ned McLean.

The story also noted "Mr. Cartier said that the duties on the diamond were well up into the thousands, but the sum paid was a matter of 'customs house confidence.' "[13]

Cartier's concern with the confidentiality of a U.S. Custom's House declaration got McLean's attention. The latter refused to pay for the diamond, prompting Cartier to file suit on March 8 in the Supreme Court of the District of Columbia. Again the Hope diamond was front-page news. SUES THE M'LEANS FOR HOPE DIAMOND, CARTIER FIRM ALLEGES IT HAS NOT RECEIVED A CENT—ASKS FOR $180,000—PURCHASE IS NOW DENIED—FRIENDS OF MCLEANS SAY JEWEL WAS TAKEN ON APPROVAL AND CARTIERS REFUSE TO TAKE IT BACK, shouted the *New York Times*.[14]

Affidavits filed by Cartier and by the McLeans and found in the archives of the Library of Congress make clear the countervailing accounts of the sale.[15] Louis and Pierre Cartier alleged that the Hope diamond was in the possession of the McLeans, who had agreed to purchase the diamond for $180,000. The Cartiers had not received any cash payment, or the pendant.

The McLeans counterclaimed that Cartier had given them the Hope diamond for inspection, but they had never actually purchased it or taken possession. They asserted that Cartier had lied about the diamond's value, claiming it had been purchased by a previous owner for $200,000 and had never been sold for under $180,000. Cartier told them he would realize no profit on the sale. Based upon information gathered by his lawyers, Ned's affidavit asserts that Cartier had bought the diamond for $80,000, basically the same price as the previous owner, and that while the new setting might have added $5,000 to its value, it certainly did not justify Cartier's excessive asking price. Furthermore, Ned's lawyers had obtained information from the Customs House in New York; Cartier had declared the Hope's value at $110,000.

Cartier in turn claimed that he'd met with the McLeans' attorney, agreed to a formal contract for the diamond's sale, and indeed celebrated it with a champagne toast at McLean's *Washington Post* office. According to Cartier, McLean said he did not have the $40,000 in cash to give him, so he took the train back to New York. Cartier then received a telegram to come back down to Washington to reset the diamond so that Evalyn could wear it on Monday, January 30. When he showed up he was told that Ned had gone to Baltimore to get the $40,000. Pierre insisted that the McLeans keep the diamond and pay up.

The popular story was not about price, but more about the reputation of the diamond. The McLeans were seen as trying to get out of the purchase because of the bad luck attending to the Hope and not because they were being gullible or being cheated over its monetary value. They received all sorts of correspondence with offers of alleviating the evil supposed to reside in the diamond. For example, Virginia Calhoun of New York City wrote to Evalyn offering to "break the spell" over the Hope diamond and to transform the "spirit" of "evil genius" making it instead into a "mascot of good fortune"—all for a "bonus" of $5,000.[16]

The Cartier suit was settled out of court on February 1, 1912. The *New York Times* published a front page story the next day, M'LEANS TO KEEP THE HOPE DIAMOND, WEALTHY PURCHASERS OF FAMOUS STONE TO RETAIN IT DESPITE SINISTER REPUTATION—ORIGINAL PRICE $260,000—WILL BE WORN FOR FIRST TIME TONIGHT BY NEW OWNER AT RECEPTION AT MCLEAN MANSION. The reporter wrongly asserted that the McLeans had not known about the diamond's reputation when they'd agreed to buy it—something a *New York Times* editorial that day also found fascinating:

> Credulity is a little strained by the report that a bargain to
> buy an enormous diamond had to be enforced by legal
> proceedings for the absurd reason that the people who
> made the bargain heard that the stone was "unlucky," and
> therefore didn't want it.[17]

The irony was that the Hope diamond, supposedly cursed and worthy of rejection, was now acceptable and would immediately crown a celebratory occasion. Evalyn wore the Hope diamond publicly for the first time for a reception honoring Russian ambassador George Bakhmatief (who was also Ned's uncle). The event was remarkable. The 40 dinner guests included the Russian ambassador and his wife, the ambassadors of Great Britain and Brazil, ministers from Denmark, the Netherlands, and Belgium, the U.S. Secretary of the Treasury and the Postmaster General, Senators Brandage and Du Pont, and several congressmen. Diners were later joined by 1,500 other guests drawn from "the smart circles of official and resident society," as the *New York Times* called them.[18] Guests were entertained by musical artists from the Metropolitan Opera Company.

A young Evalyn Walsh McLean wearing the Hope diamond on a necklace and the Star of the East as an aigrette. She often swapped the positions of these two diamonds.

For the occasion, Evalyn was adorned in a Worth gown of silver net over white charmeuse. She wore the Hope diamond on her head and the Star of the East on a necklace, in Orientalist fashion. The mansion itself was festooned with flowers—palms, roses, lilacs, pink Japanese azaleas, crab-apple blossoms with green ferns—creating an elegant springlike atmosphere. The reception, not counting the Hope diamond of course, cost over $30,000 according to the *Times* and some $48,000 according to Evalyn—the equivalent of over half a million dollars today.

The most expensive single item and highlight of the reception was the table décor. Some 4,000 yellow lilies were imported from England especially for the dinner. They were delivered to the McLeans via the *Lusitania*, the same ship that carried Pierre

Cartier and the Hope diamond to America, and whose sinking three years later on May 7, 1915 by a German submarine would provoke U. S. entry into World War I.

A record of the McLean account with Cartier reflects the 1912 settlement. The purchase price of the Hope diamond was $180,000. The McLeans made a cash payment of $20,000 on February 2. In subsequent months they turned over to Cartier a diamond *cravette* collar mounted in platinum valued at $9,000 and the emerald and pearl pendant originally agreed to and valued at $26,000. They then proceeded to make payments of $1,000 a month over the years, sometimes paying one month at a time, sometimes two or three, and sometimes accruing additional payments for interest due. They also incurred new expenses with Cartier. In March Ned McLean negotiated with Cartier's staff for a new $7,430 diamond chain necklace from which to hang the Hope diamond.

In all of the dealings between the McLeans and the Cartiers, there did not appear to be much acrimony. Suing for payment was commonplace for the ultrarich, and the Cartiers were used to it. In any event, Evalyn continued to do business with Pierre throughout her lifetime, and indeed, he and his wife were guests at her parties, including one glittering Mardi Gras celebration she gave for Harry Truman at her Friendship estate in 1945.

It was the reputed curse, not the price, of the Hope diamond that captured the public's attention. The subtitle of the *New York Times* article announcing the sale, $300,000 FOR JEWEL OWNED BY LOUIS XVI AND WORN BY MARIE ANTOINETTE AND MAY YOHE—WAS ALSO ABDUL HAMID'S— BLUE STONE, ONCE OF 112 CARATS, NOW 44½—CREDITED WITH BRINGING ILL-LUCK TO ITS POSSESSORS, brought quick responses. A relative wrote to Ned, "as you have just purchased the beautiful but awful Hope diamond, I do sincerely hope nothing will happen to either you or cousin Evalyn."[19]

Some responses questioned the accuracy of the supposed history of the diamond. The Duke of Newcastle issued a statement on behalf of his brother, Lord Francis, denying anyone had worn the Hope while in his possession. T. Edgar Wilson, the editor of the *Jewelers' Circular Weekly* responded in a letter to the *New York Times*.

> Although the writer has been connected with the jewelry
> trade press for nearly twenty years and has been especially
> interested in the history of the great diamonds of the
> world, he never heard of any stories connected with the
> Hope diamond until a sensational article appeared a short
> time after it was brought to this country in 1901.[20]

Wilson discounted any historical reports of bad luck being associated with the Hope's owners, noting the growth of made-up stories:

> It has been the custom not only to revive these stories
> every time mention of the stone appears in the pubic press,
> but to add to them fictitious incidents of misfortune as to
> alleged possessors of the stone at various times.[21]

Yet neither the reputable *New York Times* nor other newspapers around the world let the facts get in the way of a good story. The continuing saga of the Hope diamond had a great deal of public appeal and staying power.

The story of the cursed Hope diamond caught Evalyn McLean's fancy in a special way. She was not from a family of the idle rich. She believed herself to be poor at heart and in origins. Tom Walsh had worked for his money, and she had shared in that life. Her father's money was "clean money," which came directly from the earth, not from other men. McLean thus felt herself somewhat protected from the effects of the supposed curse. Simply, she did not deserve to be cursed.

But still, she took precautions. Evalyn wrote that she and her servant Maggie Buggy had gone to a church in Virginia to get a priest, Monsignor Russell, to bless the Hope diamond and thus neutralize the curse. The Monsignor donned his robes and placed the diamond on a velvet cushion in a side room of the church. Evalyn reported on the rite,

> As he continued his preparations, a storm broke. Lightning flashed. Thunder shook the church. I don't mind saying various things were scared right out of me. There was no wind or rain; just darkness and these lurid lightning thrusts. Across the street a tree was struck and splintered. Maggie was half-frantic with her fear; beads were clicking through her fingers. I wished I could have such faith; Maggie was calling on Personages with whom I rarely reckon in my thoughts. Monsignor Russell's Latin words gave me strange comfort.[22]

As Evalyn's writings indicate, she mainly found the curse of the Hope diamond to be a playful amusement in the years following the acquisition. Spiritualism and astrology were popular in her social set. Her friend Florence Harding, the wife of then Senator Warren Harding and strong advocate for women's rights, was also quite superstitious, and more apprehensive about the curse than Evalyn. The two women, Florence, the serious elder, and Evalyn, the younger firebrand, became close companions.

E valyn's somewhat playful attitude toward the curse changed in 1919. Evalyn, Ned and their three children, Vinson, John II, and Ned Jr., took up full-time residence at Friendship, the 76-acre McLean family estate in the northwest section of Washington. The property included a historic mansion visited by George Washington. John R. McLean bought the property and also purchased adjacent tracts of land. Remodeled by Evalyn, Friendship sported manicured lawns, rows of majestic cedars, fountains, and a full menagerie of donkeys,

The McLeans with Vinson and younger brother Jock.

goats, geese, ponies, and cows. It was also home to Evalyn's pet llama, monkey, and parrot.

In May, Ned and Evalyn went to Louisville for the Kentucky Derby. On May 18 Vinson, then aged nine, was playing near the road in front of the estate. A former gardener had pulled over to the roadside. He had some ferns in his car. Vinson playfully grabbed a few and was making his getaway, when a Ford—going about eight miles an hour, banged into him. Vinson was knocked to the ground, his head hitting the concrete.[23] The driver and three passengers, all women, stopped, helped get Vinson to the house, and then absconded. An army surgeon who was in the area was summoned. Vinson's condition was serious and declining. The McLeans were called in Louisville—Evalyn was apparently told Vinson had the flu. Ned was probably told the truth. They left immediately for home via a specially chartered train. A specialist from Johns Hopkins University in Baltimore, a brain surgeon from Philadelphia, and another physician from Washington all joined to help.

Despite an emergency operation, young Vinson died. A *New York Times* report noted

when news of the death of the boy spread throughout
Washington tonight, it was at once remarked that this
was another tragedy to be added to the long string of
misfortunes that had followed the successive owners of
the Hope diamond.[24]

Ned went on a drinking binge, devastated by the death of his son.
Florence Harding tried to console Evalyn. And family, friends, and
the public wondered if the Hope diamond was indeed a talisman of
evil.

21

MODERNITY'S CURSE

The *Hope diamond curse begged for* public explanation. A series
of *New York Times* editorials following the McLean purchase
both mystified and rationalized the belief in the mysterious nature
of the diamond.

> The superstitions about the good or ill luck residing in
> precious jewels and amulets has a solid basis in fact and
> philosophy.
>   We would not suggest, of course, that this bit of
> crystallized carbon differs from others except in color, size,
> and like innocent and harmless characteristics, but just the
> same, its ownership probably has often been followed by
> trouble and disaster.[1]

The explanations did not generally seek to demonstrate the existence of the supernatural. To the contrary, they sought worldly explanations, whereby seemingly irrational beliefs could be made
understandable by reference to historical traditions, economic principles, psychological anxieties, and other such naturally occurring
phenomena. In this, they reflected the scholarship of the era, the efforts by James Frazer, Emile Durkheim, Franz Boas, Sigmund Freud,
Thorstein Veblen, and others to explain religion, magic, superstition, and folklore in terms of rational principles, historical events,
or even human nature.

One explanation suggested that the possession of shining precious stones inspired a feeling of confidence in possessors who would then overachieve. Their accomplishments would provoke envy by others, and invite harm as a result. A second suggested that such large and valuable diamonds as the Hope were unlucky because "the gem meant the locking up of a large amount of capital in the very least productive of all investments."[2] They thus jeopardized the very fortunes that made its acquisition possible. Another suggested that the Hope diamond created an undue psychological burden on its owners, bringing about haunting anxieties and incidental ills. Still another suggested a form of profitable myth making to increase the value of the gem.

T he instant popularity and wide resonance of the legend of the Hope diamond curse was extraordinary, and well suited to the times. The idea of a curse fit well with increasing consciousness of colonialism and the expression of class revenge in the United States in the early 1900s.

Following Wilkie Collins's paradigmatic *Moonstone,* curses were popularly conceived of in the West as weapons in the failed arsenal of colonized peoples. Curses were punishments for the looting and pillaging of the treasures of the temples and ancient cities of Asia, Africa, and the Americas. The rapacious desire for wealth abroad paralleled such desires at home. Undeserving aristocrats, profiteering capitalists, and unscrupulous traders made or maintained their wealth off the labor or suffering of unfortunate urban masses, dirt-poor farmers, disenfranchised African Americans and marginalized others. While the wealthy might attribute curses directed their way as class envy, for the poor, curses were the moral revenge for the wasteful spending, lack of compassion, and immoral deeds of the members of "high society."

The curse resonated with the politics of the era. The Progressive movement, promoting social reform and economic fairness, struggled with vested interests seeking to preserve the privileges of wealth and class. The curse expressed the "dark side" of the reformist agenda. This sentiment was evident not only in the Hope diamond curse, but also others, including the expressions following the dramatic sinking of the *Titanic* in April of 1912, wherein 1,513 people lost their lives. A number of stories, toasts, and songs were created after the sinking, reflecting upon the disaster. Among some African Americans, there was the idea that Jack Johnson, the heavyweight boxing champion of the world, was refused passage on the prestigious ocean liner because he was Black. The sinking was seen as a curse of sorts—a form of divine retribution against the injustice of the owners and the wealthy privileged people who benefited from such prejudice. One song, *God Moves on the Water,* highlighted the punishment of the rich. One verse went:

> *Well that Jacob Nash was a millionaire,*
> *Lord, he had plenty money to spare.*
> *When the great Titanic was sinkin' down,*
> *Well, he could not pay his fare.*[3]

Similar ideas of divine or supernatural retribution energized the Tutankhamen curse in 1923. Lord Carnarvon, the sponsor of Howard Carter's archaeological expedition that unearthed the tomb of the ancient Egyptian Pharaoh Tutankhamen, fell ill and died. The London *Times* and other newspapers reported mysterious circumstances that both caused and attended his death. The famous Arthur Conan Doyle announced that the curse of the Pharaoh was the cause. The tomb had been violated and looted, and now the mummy or ancient gods or spirits were exacting their retribution. Others associated with the expedition died, their deaths also attributed to the curse. This led to hysteria in England.

The logic of the curse is that supernatural power is thought to flow through contact objects—whether gems, ships, human remains, words or other objects—from the curser to the afflicted. The contact object, whether stolen, purchased, found, or gifted is errantly regarded as valuable or even blessed. With cursed diamonds, the idea is that the energies once contained in the Indian diamonds were somehow released by Europeans and Americans. This coincides with the way Westerners brazenly applied their "technology" to "spiritual objects" by cutting into and faceting diamonds. In this ethno-logic of the curse, the desire to "open up the diamonds" for them to emit more "fire," "light," and "beauty" opened up a Pandora's box of the accumulated evil they had heretofore contained. Diamonds were in the West, named as "stars," such as McLean's Star of the East. Some, like Conan Doyle's fictional Star of Africa, become "bad stars" or literally, "disasters"—wreaking misfortune on those who possessed them.

Viewed in this way, curses of the time and type of the Hope diamond might be seen as an aesthetic commentary, a corrective to the unfairness evident in the society, both toward its own people and to others. This was not an isolated commentary. Andrew Carnegie, one of the richest men in America, had argued against the inheritance of great wealth. He thought it should be given back to society, supporting beneficial institutions and social purposes. Carnegie had written, "It is no longer questionable that great sums bequeathed often work more for the injury than for the good of the recipients." Large fortunes did their inheritors no service, "I would as soon leave to my son a curse as the almighty dollar," he declared.[4]

In this view, the new modernity—in its excessive form—was itself cursed. One extravagantly wealthy American, John D. Rockefeller, declared, "God gave me my money," much to the chagrin of millions of farmers, workers, and recent urban immigrants who had little.[5] Those masses found it an appealing act of justice if someone else's god, by way of a curse, could take that money away.

22

YOHE'S PROP

Throw away the stone and break the spell—that's what May Yohe, the former Lady Hope and divorced wife of Lord Francis Hope exhorted Evalyn Walsh McLean to do.[1]

There is, however, absolutely no evidence whatsoever that Yohe talked about, knew of, or expressed a thought about any Hope diamond curse while married to Lord Francis during the period 1894–1901, or prior to the appearance of the curse stories in the newspapers of the early 1900s, despite her apocryphal declarations to the contrary.

May Yohe was a talented and experienced actress. She knew a good story when she found one, and immediately adopted the legend as her own.

Yohe had recently divorced her second husband, Putnam Bradlee Strong. She attempted a comeback in the theater, appearing in *Little Christopher Columbus* in London. Lord Francis came for the opening night and apparently wept. May Yohe wore a replica of the Hope diamond, something she continued to do for various performances over the years.

In 1914, while performing in South Africa, Yohe met and married Captain John Smuts, the nephew of the famous Boer General Jan Smuts. Smuts was wounded during World War I and had had to retire from the military. He and May moved to Singapore, living on a rubber plantation for several years, and then to the United States. John and May tried and failed at a number of small business ventures during this period.

May finally hit upon some success with a book and silent film project in 1921. The book, *The Mystery of the Hope Diamond,* was published and a silent film *Hope Diamond Mystery* with 15 episodes released. The book, written by H. L. Gates was said to be from the "personal narrative" of Lady Francis Hope. The film was directed by Stuart Paton for Kosmik Films, with the story by May Yohe who also appears in the film along with a young Boris Karloff.

The film series played over a 15-week period. The episodes included "Hope Diamond Mystery," followed by the "Vanishing Hand," "Forged Note," "Jewel of Sita," "Virgin's Love," "House of Terror," "Flames of Despair," "Yellow Whisperings," "Evil Eye," "In the Spider's Web," "Cup of Fear," "Ring of Death," "Lash of Hate," "Primitive Passions," and finally, "Island of Destiny."

The book and the film offer a story of the Hope diamond that was much more fanciful than Cartier's—a virtual mishmash of supposed history, recollections, and bizarre imagination. The plot follows Collins's *Moonstone* story. In Yohe's ethnographically puzzling account, Tavernier is supposed to have discovered the blue diamond in the breast of Brisbun, a Tibetan jade statue of Buddha in a Sita Ram Temple in Burma. A "cult of pagan priests" is "bent on recovering the stone."[2] Its agents exact revenge on the owners of the Hope diamond as they try to steal it back in order to restore it to the " jade idol in the wilderness."[3]

Yohe inserts her own story in the tale telling, including her own, seemingly fictionalized experiences with the diamond. She finds in her failed marriages with Lord Francis Hope and then Putnam Bradlee Strong the long reach of the Hope diamond curse. Her marriage with Hope is rife with lack of affection. She is not accepted by his family and society. He is self-absorbed, and cannot give her the attention she needs. They divorce. Her affair and marriage to Strong also ends in disappointment. They travel the globe, but he hocks and sells her jewelry to pay for an extravagant lifestyle they

"The Hindu Gets the Diamond" scene from May Yohe's drama.

can ill afford. While she is on tour earning money, he takes up with another woman. She is deceived and humiliated.

May Yohe ends her 1921 story with a chapter "I Escape the Curse." Her escape is achieved by divorcing Lord Francis, divorcing Strong, putting her jewels and life as Lady May behind her, and enjoying the poverty and humility of life with John Smuts. Broke, living modestly, she cares for her infirm husband, enjoys her role as a housewife, and finds happiness in the small pleasures of life. Though herself free of the "pagan curse," she expects the diamond to continue to exert its evil upon others.

In reality, Yohe's life was harsher and even more tragic than represented in her *Hope Diamond Mystery*. She continued performing in the 1920s to support herself and her invalid husband. They settled in New England and tried to remodel a farmhouse in Marlow, New Hampshire, turning it into the Blue Diamond Inn. Unfortunately the inn burned down. During the Depression, Yohe labored for the Works Progress Administration mopping floors; she died of a heart attack in 1938.

※　※　※

Yohe's fractured history is the most elaborate tale about the curse of the Hope diamond. Bits and pieces of her story find their way into magazines for supernatural tales as well as the *New York Times, Time,* and *Newsweek* magazines. Her fantastic assertions are repeated over and over again so that decades later they become part and parcel of the tale of the Hope diamond. For example, even in 1986, the *Washington Post* would report that "hundreds of years of legends surround the curse of the Hope diamond," while a 1995 *Life* magazine reported the Hope to have come as a blazing eye from the statue of Ram Sita.[4]

With the death of Vinson McLean and the stories of May Yohe, the curse of the Hope diamond became enshrined as a popular modern legend. It was then elaborated, spread, and touted by Evalyn McLean, who had a unique ability to keep the story before an interested public.

23

HIGH SOCIETY TALISMAN

Legends are larger than life. Everything about the Hope diamond and its owners, the McLeans, was magnified in the public eye and imagination. The size, value, and notoriety of the Hope seemed to increase over the years. The McLeans became more powerful, wealthier, more outrageous, and eventually more tragic than most anyone else.

The Hardings and McLeans were already close friends at the time of Vinson's death. Warren and Ned played golf, traveled, played poker, drank, smoke, and caroused together. Florence and Evalyn did charity work and kept watch over their husbands' follies and dalliances, berating and threatening their respective spouses for those most outlandish. Florence consoled Evalyn over the tragic death of her son. Evalyn consoled Florence over the prediction of their astrologer Marcia Champney. Champney intimated that Warren Harding would win the presidency, but then die in office.

Harding did indeed win the 1920 election. He'd run on a platform of returning the country to normalcy in the aftermath of the World War. Harding made Ned the head of his presidential inaugural committee—a position for which he was totally unqualified.

Harding proved to be a weak and ineffective leader. He made some strong appointments to his cabinet—Herbert Hoover, Charles Hughes, Andrew Mellon—and expected them to make, oversee, and execute policy. Though not himself particularly corrupt or venal, Harding was nonetheless surrounded with a number of people who were. Deals were made to benefit from government policies. Indeed Ned's father's old house at 1509 H Street in downtown Washington was used as a hideaway for making such deals. Termed "the Love Nest," it was also used for sexual liaisons, card playing, and heavy boozing—now outlawed by Prohibition. Ned McLean spent $300,000 to build a nine-hole golf course at Friendship to host twice-weekly rounds for the presidential duffer.

Florence Harding, nicknamed the "Duchess" by husband Warren, and "Boss" by Ned McLean, proved an adept and inspirational First Lady. She supported women's equality, programs for World War I veterans, international relief, the causes of orphans, and the humane treatment of animals. But a cloud hung over her tenure in the White House. She continued to consult her astrologer and worry about the dismal prediction. She was frustrated with Warren's extramarital affairs. At one point, both she and Evalyn hired an unsavory character, Gaston Means, to follow their husbands and report on adulterous behavior. Florence was surprised to learn that Evalyn had allowed Warren to use Friendship for the purpose.

Jazz Age Evalyn Walsh McLean.

Nonetheless, with her best friend in the White House, Evalyn became the number one hostess in Washington. She hosted private dinner parties, massive balls and celebrations. Jazz bands and dancing overflowed the halls of the Friendship estate. Evalyn epitomized the strong, independent, almost libertine woman of the "Jazz Age."

Ned McLean drives President Harding.

Ned was made a $1 a year special agent of the FBI, a designation he relished. He handled Harding's blackmail problems with former lovers. Ned was also involved in what was to be known as the infamous Teapot Dome scandal, having written a check for $100,000 to Harding's Interior Secretary Albert Fall. Fall was later accused of improperly selling off government oil supplies to co-conspiring swindlers.

Warren Harding died on August 2, 1923. Calvin Coolidge became president. Florence sought refuge with Evalyn at Friendship, carrying with her from the White House a cache of important presidential papers, many of which she thought would sully the reputation of her husband. She stayed at Friendship for 18 days burning those papers. A year later, Florence too was dead. Evalyn had lost a friend and mentor.

Things did not go well for the McLeans after the deaths of the Hardings. The Senate Public Lands Committee found Ned to be the key link in the Teapot Dome scandal. He spilled all to the committee, sketching out the vast corruption of the administration, implicating many of its figures, and forever damning the Harding presidency to ignominy. Ned was publicly humiliated. He drank more and exhibited increasingly bizarre behavior. His dark moods are documented remarkably in Evalyn's own home movies.

The McLeans' extravagant lifestyle was also taking its toll. They owned Friendship, the Walsh mansion at 2020 Massachusetts Avenue, another mansion in Georgetown, a 2,600-acre Belmont Farm in Virginia, an estate in Newport, and Briarcliffe in Bar Harbor, Maine. They traveled regularly and employed a full retinue of servants. Most of their fortune was tied up in property and jewelry. Ned's inherited cash assets were running down and by the late 1920s could not support their lifestyle.

The most visible symbol of the McLean fortune, the *Washington Post,* was losing money—some $20,000 per month. Ill managed, it was heading for bankruptcy. Ned had never been a hard worker and served as newspaper publisher and sometime editor in chief in name only. Eugene Meyer made an offer of $5 million for the *Post* in 1929. In 1931, William Randolph Hearst offered $3 million. Evalyn did not want to sell, hoping that her sons, when grown, would inherit the paper. But the debts piled up. Evalyn expressed her willingness to put up the Hope diamond as collateral for a $250,000 loan to bail the *Washington Post* out of trouble, but it wasn't enough.

In 1932 the paper went into receivership. An auction followed, held on the steps of the *Washington Post* E Street building on June 1, 1933. Evalyn, wearing the Hope diamond, looked on from an upstairs window. Eugene Meyer, then serving as head of Herbert Hoover's Federal Reserve Board, was the winning bidder, having offered $825,000. It took years for him to bring the *Post* back to profitability and build a legacy inherited by his daughter Katherine Meyer and her husband, Philip Graham.

Ned and Evalyn did not get along. Their arguments were well known among their friends. Evalyn threatened to leave Ned back in 1916, but was wooed back with 60 telegrams from her husband professing his love. The fights, his dalliances and obsessions continued through the 1920s. Finally, Ned and Evalyn separated in 1929. Ned was openly adulterous, living in Beverly Hills with Rosie Davis, whose sister was the mistress of William Randolph Hearst. In 1930 Ned tried to divorce Evalyn, filing papers in Mexico. Evalyn countersued. As reported in the *Washington-Times Herald,* Evalyn alleged that Ned was living with another woman, drank excessively, and caused her "bodily suffering by beating and striking her, cursing and calling her vile names."

In 1932 Ned obtained a divorce in Riga, Latvia, of all places, serving the divorce papers on Evalyn wrapped as a Christmas present. Evalyn again challenged the action, claiming that Ned was hospitalized in Paris with a nervous breakdown. She sought to have Ned committed. The *Washington Daily News* reported MRS. MCLEAN WANTS HUSBAND ADJUDGED OF UNSOUND MIND. She succeeded. In October 1933 Ned was declared insane. He was committed to the Sheppard and Enoch Pratt Sanitarium in Towson, Maryland, and diagnosed with psychosis and alcohol saturation. He lived in his own cottage on the grounds. A fellow patient recalled that he went by the name of Mr. Orlo. In 1941 Ned died of a heart attack. In his will, he'd largely cut out Evalyn and his children, leaving $300,000, according to the *Washington Daily News,* to former mistress Rosie Davis.

I n the midst of dealing with Ned and the bankrupt *Washington Post,* Evalyn sought to help Charles Lindbergh recover his kidnapped son in 1932. Evalyn was empathetic. As a celebrity she had endured a number of kidnap threats. Her plan was to locate the kidnappers, pay them off, and get Lindbergh's son. She would not have to reveal their identity nor aid in their capture.

Evalyn again turned to Gaston Means. She put together $100,000 in cash for the ransom by mortgaging some of her father's property in downtown Washington. She gave it to Means in small bills. Means then led Evalyn on a wild-goose chase from South Carolina to Atlanta to Texas and Mexico trying to make contact with the kidnappers. In the end, no contact was made. The Lindbergh baby had been killed. Means made off with Evalyn's money.

By June 1933, Evalyn had to come up with funds to cover the mortgage before the bank foreclosed. Short of cash, she sent aides Elizabeth "Bessie" and Vylla Poe to New York to pawn the Hope diamond.

Bessie hid the diamond at the bottom of her handbag, covered with handkerchiefs, gloves, and watercolor painting materials. The sisters braced their feet against the door in their traveling compartment on the train. In New York they walked a gauntlet of homeless and drunk people in the tunnel between the train station and the Hotel Pennsylvania. They took the Hope diamond to William Simpson. Simpson and Evalyn McLean talked by telephone. He wanted the diamond appraised. The sisters, accompanied by a Simpson bodyguard, went to the Diamond Mart. The Hope was appraised at $200,000. Simpson loaned $37,500 on the pawned Hope. Evalyn raised the rest of the money by pawning other jewelry elsewhere.

Within two weeks, Evalyn had the cash to redeem the Hope. She herself went to New York, paid Simpson and then "gleefully" rehung the Hope by its diamond chain around her neck.[1]

Evalyn's generosity came to the fore with war veterans, a cause inspired by Florence Harding. When she moved into Friendship Evalyn had turned over some of the estate to the convalescence of recovering soldiers. She helped the Red Cross and attended to some of the needs of the Bonus Army during their march on Washington—personally bringing meals to the protesting, starving veterans. Through the 1930s and 1940s, she served GIs, entertaining them and giving them a morale boost. Many photographs show her sitting, talking, laughing, and drinking with soldiers—all while wearing the Hope diamond. She offered the use of the Hope diamond for GI charities—admission to see the "hoodoo gem" at one function was 25 cents.[2] In 1942, she hosted scores of GIs at her New Year's Eve Party. According to her personal secretary, Nannie Chase, Evalyn would visit Walter Reed Army Hospi-

Evalyn Walsh McLean with her daughter.

tal on Wednesdays, and let wounded and recuperating soldiers play "catch" with the famous blue gem.

Friends and relatives recognized Evalyn's kind and giving spirit. Wrote one cousin in her New Year's greeting:

What does the Hope diamond stand for? Not for what it is supposed to stand for—but, with you for hope—the greatest of all human emotions. That hope that you have given to others and hope it has given to you, that is why I hope and know it's spell is broken. It now stands for all good things against the sorrow of its past history. That's because it belongs to you.[3]

Evalyn's good work included renting out for a nominal fee the beloved Walsh mansion at 2020 Massachusetts Avenue after her mother died in 1932. The mansion was used in succession by the U.S. Rural Rehabilitation Resettlement Administration, the Rural Electrification Commission, and the American Red Cross.

Evalyn's personal life was entwined with her public, glamorous one as paramount Washington host and insider. Evalyn's parties were legendary, both in expense and guest list. Diplomats and dignitaries, royalty and national leaders, New Dealers and Republicans, scholars and entertainers graced her table at Friendship over the years.

While Evalyn did not marry again, she was periodically linked in gossip columns with several figures, notably Senator Henry Ashurst.

Evalyn and Ned had three other children after Vinson; Jack "Jock," born in 1916, Edward "Ned" Jr., born in 1918, and Emily, who later changed her name to Evalyn, born in 1921. Daughter Evalyn or "Evie" married North Carolina Senator Robert Reynolds, 36 years her senior. Reynolds was a flamboyant ladies' man called the "Kissing Senator," who'd been photographed years before kissing the famous movie star Jean Harlow. Evie was his fifth wife. On September 20, 1946, Evalyn Reynolds committed suicide, overdosing on sleeping pills. She left behind a four-year-old daughter, Mamie Spears Reynolds. This tragedy too became incorporated into the legend of the Hope diamond.

In popular circles, Evalyn Walsh McLean was said to have succumbed to the curse, either really or metaphorically. Evalyn herself took different positions on the curse of the Hope diamond during her lifetime. Occasionally she appeared to take it literally. Other times, it seemed to be an amusing story and conversation piece. And sometimes she took the legend as a parable or commentary on her own life. In 1936 she wrote,

> Do I believe a lot of silly superstitions, legends of the
> diamond? I must confess I know better and yet, knowing
> better, I believe. By that I mean I never let my friends or
> children touch it. Call it a foolish woman's fetish if you
> like . . . I have come to feel that I have developed a sort
> of immunity to its evil. What tragedies have befallen me
> might have occurred had I never seen or touched the
> diamond?[4]

But many of her friends and associates touched and wore the diamond; even her dog. There are still Washingtonians who recall that one or another of their relatives were allowed, and even encouraged by Evalyn, to inspect the diamond and even wear it for a wedding. And at another time she wrote, "I've worn my diamond as a charm. I kid myself, of course—but I like to pretend the thing brings good luck."[5]

At another time Evalyn McLean, perhaps a bit more pensively wrote:

There are those who would believe that somehow a curse is housed deep in the blue of the Hope diamond. I scoff at that in the privacy of my mind, for I do comprehend the source of what is evil in our lives . . . the natural consequences of unearned wealth in undisciplined hands.[6]

E valyn Walsh McLean passed away at her mansion on the night of April 26, 1947, surrounded by an intimate "who's who" of Washington society—her son-in-law senator, the vice president of Georgetown University, a newspaper publisher, Supreme Court associate justice Frank Murphy, and her attorney Thurman Arnold.

Following her death, her jewels, including the Hope diamond and the Star of the East, had to be secured. According to Arnold, he and Frank Waldrup, managing editor of the *Washington-Times Herald,* gathered up the jewels into a shoebox intending to put it in a safe deposit box in a local bank or jewelry store. But it was Saturday, and all the places they went had their safes secured by time locks; none could be opened until Monday. They ended up going to the FBI building, and after securing director J. Edgar Hoover's permission by telephone, left the jewels in his office for safekeeping.

Edward Henderson, a curator in the Department of Mineral Sciences in the Smithsonian's National Museum of Natural History, recalls an alternative version of events. He has Justice Murphy, a former Attorney General of the United States, driving around Washington all night in a taxi looking for a place to deposit the gems. This seems far-fetched. But according to Henderson, Murphy ended up at the Riggs National Bank. Bank officials questioned him as to the deposit; Murphy informed them that he wanted to secure the Hope and the other diamonds and gems. The bankers needed to know their value, and ended up calling Henderson. Henderson, re-calling the pawning of the diamond to secure the ransom in the Lindbergh kidnapping case, offered an estimate of the Hope diamond's worth at $100,000.

On April 28, the *Washington Daily News* asked, WHO'LL BE THE NEXT TO RISK WEARING 'UNLUCKY' DIAMOND? Evalyn's will requested that the jewels be held in trust, to be split among her grandchildren until the youngest, Mamie Spears Reynolds, had reached the age of twenty-five. This wish could not be accommodated. Evalyn had left a mountain of bills and debts. In 1949 the court granted a petition by the executor, trustees, and family to sell the jewels in order to settle the claims against the estate. Though several of her descendants were to later assert the value of the Hope diamond at the time at $2 million, it was appraised for only $176,920; the Star of the East was appraised at $185,000. Some seventy-two other pieces constituted the lot, the whole of which was purchased by Harry Winston. Newspapers reported the sale for $1.25 million; Thurman Arnold later wrote that it was for $1.1 million, others claimed it was even less.

McLean's 60-room home at 2020 Massachusetts Avenue was sold off in 1952 to the Embassy of Indonesia for $335,000. According to John Alexander, author of *Ghosts: Washington's Most Famous Ghost Stories,* embassy personnel have occasionally glimpsed a young nude woman gliding down the elegant stairway. The speculation is that it is the ghost of the young Evalyn, unmarred by the curse of the diamond. Unfortunately no one has been able to get close enough to the "ghost" either to see clearly any features or to see if she is wearing the diamond. Some years ago I asked a number of Indonesian embassy personnel about the ghost. I finally found one staffer who claimed he'd seen the ghost. He strongly asserted, however, that she was attired in white flowing robes—a perception that I took to be a concession to Islamic ideas of female modesty.

24

WINSTON'S BABY

As *Evalyn Walsh McLean acquired the* reputation as the queen of diamonds, Harry Winston was proclaimed the king. They were contemporaries who both loved diamonds, but as owners of the Hope they charted very different courses for it in American society.

Harry Winston was born in New York City in 1896, the son of a jeweler. His mother died when Harry was seven. Family folklore had it that at the age of twelve Harry was walking down a Brooklyn street when he spotted a tray of junk jewelry in the window of a pawnshop. He bought a ring with a green stone for twenty-five cents and raced back to his father's jewelry shop announcing he'd just purchased a two-carat emerald for less than a dollar. Two days later, Harry supposedly sold the ring for $800.

Harry's dad had asthma, and so the Winston family shifted from New York to California. Harry's father ran a modest jewelry store on Figueroa Street in Los Angeles.

Harry dropped out of school at age 15 to help out in the store. He exhibited a natural eye for gems and talent as a salesman early on. Harry would bring gems to area saloons trying to entice oil drillers and other newly wealthy Californians to invest their money in his wares. The business was successful enough for Harry to save $2,000 and head back east. Suffering from what he called "diamonditis"—a lifelong devotion to the brilliant gemstones, he established a one-man wholesale operation, the Premier Diamond Company at 535 Fifth Avenue in New York.[1]

Winston found a strong niche working with antique and estate jewelry that had been sold for a fraction of their worth in the postwar period. The women's suffrage movement and the "Jazz Age" were encouraging a new type of self-assured woman, like Evalyn Walsh McLean, who found the older nineteenth- and turn-of-the century jewelry a bit dated. The "Roaring '20s" occasioned popular Art Deco styles in fashion, architecture, graphic design, and jewelry. As a result of a booming economy, Americans had more disposable wealth for transforming the old gems into new jewels. Winston took advantage of this trend, systematically identifying jewelry estates, bidding on them, and reselling their gems for a profit. With his good eye for gems and an instinct for their true value, as well as bank support, Winston prospered. In 1932 he formed Harry Winston, Inc.

In 1933 he married Edna Fleishman. They'd met on a train to Atlantic City a few years before—she was off to recuperate from a tonsillectomy accompanied by her father, a physician and sociologist; he was on a selling trip. They'd been seeing each other for some time, but Edna had broken off the relationship finding Harry too occupied with diamonds—his "babies," as he called them. She became engaged to another man. Harry called her just before the wedding and convinced her to marry him instead; she agreed, provided the wedding went ahead quickly. On their Palm Beach honeymoon, Harry supposedly spent a good deal of time talking about diamonds and making arrangements for their sale. Edna gave in and became part of the business, advising on the creative side of the enterprise over the years. She also wore Winston jewelry, but never ostentatiously so.

The Depression was not particularly good for the diamond business, nor were the war years. Harry Winston was, however, a savvy businessman and a vocal advocate for diamonds—earning him the accolade of Damon Runyon as the "diamond champ" in 1936.[2] Winston worked on both sides of the Atlantic, making contact with European royalty as well as sultans and maharajas from Asia. He had a particularly long and close relationship with the

Duke and Duchess of Windsor. Memorably, during the early days of World War II he and Edna were in the south of France, selling their diamonds. Fearing for their safety and worried about losing their prized possessions, they secreted diamonds in Edna's shoes, wigs, and clothing for a trans-Atlantic voyage, bringing their "babies" safely home.

After the war, Winston was well positioned to take advantage of the new demand for diamonds, and indeed, to help fuel major expansion of the industry. He'd built a strong network of suppliers through the De Beers cartel, diamond cutters, salespeople, and of course, customers. Harry Winston also brought a new style to the industry. He was not satisfied with ornate post–Art Deco jewelry with its cumbersome settings. He looked for styles of cuts and designs that would show off diamonds in a stronger, flashier, though elegant way. "No two diamonds are alike. Each diamond has a different nature. Each diamond must be handled as you handle a person."[3] He thus urged designers to develop "hidden" platinum settings so the character of each diamond could come to the fore. Winston pioneered the popular use of intricate pear- and marquise-cut diamonds to create more light and fire and created ensembles of matching necklaces and bracelets intended to dazzle viewers.

Harry Winston was particularly interested in large diamonds, and had an extraordinary knowledge of gems. Most important, Harry Winston had a mission. Particularly after World War II, Winston saw the American use of diamonds as affirmation of their place in the world, a deserving population that had worked hard for its wealth and should not shrink from showing it off.

Stimulating the post–World War II American market was vital to the survival of the diamond industry. Following the War, the British-owned De Beers cartel that controlled most worldwide diamond production and distribution realized that it had to get into the business of marketing and promoting their product in order to revive the industry. New markets had to be opened up. A whole generation had come of age in England, America, and on the Continent and was ripening as a consumer class for diamonds.

De Beers sought images and celebrity for their product. The English royal family provided De Beers with the ideal form of celebrity identification and endorsement. The royal family was seen as heroic and strong as a result of their actions during World War II. They'd stayed in London during the bombing and provided moral support to the population. They were riding high as extremely well loved and respected by the British population.

In addition, young Princess Elizabeth was glamorous. In April 1947, the royal family visited South Africa. Princess Elizabeth visited the grand source of the modern diamond industry, the Big Hole at Kimberley, for her 21st birthday. De Beers hosted a luncheon in her honor and gave her a diamond jewel. The South African government gave her a necklace with 21 diamonds; Rhodesians gave her a diamond brooch. Later in the year Elizabeth married the Duke of Edinburgh, and the royal jewelry was displayed at the British Industries Fair in London. Full-page newspaper advertisements featured the gems. The association between popular, loved, high-status, glamorous royalty and jewels was designed to encourage consumers to participate in a similar relationship, albeit at a price they could afford.

In the United States, the monopolistic De Beers could not operate given the strong antitrust laws. Diamond industry public relations were handled by N.W. Ayer, who worked closely with De Beers. Ayer ran advertising campaigns and public relations promoting diamond use, and giving out information about jewelry and diamond mining. They arranged product placements by having famous actresses wear diamonds for their screen roles. In 1948 they were looking for a tag line, a memorable phrase for their ad campaign to present to De Beers. The night before the presentation Ayer's Frances Gerety, exhausted and praying for help, came up with the line "Diamonds are forever."[4]

The phrase had a history. Anita Loos, author of the 1925 novel *Gentlemen Prefer Blondes,* had written, "French gentlemen are really quite deceiving. American gentlemen are best after all, because kissing your hand may make you feel very, very good, but a diamond and sapphire

bracelet lasts forever."[5] Well before that, in 1761, Stanislas Jean de Boufflers authored a short story, "The Queen of Golconda." In this love
tale a boy and girl develop affection in their childhood, but their in-
nocence is corrupted as they grow. The boy fights in a war; the girl is
sold into prostitution. The girl eventually becomes the successful
Queen of Golconda. Aged, she withdraws from the splendor of the
court and returns to her beloved childhood friend declaring,

> delight has but a momentary existence, but a settled
> enjoyment can last a lifetime. The former may be likened
> to a drop of water, the latter to a diamond. Both shine with
> equal brilliance, but the merest breath can extinguish the
> one, while not even steel can deface the other.[6]

The sentiment and the phrase proved to be an advertising marvel,
combining the history and durability of diamonds with the idea
that love is eternal. De Beers commissioned a series of diamond ads
in which great artists such as Pablo Picasso and Salvador Dalí and
others linked their work to the theme.

The mass market for diamonds during the postwar years was for
diamond engagement rings. Huge numbers of American servicemen
were returning home. Many had delayed engagement and marriage.
These postwar courtships, romances, and marriages were to fuel the
baby boom and contribute to the image of the American dream success story. But the first stage was engagement, and the diamond industry did everything it could to exploit the need and grow the desire for
the diamond ring as a symbol of stability in what had been a hellacious
era of war. Young couples were eager to buy love and permanence.

Jewelers, gem merchants, and suppliers wanted consumers to
buy the best product they could afford. This required an education
and promotional campaign so that such consumers would understand diamond price and quality standards. The industry thus
stressed the "four Cs" of diamonds—clarity, color, cut, and carat
weight. These characteristics were particularly important for diamond engagement rings where one single stone had to show off

extremely well. The clearer the stone, the purer the color, the more fiery the cut, and the greater the carat weight, the higher the price. Jewelers, in essence, provided a calculus for the American middle class to measure love. Recalling the sentiment that fueled the onset of the more elite Diamond Circle in the late 1800s, jewelers promoted the notion that the bigger and better the diamond, the larger and deeper the love, the smaller and poorer the engagement ring, the more such love was tenuous. Of course the ring had to be quite conspicuous, so that love could be exhibited to friends, family, coworkers, and others. Intimacy could be publicized and even compared.

With the acquisition of the McLean diamonds and other significant large diamonds in the post–World War II period, Harry Winston hit upon a great idea to increase the popularity of fine quality gems among his buying audience. On November 16, 1949, Winston asked Mrs. Thomas Phipps, a well-known figure in New York's high society crowd, to wear the Hope diamond at the *Bal de Tête,* a charity ball for the Veterans Music Service at the Ritz-Carlton Hotel. It marked the prelude of what was to become Winston's Court of Jewels. The following week, the Court of Jewels exhibit opened in Rockefeller Center for the benefit of the United Hospital Fund.

The Court of Jewels consisted of a traveling exhibition of a collection of gems supplemented by a jewelry "fashion" show. The collection, valued at $10 million, featured large and famous diamonds—the two most notable of which were the Hope and the Star of the East. Other diamonds included the a 60-carat emerald-cut diamond ring from the collection of Mabel Boll, the Indore Pears, a matched set of two 44-carat diamonds, the 72-carat Idol's Eye, the 127-carat Portuguese diamond, the Dudley necklace, the Inquisition necklace, and the 31¼-carat McLean diamond. Over the years, some of the gems in the Court of Jewels were sold, replaced by other stellar gems. The McLean diamond, for example, was purchased by the Duchess of Windsor. Evalyn's Star of the East went to King Farouk, as did the 126-carat Jonker diamond.

The Court of Jewels traveled throughout the United States, but also made visits to Canada and Cuba. It served civic and charitable functions—the United Hospital Fund ball in New York, the Symphony Jewel ball in San Antonio, and the National Foundation for Infantile Paralysis, for example. It was typically sponsored by nonprofit cultural and social organizations as a fund-raiser. Audience members would pay a fee to the event. Song, music, speeches, and food would be part of the program, but the main feature was to have local socialites and members of the local cooperating organizations modeling Harry Winston's Court of Jewels jewelry. The models, decked with jewels, could be "queen for a day." Venues were as wide ranging as Rockefeller Center and the Texas State Fair.

As Winston stated, "I want the public to know more about precious gems. With so much expensive junk jewelry around these days, people forget that a good diamond, ruby, or emerald, however small, is a possession to be prized for generations."[7]

Winston and his Court were amazingly effective in bringing diamonds to the attention of the American public. Indeed, to illustrate the point, *Life* magazine titled its 1952 profile of Winston's operation, "Golconda on 51st Street."[8] Here, thanks to Winston, the prized treasures of far-off, historical, almost mythological kingdoms could be purchased by many Americans at an affordable price.

Harry Winston's Court of Jewels provided an Americanized version of the British one. The 1953 coronation of 27-year-old Queen Elizabeth II was widely covered in the United States. Her court, with its pomp, circumstance, and Crown Jewels drew great attention in the American media, with major pictorials in *Vogue, Life,* and *National Geographic,* and plenty of stories in the newspapers and popular magazines like *Reader's Digest.* No one could miss the stunning, elegant display of Britain's big and historical diamonds. Their flash and glamour resonated with Harry and the Court of Jewels tour. Harry Winston was described as having the largest collection of large, historical, famous gems after the British crown. Winston, called the "King of Diamonds" in a 1947 *Cosmopolitan* story, was firmly ensconced in his throne at the pinnacle of the American diamond market.[9]

Mrs. Thomas Phipps wears the Hope diamond at the Bal de Tête in New York.

Even though the Court of Jewels became attenuated by the mid-1950s, Harry continued to tour the Hope diamond for charity balls and popular exhibitions. Among the most popular was a 1958 visit to the Canadian National Exhibition in Toronto. Reminiscent of the popular Crystal Palace display in London over a century earlier, the Hope was viewed by many of the three million visitors over a 16-day period.

For the Court of Jewels in New York, Eleanor Steber of the Metropolitan Opera sang the "Jewel Song" from Faust. Fine as it was, that song did not tell the story of diamonds in the early 1950s. "Diamonds Are a Girl's Best Friend," sung by Marilyn Monroe for the 1953 film *Gentlemen Prefer Blondes,* based upon the Anita Loos novel, did.

Monroe plays an exuberant, optimistic young woman who clear-mindedly appears to know what she wants—to marry a rich guy who can shower her with wealth. She appears as a shallow, gold-digging, diamond-seeking American woman caught up in the prevalent materialism and consumerism of the times, singing:

Men grow cold as girls grow old
And we all lose our charms in the end.
But square-cut or pear-shaped
Those rocks won't lose their shape
Diamonds are a girl's best friend.[10]

In the film, Monroe pauses in the song. She poses with lips moist in her diamond-sparkling, slinky-tight, red dress and says seductively to the camera, "Talk to me, Harry Winston. Tell me all about it."

The film's story line proceeds with an irony so appropriate to the times. The Monroe character doesn't permit herself to marry the rich guy for his money. Instead, she falls in love with the poor guy. Diamonds, she realizes, are just a false desire and provide only counterfeit salvation. But wait! All is not lost. The poor guy is actually rich. Love is reaffirmed, you don't have to be rich to be happy, but if you're happy you might get rich, and if your desires are good and normal, rather than venal and extreme, you might just get that big diamond ring after all.

The juxtaposition of Winston and Monroe is striking. Harry Winston was a rather humble, humorous, down-to-earth businessman who loved diamonds. Physically, he was short and stocky, though of a dignified and disciplined bearing. He enjoyed beautiful things and surroundings—his French Louis-style office, his elegant Fifth Avenue townhouse, and his finely decorated Scarsdale home. Personally, he avoided the limelight. Early in his career he used a more debonair front man for pitches to banks and major business partners. His insurance company discouraged photographs and public appearances for fear he would be threatened and kidnapped.

Harry's love of diamonds was notorious, though he did not wear them in any ostentatious way. He was a connoisseur. Sometimes he took out diamonds to contemplate their character and register their features in his legendary gemological memory. Harry translated this aesthetic sensibility into commercial success, most famously so in the

Harry Winston.

case of the Jonker diamond. Purchased in 1935, the Jonker was then one of the largest raw diamonds ever found, weighing in at 726 carats. Harry kept the stone for almost a year, contemplating its features. He had Belgian diamond cutter Lazare Kaplan study the diamond. Between the two, they came up with a bold plan to cut it into 12 smaller diamonds, which they did, earning both acclaim and profit.

Harry also used his infatuation with diamonds to sell them. With big diamonds, he saw his job as matching up the diamond with the "right" customer. He could become so focused on salesmanship as to be oblivious to the presence of his own family and friends. But he was generally apologetic and on best behavior after such episodes.

Harry Winston was good-natured on the subject of the Hope diamond curse, taking it in a rather humorous vein. Edward Wharton-Tigar, a colleague in the diamond industry, tells a story told to him by Harry. Harry and wife Edna had been to Portugal. Like many couples of the day, concerned with air travel safety, the Winstons booked separate flights for their return. Edna was booked on a Pan Am flight from Lisbon, stopping in the Azores for refueling; Harry was scheduled for the same flight the next day:

> When Harry's plane arrived in the Azores the seat next to his was taken up by a fellow American who told him that he had been on the previous day's flight but had been obliged to stop off at Santa Maria for the night and catch the present one. Harry asked what had caused him to change his plan.
>
> "I'm not usually a superstitious man," explained his companion, "but yesterday I found myself sitting next to the wife of the man who owns the Hope diamond, and I just was not prepared to take the risk of sharing in the bad luck which that thing is supposed to bring."
>
> "You're out of luck again," said Harry. "You are now sitting next to its owner!"[11]

In the 1950s, no curse threatened Winston. But science did.

Since the late 1800s there had been several attempts to create diamonds artificially through the laboratory application of great heat and pressure. J. Ballantine Hannay produced small stones in his laboratory in 1880 that were then donated to the British Museum.

The idea of man replicating in short order the almost unimaginable feats of nature was popularly known. After all, *Superman* comics featured the "Man of Steel," who could squeeze a piece of coal into a glowing diamond. Still, this was thought to be more fantasy than reality, with various scientific experiments either unsuccessful or discredited. Indeed, Hannay's diamonds were not recognized as such until the 1940s.

Interestingly, Evalyn Walsh McLean trumpeted the creation of synthetic diamonds for commercial uses. As she opined in a "My Say" news column she wrote for the *Washington Times-Herald,* their use in drills could "open up untold wealth for the country."[12]

World War II heralded the atomic age, and with it all sorts of new experiments with nuclear energy. Some involved diamonds. In the early 1950s, such experiments were conducted by scientists from Harvard, the Argonne Laboratories, and the American Museum of Natural History. They found that by putting diamonds in cyclotrons, they could alter their colors, at least temporarily. Others, like General Electric, experimented with the artificial fabrication of diamonds.

These efforts made the diamond industry exceedingly nervous. Manufacturing diamonds might be cheaper than mining them. Manufactured diamonds might be engineered to be larger and more finely finished than natural diamonds. Manipulation of color through nuclear radiation could upend the whole market for rare colored gems. In short, these experiments threatened to undermine the supply, demand, and price structure of the multibillion-dollar diamond industry.

The diamond industry went after the scientists through various lobbying efforts. Due to industry action, the Atomic Energy Commission in 1953 forbade the use of its equipment to radiate gemstones. It later relaxed this ban under specified conditions. The industry prevailed in its efforts with the Federal Trade Commission of the time, which favorably ruled that man-made products could not be called "diamonds," or even "artificial diamonds," or "synthetic diamonds." Hence, today, we have "zircon," or "zirconia," which, while named after a naturally occurring gem, denotes, at least on the American market, an "artificial, manufactured diamond."

In 1954 however, General Electric scientists successfully produced synthetic diamonds using a secretly patented process. On February 15, 1955, General Electric revealed its accomplishment. General Electric stock rose and De Beers shares dropped.

On May 28, 1956, C. Guy Suits, General Electric's director of research, presented a 100-carat cluster of the synthetic, industrial diamonds that had been produced in Schenectady, New York, to the Smithsonian Institution. The development of synthetic diamonds for use as jewelry followed.

The industry sought to portray such diamonds in an unfavorable light. Manufactured diamonds were characterized as "artificial," mutants of a sort, produced by "unnatural" processes. As diamond expert Marcus Baerwald noted,

> The acceptance of natural diamonds is rooted in centuries of history and tradition, world-wide romance, the approval of kings and queens, and the blessing of fashion. Winning similar acceptance for synthetics would be a long and incredibly difficult task. It is hard to imagine British royalty being crowned with stones from a laboratory.[13]

Synthetic gems were anathema to diamond lovers like Harry Winston. Winston's whole philosophy was to deal with diamonds in a much more personal, biographical way. The gems in his Court of Jewels all had names, personalities, and biographies.

Harry Winston, knowledgeable about and conversant with the great national jewel collections of European countries, long felt that the United States needed and deserved a national collection. There was one at the Smithsonian Institution, though it was not very impressive. The collection had begun in 1884 by Frank Clarke, chief chemist with the U.S. Geological Survey, who acquired about a thousand specimens for $2,500. The collection had grown with subsequent small purchases and donations, including the collections of Isaac Lea, Leander Chamberlain, Fredrick Canfield, and Colonel Washington Roebling, the builder of the Brooklyn Bridge. In 1917–19 it moved from its original home in the National Museum Building (now the Arts and Industries Building) to the new National Museum, now known as the National Museum of Natural History. The collection was generally weak in rarer, higher priced historical stones.

By the mid-1950s the Smithsonian was actively seeking to enhance the collection. George Switzer, the acting curator of mineralogy, shared Winston's goal of encouraging a first-class gem collection in the national museum, primarily for research and educational purposes. Leonard Carmichael, the secretary of the Smithsonian, had agreed to major construction of a new mineral hall for the collection as part of a larger modernization program at the institution. The museum set its sights on acquiring significant famous gems, the Hope diamond in particular. It had even secured from the General Services Administration a commitment that gems, confiscated by the federal government, would be turned over to the Smithsonian to aid in acquisition purchases.

Harry Winston was a patriotic guy, who believed in the greatness of the American way of life. He was no extremist, but a mild chauvinist. He wanted something to rival the Crown Jewels of European nations. He agreed with the sentiment expressed by friendly newspaper columnist Ilke Chase, "What would the woman President of the United States wear when confronted with her jewel bedecked counterpart from the Soviet Republic of Whatistan?"[14] Winston and others envisioned First Ladies of the United States wearing superb gems from the collection to various international functions and White House events. It was through such display that the United States could help affirm its status in the world. Others objected to this vision, worried that such use of jewelry could create the wrongful appearance of an aspiring aristocracy in a strongly democratic nation.

For Winston, the collection would also be educational. At his Fifth Avenue store, Winston had instituted demonstrations and workshops so that customers, visitors, and apprentices could learn about diamond craft. He could easily imagine Smithsonian displays that could inspire visitors about the history, science, and artistry of diamonds.

Also, the acquisition by the Smithsonian of truly important, valuable, historic, and famous gems would help affirm the value of diamonds as natural and historically biographical, rather than synthetic and anonymous. Whatever the status of the General Electric artificial diamond cluster, it would surely be trumped by the Hope.

25

TAX DEDUCTION

Negotiations for the Smithsonian to acquire the Hope diamond from Harry Winston took more than a year and reveal the complexities and intricacies that go into a high stakes acquisition for the national museum. There is an advantage in working in the "Nation's Attic," as the Smithsonian is sometimes called—a lot of old records about the collections are available, though you have to know where to look. Aided by my colleagues in the Smithsonian's Institutional History Division, I obtain folder number 225042 from box 667 in unit 192—*United States National Museum, Permanent Administrative Files, 1877–1975.* The file encased by this dry bureaucratic designation is a treasure trove.

The record began with a letter from Frederick Pough, the respected retired curator of gems at the American Museum of Natural History in New York to George Switzer, acting curator of mineralogy, Division of Mineralogy and Petrology, National Museum of Natural History, Smithsonian Institution. Fred had obviously had prior discussions with George about a possible acquisition.

March 26, 1957
LETTER FROM FRED POUGH TO GEORGE SWITZER
I asked him [*Winston*] about the Hope and he said he
would be glad to dispose of it. I explained your situation

and he thought that you and he might be able to work something out, if you can save up a little more stuff, and that he might make a contribution of part of the price to the Museum, for he could, after all, take it out of income tax and so it wouldn't cost him so much. He seemed to rather like the idea of having the stone end up at the National Museum . . . Next step is to try to get some indication of how much value he does want and how much of a contribution he would be willing to make. It is hard to put an exact value on something as unique as the Hope.[1]

April 1
LETTER FROM SWITZER TO POUGH

Thanks . . . our exhibit is being modernized, and the new gem hall is going to be, we believe, quite unique. It will be nearly a year before it will be reopened. I would like to discuss with Mr. W. the possibility of working out a deal by that time, so that the Hope could be the feature attraction of the opening of the new hall. I believe we could both get a tremendous amount of publicity out of it . . . I could bring some sketches of the hall, and describe how we would exhibit the Hope if we could get it.

April 11
LETTER FROM SWITZER TO POUGH

I have spoken to both Dr. Kellogg [director of the museum] and Dr. Carmichael about the possibility of getting the Hope, and they are enthusiastic. We all feel the Smithsonian would be the best permanent home for it, and that Mr. Winston would be performing a great public service in making it possible for the Smithsonian Institution to acquire the stone . . . I am telling you this so that you will know that I have official sanction to pursue the matter.

Switzer laid out the possible deal in this internal memorandum copied to Tom Clark, the Smithsonian's treasurer. He proposed to use some of the diamonds confiscated by the federal government from smugglers to pay for the Hope diamond.

April 29

MEMO FROM SWITZER TO CLARK, COPY TO KELLOGG

I have approached Mr. Winston with a proposition . . . He is definitely interested . . . and has asked that we inquire into the tax situation . . . Mr. Winston values the Hope diamond at $500,000. (It was sold in 1911 for $300,000 [sic]). Its value has been estimated by various people, some higher and some lower . . . In my opinion . . . $500,000 is a reasonable and justifiable figure . . . The Smithsonian has obtained recently from the General Services Administration, 1,540 carats of small loose cut diamonds valued at $170,000 . . . we shall soon receive an additional shipment valued at $80,000. We also have received . . . permission to use this material (confiscated from smugglers and awarded by court order to the U.S. government) to exchange for important, large, gems for the collection . . . My proposition to Mr. Winston was that we exchange our $250,000 of small loose diamonds for the Hope diamond. He countered with the statement that the Hope diamond is worth $500,000 . . . However, he has stated that he would like to receive the $250,000 of diamonds in exchange, and would like to present to the Smithsonian a gift amounting to the balance of the value of the gem, or $250,000, provided this gift of half the value could be used as a tax deduction . . . Mr. Winston wishes the Institution to ask the Internal Revenue for an opinion in this matter.

May 3

LETTER FROM SWITZER TO POUGH

I have just returned from the Internal Revenue where Mr. Tom Clark . . . and I received a favorable response . . .

Mr. Winston can get a deduction on the difference in value
between what he gets and what he gives . . . The value
placed on the Hope would have to be established as fair
market value. The examiner . . . would probably ask for
opinions . . . The $500,000 value seems perfectly fair . . . A
letter should be written by Mr. Winston or Mr. Frey
[*Winston's associate*] addressed to the Commissioner of Internal Revenue . . . explaining what is contemplated and
asking for an opinion . . . Internal Revenue promised
prompt attention.

Winston's associates let Switzer know that they weren't keen on
going to the Internal Revenue people directly, and asked for Smithsonian intercession. Secretary Carmichael's suggestion about a
staged gift became very important.

May 21

LETTER FROM SWITZER TO HARRY WINSTON

I have just spoken to Dr. Leonard Carmichael . . . He is very
enthusiastic about the prospects . . . this would be one of
the most important acquisitions ever to be received by the
Institution . . . Carmichael wishes to . . . bring the matter
to a close to your satisfaction. He is a close personal friend
of one of the Assistant Secretaries of the Treasury and
wishes to discuss the matter with him informally. This, of
course is ideal, because he will be talking at a level higher
than that of the Commissioner of Internal Revenue . . . Carmichael would now like to receive a letter
outlining your thoughts . . . Carmichael says that gifts to
the Institution are frequently spread over a period of years
in order for the donor to be able to take full advantage of
the gift tax allowance . . .

It is unclear whether or not the following was actually sent as a letter, but its content captures the importance of the acquisition.

Undated, probably May
DRAFT LETTER FROM CARMICHAEL TO WINSTON

I was overwhelmed . . . that you were considering presenting
the Hope diamond to the Smithsonian. Now he [*Switzer*] tells
me . . . you have obtained for the Smithsonian the offer of a
gift from Sir Ernest Oppenheimer [*Director, De Beers*] . . . I am
tremendously excited about the Hope diamond. This is the
only great historical diamond that the Smithsonian could
conceivably acquire, and thus the gift you are contemplating
is especially notable. It will be a most worthy nucleus for what
I hope will become one of the world's finest gem collections.

A transfer of the loose, confiscated diamonds was made from the
Smithsonian to Harry Winston, as Switzer wrote to Daniel Frey.

May 21
LETTER FROM SWITZER TO FREY

I suggest you keep the diamonds until we have seen
Internal Revenue. I hope they never come back.

The Hope diamond was to be tested. Security concerns, even in the
case of an internal memo, were clear.

June 3
MEMO FROM SWITZER TO KELLOGG

. . . Bureau of Standards examination of a certain
diamond we hope to get . . . Van Valkenburg says he
plans photoconductivity, density, and similar non-
destructive tests which would require a few days to
perform . . . Shepard says he can arrange for an armored
truck or police escort or both.

A few weeks later, Switzer went to Brooklyn, met the U.S. marshal,
and received a shipment of confiscated diamonds totaling about 807

carats. He made plans to meet Winston representatives so they could then take those diamonds off his hands and assume insurance liability for them.

June 21

MEMO FROM SWITZER TO KELLOGG

The attached travel voucher covers my trip to New York . . . I received the 807.81 carats of diamonds from the United States Marshall . . . then turned the diamonds over to Harry Winston, Inc . . . We have now loaned to Harry Winston, Inc., cut diamonds valued at $244,000. Mr. Winston seems quite positive about his intention of carrying out a part exchange—part gift of the Hope diamond to the Smithsonian.

Switzer had now transferred to Winston 2,335 carats of diamonds. Robert Hodes, Winston's lawyer, then wrote to Switzer pointing out the necessity of making the contribution over a number of years.

June 24

LEETER FROM HODES TO SWITZER

Section 170(b)(2) of the I.R.C. limits a corporation's deduction for charitable contributions to 5% of its taxable income . . . The excess of value of the Hope over the customs service seizures will be greater than 5% of the taxable income of Harry Winston, Inc. during the current year and the two succeeding years. Accordingly, some method must be devised by which the contribution can be spread over a number of years . . . The contribution also has a bearing on the question of valuation . . . The Hope diamond has different values at different times . . . It therefore seems necessary for us to arrive at an agreement with the Treasury Department.

Carmichael now took the matter to W. Randolph Burgess, Under Secretary of the U.S. Department of the Treasury, asking for Treasury help in outlining the procedure for the tax write-off.

Switzer offered his estimate of the value of the Hope diamond.

July 9
MEMO FROM SWITZER TO KELLOGG

Various figures have been mentioned in the newspapers and elsewhere, ranging from $500,000 to $2,500,000. Mr. Winston told me he had received a firm offer last year of $750,000. In the publicity released about the stone when it is exhibited a figure of $1,000,000 is usually given. Mr. Winston has indicated that he is willing to accept any reasonable figure, and has suggested that the appraisal be made by the U.S. Customs Appraisers in New York.

Everything seemed to be going fine. *National Geographic* magazine was planning an article on diamonds, written by Switzer, for its April 1958 issue. Melvin Bell Grosvenor, president and editor of *National Geographic,* wrote to Carmichael.

December 26
LETTER FROM GROSVENOR TO CARMICHAEL

We have been advised on a confidential basis of the proposed donation of the Hope diamond by Mr. Harry Winston to the Smithsonian. Appropriately, we have placed a color picture of the Hope diamond as the lead illustration with this article, and have hoped to be able to announce this impressive gift to the American people . . . We understand that Mr. Winston's lawyers and the Government have not yet completed arrangements for the transfer of ownership of the gem. . . From what Mr. Winston told Mrs. Patterson [*a National Geographic staffer*] it would seem that in his mind, at least, there is no doubt that the transfer will be made . . . When told that our article would not appear until April, Mr. Winston gave us uncategorical permission to report the gift. 'Certainly,' were his words, 'The Smithsonian will want to publicize the fact that the Hope will be on display in its collection.' . . . However, we want to be absolutely sure, of course, that we will not be jumping the gun for you . . . Because of our necessary early release of color plates . . . we must complete all caption material by January 13. Does it meet with your approval to make this announcement of the gift of the Hope in the April issue, making any last minute changes before January 13?

Carmichael was excited by Grosvenor's report. He wrote to Winston seeking direct approval for the announcement in *National Geographic,* enclosing a copy of Grosvenor's letter.

December 31
LETTER FROM CARMICHAEL TO WINSTON

I am sure that you know that Mr. Hodes has been informed that a final [*Internal Revenue Commission*] ruling in regard to the gem cannot be expected before January 15, 1958 at the earliest.

Absent the ruling, *National Geographic* could not announce the acquisition. The magazine printed its issue with the article, but did not announce the Hope diamond gift.

In the months that followed, Hodes and Switzer exchanged notes bemoaning the delay. Switzer wrote Hodes in March 1958, "We are still hoping to open our new hall in late April, but I am worried about the diamond. We still have no word from Internal Revenue." Hodes responded that he had heard from Justin Winkle, who was in charge of the matter at Internal Revenue. Apparently they had had one appraisal but the commissioner wanted another independent evaluation. He too wrote, "We are anxious to do anything we can to speed up the matter." Switzer informed Kellogg and

Carmichael, adding, "It would be very unfortunate if we were unable to combine the publicity certain to result from the acquisition of the diamond with the opening of the hall."

By early April there was still no word from Internal Revenue. The irritated Switzer informed Hodes that the new hall "won't open at the earliest before the end of May." He also noted that the museum had ordered a "special safe-case" for the Hope diamond.

In May, the roof fell in on the deal. First, a letter came from Russell Harrington, the Commissioner of Internal Revenue.

May 2, 1958
LETTER FROM HARRINGTON TO CARMICHAEL

We have reached a point in our consideration of the proposal where we feel that we cannot go forward until we have received a formal request from Harry Winston, Inc. The request should set out all the details of the proposed transaction and should be accompanied with copies of the proposed instruments which would effectuate the transfer. This suggestion is occasioned by the fact that an exchange of property is involved, a circumstance not present in the published Revenue Ruling which previously was believed might cover the proposed transaction . . . As a result of the work we've done . . . and after very careful and extended consideration, we have concluded that we cannot make an advance valuation of the gem as we had originally thought we might be able to do. This is primarily by reason of the unique character of the gem, and the relatively unsubstantial and incomplete evidence before us of firm offers to buy it . . . if a formal request for a ruling is submitted, as indicated above, we will make every effort to process it as promptly as possible . . . Should the corporation in any event decide to proceed with it, we will, of course, be obliged to determine the value of the gem incident to our audit of the tax return which reflects the transaction.

Harrington's letter was frustratingly bureaucratic.

On May 5, Kellogg, who had a reputation within the Smithsonian of stymieing initiative, wrote a confidential memo to Carmichael. He was concerned about money. The proposal on the table was for Winston to transfer over to the Smithsonian ownership of a certain percentage of the Hope diamond each year. In effect, Winston would continue to own part of the Hope diamond even though it would be in the possession of the museum. One question was how much would he own, and what percentage of the diamond would the $250,000 in diamonds that the Smithsonian had already transferred to Winston buy? If the Internal Revenue valued the Hope diamond at $1 million, Kellogg did not want to have to come up with another $250,000 to pay for "half" of the diamond. His concerns exposed the most fundamental "contradiction" at the heart of the Smithsonian itself. The letter was written on the standard "Office Memorandum" stationery used by the Smithsonian, which at the top of the page in bold letters says, "United States Government."

May 2, 1958

MEMO FROM KELLOGG TO CARMICHAEL

Who will own the diamond, the Government or the Smithsonian Institution? . . . either the Government or the Smithsonian Institution has liability while in possession of the Hope diamond. It would be preferable to have the Hope diamond transferred to the United States Government. This would free the Smithsonian Institution from liability in the event it was lost or stolen. Winston could then seek to recover in the Court of Claims for whatever loss was involved. The Secretary of the Smithsonian as a contracting officer could sign the contract for the Government . . . No insurance for the Hope diamond is provided in the contract . . . A special policy of this type may cost $60,000 a year.

Kellogg's memo pointed to just how complicated the deal was in the context of the Smithsonian and the government. The Smithsonian is a unique institution called a public trust establishment. A portion of its funds comes from the original bequest of James Smithson, an English scientist who gave the institution its name. Other funds for the Smithsonian museums and operations come from appropriations bills passed by the U.S. Congress and signed by the president. The Smithsonian is not a federal agency; it is governed by a Board of Regents consisting of representatives of all three branches of government, and private citizens who form the majority of its members. The secretary is appointed by the Regents, not the president, and is by statute not a federal employee, though he has the authority to contract federal funds. The Smithsonian can thus operate in both worlds; it is often considered to be the government, but is under the Internal Revenue regulations, treated as having the status of a nonprofit organization. The secretary of the Smithsonian could make the decision for either the use of government, i.e., federal funds, or for the use of Smithsonian, i.e., trust funds, or both to acquire the Hope diamond. Kellogg was suggesting that to minimize the liability and the payment of insurance the secretary use federal funds for the acquisition and to consider the diamond federal property, not Smithsonian property.

For his part, Winston did not want an actual cash payment from the Smithsonian. Winston proposed that the transfer of the Hope diamond to the Smithsonian be effectuated in two parts, one part through a Bill of Sale and the other through a Deed of Gift. Winston would value the Hope diamond at $1 million. For the sale, Winston would get $250,000 in the government-confiscated diamonds he'd already been given by the Smithsonian. In return, the Smithsonian would then own one-fourth of the diamond. For the gift, Winston would transfer over to the Smithsonian a one-tenth interest of his share in the diamond each year for ten years. That is, out the outset, the Smithsonian would own 32.5 percent of the diamond—25 percent from the sale and 1/10 of the remaining 75 percent donated by Winston for year one.

Winston was willing to turn over the diamond to the Smithsonian immediately, without waiting for an Internal Revenue ruling on the tax consequences. Presumably, Harry Winston would be able to deduct whatever portion he was legally entitled to of the donation he gave each year. He might value that at the full $75,000, but he could always choose a lesser amount. Furthermore, Winston proposed that neither side would be responsible for any liability with respect to the diamond.

Elisha Hanson, operating for Carmichael as legal counsel to the Smithsonian, was asked for his opinion. Finding "the proposal is unique indeed," his recommendation was harsh.

May 27

LETTER FROM HANSON TO CARMICHAEL

In the event of the sale of the Winston company, or its business, or in the event of a bankruptcy or receivership proceeding, these undivided interests [*the undonated percentage of the diamond*] would become matters of real legal concern to the Smithsonian . . . Also, even though the instrument as submitted by Winston proposes to absolve both parties from responsibility for any loss of or damage or injury to the Hope diamond, regardless of cause, nevertheless the law of negligence undoubtedly may be applied to the party in possession . . . The Winston Corporation . . . is owned outright by Harry Winston . . . His death, should it occur before complete ownership is transferred might create . . . legal controversy over the settlement of his estate . . . Whatever the Hope diamond may be worth today, . . . it was acquired by Winston for far less than the $250,000 appraised value of the Smithsonian's melee of diamonds. For this melee, Winston would exchange but a one-quarter interest in the Hope diamond—not a $250,000 interest— on a value to be fixed by the Commissioner of Internal Revenue . . . The tax consequences are those not only of Winston, but of the United States. The higher the value fixed on the diamond, the greater the saving to Winston over a period of years and the greater the loss in tax revenues to the United States . . . If the transaction is completed, questions certainly will be raised both in the Congressional and public minds. From a purely legal point of view . . . the Smithsonian should not enter into an agreement with Winston whereby it would acquire anything less than full and complete ownership of the diamond immediately, and not at some indefinite time in the future. Only if Winston should propose an immediate transfer of full ownership, would it become necessary to consider the further question as to whether the transfer would be in the sound interest of both the Smithsonian and the United States.

In Hanson's opinion, Winston was ripping off the Smithsonian and the government. The next day, Carmichael had to write a difficult letter to Winston's attorney.

May 28

LETTER FROM CARMICHAEL TO HODES

I regret to inform you that . . . I am convinced that the Smithsonian has no option but to ask you to inform Mr. Winston that we deeply appreciate all that he has done in his effort to work out financial and other arrangements by means of which the Hope diamond could be transferred to the Smithsonian Institution, but because of a number of special considerations related to the Smithsonian itself it seems inadvisable for us to proceed further in connection with these negotiations.

As I read this letter from the Smithsonian's archives I am amazed. Even as a staffer who has intimately known the Smithsonian bureaucracy over some decades it is hard to imagine how the negotiations could get to such a point. Incredibly, the Smithsonian was about to lose the Hope diamond!

Hodes received Carmichael's letter on Thursday, May 29, and called the Smithsonian secretary from New York. Hodes asked Carmichael to telephone Harry Winston at PL(Plaza) 3-1510 and speak with him directly. The folder contains Carmichael's typed notes from the conversation.

> Mr. Winston said that he was sorry, but he could understand how such decisions arose. He was still anxious to have the Smithsonian Institution own the Hope diamond. He suggested I ask the Smithsonian lawyer to draw up a statement of the conditions under which we would be willing to accept the diamond. I told him that I thought this reply should be made directly to Mr. Hodes rather than to him. Mr. Winston agreed. I told Mr. Winston that the only condition under which the Smithsonian could accept the diamond would be as an outright gift, without any evaluation or requirement that we express a valuation for the gem.

Negotiations continued between Hanson and Hodes over the next two months. Winston was willing to give up the cash sale part of the deal. The Smithsonian wanted complete and full ownership from the outset, something Winston couldn't give up without serious loss of his tax deduction—now made more important given the lack of the cushion provided through the sales part of the deal. Winkle from Internal Revenue expressed an informal opinion that if Winston formally gifted the full ownership of the Hope diamond to the museum at once, he would not be allowed to take the deductions spaced out over a number of years. Hodes, relying on Internal Revenue case law, suggested a "tenancy in common," whereby Winston would transfer the diamond by absolute gift to the Smithsonian, not the U.S. government, a one-tenth portion of the diamond each year over a decade. After all, Carmichael himself had originally suggested taking a tax deduction over the years.

Finally, Winston and the Smithsonian agreed on the deal.

DEED OF GIFT

KNOW ALL MEN BY THESE PRESENTS that the undersigned, HARRY WIN-STON, INC., a New York corporation with offices at 7 East 51st Street, New York, N.Y. (hereinafter called "Donor"), has given, transferred and delivered and does hereby give, transfer and deliver unto the SMITHSONIAN INSTITUTION, an establishment of the United States of America located in Washington, D.C. (hereinafter called "Donee"), as and by way of an absolute gift, an undivided one-tenth (1/10) interest in and to a certain historic 44½ carat blue diamond generally known as and hereinafter called the Hope diamond.

TO HAVE AND TO HOLD the said undivided one-tenth (1/10) interest in and to said Hope diamond forever, subject to the following terms and conditions.

I. Ownership of the Hope Diamond

From and after the execution of this deed of gift, the ownership of said Hope diamond is and shall be as follows: an undivided nine-tenths (9/10) interest in Donor, and an undivided one-tenth (1/10) interest in Donee.

II. Possession of Hope Diamond

(a) The Donee shall have the right to possession, dominion and control of the Hope diamond during such days as it may designate, provided that the total number of such days in any year shall not exceed thirty-six and one-half (36½).

(b) The Donor shall have the right to possession, dominion and control of the Hope diamond during such days of the year as are not designated by the Donee, pursuant to Paragraph II (a) above.

(c) The party having possession of the Hope diamond shall not be required, upon expiration of its period of entitlement to possession pursuant to the provisions of Paragraph II(a) or (b) above, to deliver the Hope diamond to the other party, except upon a week's notice in writing.

III. Responsibility for the Hope Diamond

Neither party shall be responsible to the other party for any loss of or damage or injury to the Hope diamond, regardless of the cause of the injury, loss, or damage.

IV. Receipt

Donee hereby acknowledges delivery of one-tenth (1/10) interest in the said Hope diamond and that it has received possession of

said diamond and that it will hold said diamond and said part interest in said diamond pursuant to the terms and conditions of this
deed of gift.

IN WITNESS WHEREOF, the parties, by their duly authorized offi-
cers, have hereunto set their hand and seal this 17th day of July, 1958.

The agreement was signed by Winston and, for the Smithsonian, by
J. L. Keddy, the acting secretary at the time. In subsequent years, annual supplementary deeds transferred additional one-tenth interests in the Hope diamond until the Smithsonian assumed full
ownership in 1967.

Of course the agreement misstated a key fact, as agreements
often do. The Hope diamond was not delivered by the date of sig-
nature. It did not come to the Smithsonian for several months.
And, the agreement was silent about one important matter that
Elisha Hanson raised with Carmichael on August 18, the day before
the attorney left for vacation. "Incidentally," he reminded the secretary, "Winston has in his possession a melee of diamonds belonging to the Smithsonian." Arrangements had to be made to get those
back.

AMERICA'S
DIAMOND

26

MUSEUM SPECIMEN 217868

O*nce captured by the museum, the Hope diamond* becomes an object of history—natural and cultural. Its treatment is officially ritualized. Given the Hope's presence in a science museum, it is regarded as a scientific specimen. Its every movement is scrupulously monitored and recorded. It is surrounded by rationally construed operations, scientific discourse, and a multiplicity of institutional systems. It is not that culture stops at the door to the museum, but rather that the museum world itself constitutes a new cultural system within which its objects are made meaningful.

The Hope, like every other museum object, was given a unique accession number, in this case 217868. The standard Smithsonian Accession Memorandum is decidedly bland. It was accessioned into the Department of Geology, Division of Mineralogy and Petrology on December 22, 1958, as a gift acquired from Harry Winston, Inc. The accession consisted of the Hope in a diamond and platinum setting and necklace of 62 diamonds.

In December 1988, the Hope was graded and tested by the Gemological Institute of America—a procedure repeated again in September 1996. It was described as a cushion antique brilliant cut with 58 facets (plus 2 extra on the pavilion and several on the girdle), VS_1 clarity—slightly included, with whitish graining, of a fancy dark grayish blue in color, and with measurements of 25.6 mm by

21.78 mm with a thickness of 12 mm, and weighing 45.52 carats. Microscopic inspection also revealed a good bit of wear and tear on the diamond, with numerous fissures and imperfections not apparent to the naked eye.[1]

A few things came to light as a result of such examination. For one, the historic weight given to the diamond—44½ carats—actually turned out to be 45.52. This difference was due to the fact that the old weight was given in English carats (about 205.3 milligrams per carat) and the new in metric carats (200 milligrams per carat).[2] Another finding was that Harry Winston had altered the Hope diamond to make it look better by slightly cutting the culet. The Hope was ground on a Harry Winston wheel.[3]

The diamond has been examined a number of times for various studies. Herbert Tillander, a Finnish gemologist, scrutinized its faceting to understand the history of diamond-cutting technology. Historically, such studies follow upon French scientist Brisson's use of the diamond to understand specific gravity. Current curator Jeff Post argues that the Hope diamond represents a biopsy of the earth's mantle. Given the rarity of large blue diamonds, the Hope represents a significant scientific specimen for understanding the characteristics and formation of diamonds.

For just over a century, scientists have sought to understand the relationship between a diamond's atomic structure and the way light moves through it. Subjecting diamonds to different light and energy sources and monitoring the results helps scientists form and test hypotheses about its composition. Researchers learned early on that exposing a diamond to radioactivity would affect its properties, and thus change its color. Another technique has been to place diamonds under an ultraviolet light. The ultraviolet waves stimulate subatomic movement that may allow for the momentary storing of energy, which, if released immediately, allows the diamond to shine, or fluoresce. Sometimes, diamonds will hold the absorbed energy and release it slowly over longer periods of time—minutes or even hours. Termed phosphorescence, to an observer in a darkened room this looks like the diamond is literally glowing from within.

Studying the Hope diamond under ultraviolet light has proved intriguing. The Hope, as other blue or blue-grayish diamonds, is categorized as a type IIb diamond. These diamonds are quite rare. The blueness of the Hope and other such diamonds is due to the presence of the element boron in the crystalline carbon, the color saturation depends upon the quantity, with more boron making for a deeper bluer gem. All type IIb diamonds are semiconductors of electricity. When exposed to short-wave ultraviolet light, blue type IIb diamonds typically phosphoresce blue for some time, indicating their slow release of internal energy. But there is a notable exception. The Hope diamond exhibits a very special characteristic. When it was first exposed to ultraviolet light in a 1965 test, it phosphoresced a deep, strong *red*. "No such phenomenon has ever before been recorded for blue diamonds," remarked curator George Switzer at the time.[4]

The test has been subsequently repeated a number of times. The reason for the Hope diamond's red phosphorescence is as yet not fully explained by scientists. Switzer's successor, John Sampson White, demonstrated that phosphorescence depends upon the size of the diamond; a large diamond might phosphoresce, while a smaller portion, even if cut from the same original stone, might not. Furthermore, a single diamond might be formed in sections, each of which may phosphoresce differently.[5] Current curator Jeffrey Post has not witnessed those phenomena, but he has subsequently found several small blue diamonds that phosphoresce red. However, no diamond matches the long, deep red phosphorescence of the Hope.

Is this unique deep red ultraviolet-induced glow emanating from the Hope diamond indicative of some supernatural power? Not likely. But with this as yet unexplained quality, the Hope diamond has a kinship with a magical stone mentioned in an old English ballad, *Hind Horn,* recorded by folklorist Francis Child and traced to the 14th century. In that ballad, the gemstone typically glows pale, but changes color to blood red as a sign of misfortune.

❀ ❀ ❀

Within the Smithsonian, the diamond has not only been subject to study, but also to tale telling over the years. Dan Appleman, chair of gems and minerals, shared an embarrassing story with the press. "Someone was weighing it once and dropped it," he recalled. "It bounced."[6]

In 1985, I was serving as the coordinator for an exhibition, *Aditi: A Celebration of Life,* mounted in the National Museum of Natural History for the Festival of India—a major binational cultural program. The Festival's U.S. chairman was S. Dillon Ripley, the just-retired secretary of the Smithsonian. He and then-current Secretary Robert McCormick Adams wanted to host Indian Prime Minister Rajiv Gandhi and First Lady Nancy Reagan, among other dignitaries, for an opening luncheon in the Gem Hall, with the head table directly in front of the Hope diamond.

How would the prime minister regard the Hope diamond? Would he ask Nancy Reagan to return it to India? After all, Pakistan had in 1976 officially asked Great Britain to return the Koh-i-Nur diamond. And we did have on file in the Smithsonian's archives a letter from a member of the public urging the diamond's repatriation:

> It is my understanding that this stone is part of a much larger stone which was stolen from a temple of Kali in India. The priests of the temple of Kali, or possibly the government of India have a claim to this diamond superior to that of the United States. Therefore I request that the Hope diamond be given to the government of India to be restored to the appropriate temple of Kali.[7]

I cautioned my boss, Ralph Rinzler, a Smithsonian assistant secretary. Maybe the dignitaries should dine elsewhere. In the end, the luncheon was held in the Gem Hall. Rajiv Gandhi sat next to Nancy Reagan and Bob Adams. At one point, Mrs. Reagan realized

Nancy Reagan and Rajiv Gandhi dine in front of the Hope diamond.

she was sitting in front of the Hope. The Prime Minister, nonplussed, did not ask for its return.

Other stories among Smithsonian staff include tales of coincidences and misfortune, whispered anecdotes that sometimes seriously, sometimes playfully use the curse as a motif of institutional lore. During the period of the reinstallation of the diamond in the new, renovated Hooker Hall, curator Post was hit by a car. He was seriously but not fatally injured. Staff members in the museum "confidentially" shared their assessment—"The curse is real." Another Smithsonian senior staffer, Mary Rodriguez, was given the chance to try on the Hope diamond necklace. She did. Within a month she had a stroke. She half-seriously wonders about the diamond's effect.

In 1971, curator George Switzer wrote an article for *National Geographic* magazine that repeated much of May Yohe's and Cartier's curse story, taking it, without comment, as an accurate historical account of the misfortunes that have beset the blue diamond's owners.[8] He and other Smithsonian staff would have a much tougher time publicly asserting belief in a curse from a scientific perspective. But some do enjoy entertaining the counterstructural idea that in the midst of the supposed rationality of the museum there are still unexplained mysteries.

These and other such stories indicate that while a scientific specimen, the Hope diamond has not been placed in a sort of cultural formaldehyde since coming to the Smithsonian. Instead, it has been repeatedly connected to its history and subjected to an ongoing occupational folklore. Inspected, exhibited, manipulated, and even loaned, its biography has continued to grow and become increasingly elaborated since it became a national treasure.

27

NATIONAL TREASURE

T*he Hope diamond became a national treasure* upon its acquisition
by the Smithsonian. Its status as such was bolstered in 1962
with the attention of the French and Jackie Kennedy.

On January 26, Pierre Verlet, the chief conservator of the Louvre,
wrote to Richard Howland, the head curator at the Smithsonian's Museum of History and Technology, requesting the loan of the
Hope diamond for an exhibition on the historic jewels of France.
The exhibition, Verlet wrote, would be held in the famed Apollo
Gallery of the Louvre for one month in May. The Hope was requested, as it was the larger part of the famed French Blue. In the
exhibition, it would be united with the Côte de Bretagne, the ruby
that had formed the dragon in the colored version of the insignia of
the Order of the Golden Fleece.

What Napoleon could not achieve in war, the government of
Charles de Gaulle would try to achieve in peace.

Howland was not the curator in charge of the Hope. George
Switzer was. Both Howland and Switzer worked in the Smithson-
ian, but in two different museums. Howland sent the request to
Secretary Carmichael. Carmichael did not share the request with
Switzer. Instead he instructed Howland to reply, as he did on
February 6:

We have considered very carefully your request to borrow the Hope diamond for one month's exhibition at the Louvre. My colleagues and I have discussed the matter, hoping that we might find a way to send the diamond to you. Unfortunately, we reluctantly must inform you that we cannot arrange for its transfer at this time.

The months of April, May, and June are the months when the greatest number of visitors come to the Smithsonian Institution, and for many of them the Hope diamond is a major attraction. It has attained a rather remarkable amount of publicity through the United States, and is the goal of many peoples' visit. Our customary practice prevents us from lending an object of such importance during the height of our visiting season.

In addition, the transfer of an object of such value, outside the territorial limits of the United States, would pose a number of problems that might involve us with complicated governmental regulations.

I realize the importance of this stone, knowing that it is part of the great blue diamond of Louis XIV, and wish personally that it might be restored to its former home, the Galérie d'Apollon, for a month's exhibition.[1]

Verlet responded, reiterating the request. He diplomatically suggested that his good friends might intercede with President John F. Kennedy in facilitating its fulfillment. Verlet also sweetened the offer—perhaps the Louvre could lend the Smithsonian something important. Memos and letters went back and forth in March and April figuring out what to do.

March 1
MEMO FROM HOWLAND TO CARMICHAEL

Shall we reconsider? . . . the publicity of the diamond's trip back to the Louvre and then home again would be of considerable importance. Tourists for a month could see a picture of the diamond, a full-size model of it, and of course the dazzling Jubilee diamond. International cultural collaboration could be stressed, as well as our close ties with the Louvre.

Then, when we really want to borrow something splendid, we have an "in." Perhaps the National Gallery would like to borrow a great painting, or we could borrow important portraits for the opening of the National Portrait Gallery, of personages like Lafayette, Louis XVI, etc.

Dr. Switzer has been out-of-town, so I have not yet discussed the matter with him. Is it possible to re-consider, in the light of worldwide collaboration and unity?[2]

Carmichael's response was brief. He scrawled a short note on the memo. "Dr. Howland: I am afraid we must say a nice *no*."[3]

Howland drafted a letter, but Remington Kellogg, the Natural History Museum director, raised objections. He noted a complication arising from the acquisition deal with Winston; the Smithsonian, at this time, did not fully own the Hope, but only a fraction thereof. He and fellow director Frank Taylor, head of the Museum of History and Technology, thought the draft made it sound that the decision to refuse the loan of the Hope was a close call. It was not. The Smithsonian did not want to disappoint the museum nor risk sending the diamond to France.

Howland pushed Carmichael on the possible intercession of President Kennedy.

March 14

MEMO FROM HOWLAND TO CARMICHAEL

You will note that Verlet suggests the possibility of his getting his good friends Mr. and Mrs. Charles Wrightsman to ask President Kennedy (their intimate personal friend) to intercede on his behalf. Do you feel our reply to Verlet should take note of this?[4]

Carmichael again scrawled on a Howland memo—"John Walker [director of the National Gallery of Art] will tell the Wrightsmans to say 'no.'"

André Malraux, the famed author and French Minister of Culture, then got into the act. He and Jackie Kennedy had met the previous May. They had spoken about how France and the United States organized government support for cultural activity, and specifically about cultural exchange between the two nations.[5] He now lobbied American government representatives. He offered a personal convoy of the Hope from and to the United States, and extraordinary security precautions at the Louvre. Morrill Cody, Assistant Director for Europe for the United States Information Agency, wrote to Carmichael.

March 21, 1962
LETTER FROM MORRILL TO CARMICHAEL

The Ministry [of Culture] believes that their juxtaposition [that of the Hope and the Côte de Bretagne] in the exhibit provides a most effective symbolic evidence of the cultural affinity of our two countries . . .

No other country, to my knowledge, has ever been so favored, and it is to Mr. Malraux's warm friendship for the United States that we owe his personal authorization to display priceless samples of France's cultural treasures [in the United States].

. . . The loan of the Hope diamond offers a unique opportunity for the U.S. Government to reciprocate for past good-will gestures from the French Government and to sustain the flow of cultural exchange which is so important to our own interests. A refusal of the request at this time would be misunderstood and could constitute a serious blow to the cordial relations we have been enjoying with our French colleagues.[6]

Meanwhile, Carmichael wrote to John Walker, asking him to mention to the Wrightsmans the Smithsonian's reluctance to lend the Hope. But the Smithsonian's effort was too little too late. Malraux had gone back to Jackie Kennedy directly and prevailed upon her to support the loan of the Hope diamond for the Louvre exhibition. The Hope loan was crucial if indeed France were to send one of its treasures to the United States. Jackie Kennedy called Carmichael to urge him to approve the loan. Carmichael did not make a decision on the spot, but apparently agreed to put the proposition to the Smithsonian's Board of Regents, its executive body.

April 10

LETTER FROM CARMICHAEL TO REGENT CLARENCE CANON

> Mrs. John F. Kennedy, however, has been directly appealed to at the White House, to ask that the gem be loaned. She spoke to me on the telephone at considerable length about her feeling that from an international and cultural point of view it was very important for us to accede to this request.
>
> I have discussed the matter with the Chancellor, Chief Justice Warren, and he says that he feels Mrs. Kennedy's request is essentially a command, and so he favors the loan. I feel that it would be very difficult for the Smithsonian not to do as Mrs. Kennedy has requested, but before authorizing the loan, I should like to ask you, as a member of the Executive Committee of the Board of Regents, for your approval or disapproval.[7]

It did not take long to come to a decision. The next day, Carmichael issued a memorandum to staff informing them of the loan of the Hope diamond to the Louvre. He also received a note from Jackie Kennedy along with the copy of a letter from Charles Wrightsman.

April 10
LETTER FROM JACKIE KENNEDY TO CARMICHAEL
<u>Thank you</u>. <u>Thank you</u>. <u>Thank you</u>.[8]

Mrs. Kennedy now had good news to report to Malraux, who would be arriving in Washington the next month as the guest of honor for a glamorous state dinner at the White House.

Switzer expressed his disappointment with the decision.

April 11
MEMO FROM SWITZER TO CARMICHAEL
We are all unhappy about the circumstances that have led to the decision that the Hope diamond be loaned to the Louvre. However, everyone understands that it is now unavoidable.

I gather . . . that there was, without my knowledge, correspondence regarding this matter between Dr. Howland and a curator at the Louvre. I do not believe that anyone in the Institution has the right to carry out negotiations, even of a preliminary nature, about a loan (or refusal to loan) without first consulting the curator in charge. In this case, I should like to make it clear that the Hope diamond is assigned to the Division of Mineralogy and Petrology, and is, therefore, my direct responsibility.[9]

Howland went to see Switzer, explained the circumstances of his involvement, and apologized, as did Carmichael.

The French government agreed to cover the transportation and insurance costs for the Hope diamond, and take care of all customs clearance and security matters. The plan was for Switzer to transport the Hope diamond via Pan Am flight 116 arriving at Orly airport at 8:50 a.m. on May 1. He would be met and then driven under escort to the Paris office of Harry Winston at 29 Avenue Montaigne, where the diamond would be removed from its setting by one of Winston's experts. He would then take the unset blue diamond to the Louvre, turning it over to Verlet. The Hope was insured for $1,000,000; Switzer for $250,000.

Switzer, years later, described the low-tech security plans for carrying the diamond. "My wife sewed a small cloth pouch for the diamond and I pinned it with a safety pin to the inside of my right pants pocket where I carry my money."[10] Switzer carried no gun. He was driven to the airport with a security escort. He boarded the flight that was making stops at Philadelphia and Boston before continuing on to Paris. But the plans went awry. "Coming into Philadelphia," recounted Switzer, "the pilot made a bad landing and we hit with an awful thump."[11] The plane was damaged, and the flight was canceled. Switzer took another flight to Idlewild in New York to transfer to Pan Am flight 72 to Frankfurt and then on to Paris. He called the Smithsonian to alert officials to the changes and asked them to send cables to Verlet. Switzer worried about having to go through customs in Frankfurt, but was assured that would not be necessary. He sat in the transit lounge until catching an Air Maroc flight to Paris. Verlet and a security man from Harry Winston's met him at the airport. Given the delay, they proceeded directly by car to the Louvre. En route, he got into a minor auto accident. Again, Switzer recounted, "I don't believe in any of the bad luck story that goes with the Hope diamond, but at that point I couldn't help wondering."[12]

The Hope finally made it to the Louvre. Tens of thousands of museum visitors came to the exhibition *Dix siècles de joaillerie française,* "Ten Centuries of French Jewels." The request of the Louvre curators, as well as the exhibition catalog, signaled the unequivocal acceptance of the Hope diamond as derived from the French Blue. The catalog recognized the Hope diamond as being famous for its royal history and even supported the Brunswick bribe hypothesis:

It was the diamond of Louis XIV stolen in September 1792, and it is said, aided in the victory of Valmy by coming into the possession of the Duke of Brunswick a few days later. The diamond weighed 44 carats when it came into the possession of the Dutch banker Hope after 1830, having been re-cut. The complementary stone formed a blue diamond sold by the Brunswick family in Geneva in 1874.[13]

Also in the exhibit was the ruby-red spinel dragon of the famed *Toison d'or,* temporarily reunited with the Hope. The Hope was put in a vitrine, in between two others—one holding the Regent diamond and the other the Sancy—the other two most valuable of the French Crown Jewels.

The catalog explicitly thanked President Kennedy for his personal involvement in securing the blue diamond.

In Washington, Carmichael wrote Jackie Kennedy,

> We at the Smithsonian are most grateful for your kindness in sharing your wisdom and your deep understanding of international cultural affairs with us so that we could make the correct decision in regard to the loan of this jewel.[14]

At the conclusion of the exhibition, James Bradley, the assistant secretary of the Smithsonian, picked up the diamond and brought it home. By October the Smithsonian had received numerous accolades, official and unofficial, that the loan of the Hope diamond had been a big hit in Paris and that it would be reciprocated.

The next year, a newspaper article titled JEWELS FOR JACKIE speculated that the Smithsonian's national gem collection could become a kind of repository from which presidents' wives might choose pieces to wear on formal occasions. It suggested,

> One of these days, Jacqueline Kennedy may pick up the telephone and call the custodian of national jewels. "Send over the Napoleon necklace and that sapphire brooch," she could say, "and . . . no, not the Hope diamond this time. I wore it last week at the French Embassy."[15]

Several editorials took up the topic of Jackie Kennedy wearing the national jewels, including the Hope, and opined on the wisdom of an American royal presidency. Jackie Kennedy never did wear the Hope diamond.

In 1963, the French promise to reciprocate the loan of the Hope was more than fulfilled. Another beautiful, enchanting lady with an enigmatic smile was sent by the French for a Washington sojourn. It was *Mona Lisa,* Leonardo da Vinci's famous painting. Exhibited at the National Gallery of Art in Washington, D.C., it drew large and appreciative crowds.[16]

The trip to the Louvre was one of the rare times the Hope diamond traveled beyond the Smithsonian. The next was in late March 1965 when it was loaned to De Beers for the Rand Easter Show in Johannesburg, South Africa. The diamond was picked up in Switzer's office by a courier for the Anglo-American Corporation of South Africa, who secreted it on his body by wrapping it in surgical tape. Switzer, who initially did not want to make the trip, did. The Hope was insured by Lloyds of London. When he reached South Africa, the curator cabled back to the Smithsonian "Switzer and Baby Doll arrived safely."[17]

The exhibition placed the Hope, in its setting, upon a gold rosebush. As Susanne Patch writes, "In keeping with its legend of bad luck, the diamond rested in the center of a golden web, like a fat blue spider."[18] A replica was put in its place at the Smithsonian for the six weeks it was gone.

The only other time the Hope was displayed outside of the Smithsonian was in 1982, when it traveled to New York's Metropolitan Museum of Art in November for the 50th anniversary celebration of Harry Winston, Inc. Ronald Winston hosted some 1,200 guests in the museum's Engelhard Court. For that fête, the Hope was reunited with the Star of the East and the Idol's Eye diamonds. The Hope rested—some said appropriately—at the foot of Rodin's *Gates of Hell*.[19]

In 1996, for the Smithsonian's 150th anniversary, the Institution produced a traveling exhibition, *America's Smithsonian*. The show contained the treasures of the Smithsonian: Abraham Lincoln's stovepipe hat, George Washington's sword, the Apollo mission moon-lander, a pair of ruby slippers made for Dorothy in *The Wizard of Oz*, paintings by Georgia O'Keeffe and Picasso, and hundreds of other objects. When curators were putting the show together, Secretary I. Michael Heyman instructed them that any of the 140 million or so things in the Smithsonian could be included in it—except for three—"The Star-Spangled Banner," the original Wright Brothers airplane, and the Hope diamond. The first two were too fragile to make a journey across the nation. The latter, the Hope diamond, was too valuable.

Just how valuable is the Hope diamond?

Its value, as the taxmen told Winston, would have to be determined by what it could actually fetch at sale on the open market. But that hasn't stopped either speculation or an occasional offer. A magazine that interviewed curator Paul Desautels in 1978 suggested $10 million had been offered. A letter the next year to Desautels from the Reid-Dureas Corporation representing a client offered $18 million. Ronald Winston, in 1995, estimated its value at $200 million. In 1999, Susanne Patch cited the price of blue diamonds sold during the decade—about $300,000 to $600,000 a carat. Allowing for inflation, a blue diamond the size of the Hope without historical significance might be expected to bring in anywhere between $25 to $40 million.[20] With its history and status, Ronald Winston might be right about its price—not that the Smithsonian is looking to sell this national treasure.

28

COLLECTION KEYSTONE

T*he donation of the Hope diamond* enhanced the newly opened Gem Hall of the museum. It brought the Smithsonian unprecedented publicity. And it endowed the National Gem Collection with a value and standing it would not have otherwise achieved.

As Harry Winston foresaw, his gift of the Hope diamond stimulated others to provide outstanding gems to the collection. Mrs. John Logan donated the 423-carat Logan Sapphire in 1960; Marjorie Merriweather Post donated the Napoleon necklace in 1962, the 31-carat Blue Heart diamond in 1964, the Marie-Louise diadem in 1971, and the Maximilian emerald in 1973; Victoria and Leonard Wilkinson gave the 68-carat Victoria-Transvaal diamond in 1977; Rosser Reeves gave a spectacular 139-carat star ruby; Janet Annenberg Hooker gave a large emerald in 1977 and a suite of yellow diamonds in 1994, and so on. Donations according to Jeff Post turned the National Gem Collection into the world's "greatest public display of gemstones."[1]

The impetus to expand and enhance that collection and its educational impact drew the National Museum of Natural History toward plans in the 1990s to redo the Hall again. This resulted in about $4 million of congressional and $13 million in private support for the making of an outstanding presentation of gems both in their natural crystal state and in the form of finished jewels. A major donation from Janet Annenberg Hooker placed her name on the new Hall, opened in 1997.

The new Hall included the Harry Winston Gallery to house the Hope diamond. For almost forty years, the Hope was displayed rather simply, hanging on its diamond necklace against a plain background, viewed in a vault through a one-inch-thick glass porthole, with a small unassuming label.

In the new gallery, the diamond rests on a rotating column, surrounded on all sides by glass. The lighting is superb; it is a fiber-optic system created by Absolute Action Ltd. of London to make the gem "sparkle, dazzle, and glow."[2] The state-of-the-art display case is designed to attract attention, while also providing for security needs in a vault below.

There was considerable debate over the style and tenor of the new Hall and the Winston Gallery in particular. Years before, Daniel Appleman, chairman of gems and minerals overseeing the collection, had said that when setting up an exhibition, "you try for a cross between a textbook and an amusement park."[3] That tension now came to the fore. How melodramatic to make the area? Should the design enhance the sense of mystery and glamour? Should it provide a dispassionate science lesson? The result bespeaks of a dignified, dramatic presentation, part museum, part mystery-temple, part elegant jewelry display worthy of Harry Winston, Inc., Cartier, and other elite firms. As the secretary of the Smithsonian, Lawrence Small, wrote in *Smithsonian* magazine:

> The [*Hope*] diamond has the place of honor at the head of the gem collection. It rests on a small column that turns slowly to show the jewel in four directions. There's an eerily human aspect to this stately rotation, as if a wearer were showing off the gem, and viewers fall silent under its spell. It's one of the great Smithsonian experiences.[4]

The Hope itself had to be prepared for the new display. In 1996, the Hope diamond was carried to Harry Winston's in New York. A 40-person SWAT team equipped with Uzis provided a diversionary delivery. The diamond was cleaned and the links on the necklace

The Harry Winston Gallery.

tightened so that the jewelry would not be affected by the new installation.

Harry Winston himself did not live to see the new display. He died in 1978. His son Ronald took the helm of the company after his death and continued to work closely with the Smithsonian on matters concerning the Hope specifically, and the gem collection more generally.

In July 2000 Ronald settled with his younger brother, Bruce, who gave up his share of Harry Winston, Inc. in return for $54 million. Fenway Partners bought a major stake in the Harry Winston group in December 2000 for $100 million. The money helped pay off liabilities and expand the business. In May 2004, Aber Diamond Corporation bought 51 percent of Harry Winston, Inc. for $85 million, with Ronald and Fenway remaining minority partners. Winston continued its flagship store at 56th Street and Fifth Avenue in New York, and also maintained shops in Beverly Hills, Paris, Geneva, and Tokyo.

Ronald's association with the Hope and the museum continues. He was instrumental in the effort of the museum to display the

Dresden Green diamond for an October 2000 exhibit. That 41-carat gem is the largest and best-known green diamond in the world. It too came from India, likely from the Golconda mines. It had been set in the Austrian Order of the Golden Fleece in the 18th century. Its joint display with the Hope was an historic occasion.

29

MISSING PIECES?

Do other diamonds share a kinship with the Hope?

Though the Hope has long been thought to be derived from the French Blue, that supposition was not conclusively demonstrated until 2004 with detailed measurement and photography of the Hope at the museum and the application of contemporary computer modeling and simulation processes.

The overwhelming consensus of competent authorities has always been that the Hope was fashioned from the French Blue, ever since it was first suggested in writing by Barbot in 1858. There has been a good deal of professional disagreement about how. Streeter argued that the Hope had to have been created by cleaving the French Blue given the technology of the late 18th and early 19th century. Considering the heart shape of the French Blue and the oval shape of the Hope, he believed that the triangular piece, where the "heart comes to a point" was cleaved off the former to make the latter. For him, this accounted for one edge of the Hope being straighter and less curved than the other. And the cleaved-off piece survived as a satellite stone—the Brunswick Blue—and then another smaller stone, the Pirie.

Herbert Tillander, who studied the Hope at the Smithsonian in the 1970s, disagreed with Streeter. Tillander made quartz models of the Tavernier Violet, the French Blue, and the Hope in order to

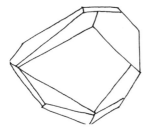

*Faceting of the blue diamond (from left to right): Tavernier Violet,
French Blue, Hope.*

compare their facets. He found that none of the facets on the French
Blue and the Hope, save only for the culet, matched up. That is, the
Hope had to have been completely refaceted from the French Blue.
This involved not cleaving, but cutting and grinding. Thus, he concluded, there could be no satellite stones. You'd get a lot of diamond
dust, but nothing that could qualify as a finished diamond. This was
consistent with the findings of Bernard Morel, the French authority
who carefully looked at the faceting of the French Blue and the
Hope; English expert Ian McGlashan sided with Streeter.

To settle the matter, Jeff Post tried a new approach for a project
proposed with the Discovery Channel's *Unsolved History* series. Joining the team was gem cutter and re-creator Scott Sucher, who had
made a cubic zirconia replica of the Hope diamond years before, and
jewelry designers and computer adepts Steven and Nancy Attaway.[1]

Working from the drawing of Tavernier's Violet from the chart
of his historic sale to Louis XIV, they made a digital model of the
gem, and then a physical replica out of cubic zirconia. They then did
the same for the French Blue, using the drawings of 19th-century
expert Hirtz and the measurements of Bernard Morel, who had
studied those renditions. When they then tried to fit the digital
models together, they found that the French Blue fit into the Tavernier, but that the Hope did not fit into the French Blue.

Believing the old measurements of the Hope to be slightly inaccurate, they digitally photographed the diamond in an extraor-
dinarily detailed way in order to render them more precise.

Retrying the process digitally, they found that the Hope fit into the French Blue that fit into the Tavernier Violet. There was only one position in which they matched up. That position keeps the table surface constant. It also preserves the thickness of the gem throughout its transformation, allowing for some polishing and refashioning. Most convincing, according to the research team, several extra facets on the Hope match up with those on the French Blue.

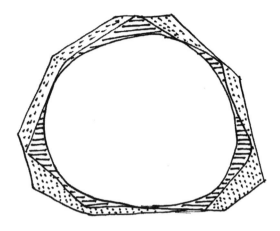

Hypothetical overlay of the three diamonds based upon the model of Bernard Morel.

Granting that there was some trial and error in making some assumptions about the faceting and angles of the Tavernier Violet and the French Blue—as neither was available for physical inspection—this simulation provided the most convincing demonstration to date of the Hope's derivation from the French Crown Jewel. Given such assumptions, and absent a direct comparison of color and a record of the cutting, the proof cannot be absolute.

What about other pieces? Could any small diamonds have resulted from the refashioning of the original Tavernier Violet into the French Blue into the Hope?

The research team carefully made a rubber mold of the French Blue from their cubic zirconia model. They then placed the model Hope in the mold. They pumped in hot wax that dried in the interstitial space between the model and the mold cavity. When opened, the wax took the shape of the diamond material that would have been removed from the French Blue to form the Hope. This wax material was very thin—less than three millimeters thick at its

Replicas of the three diamonds (from left to right): the Tavernier Violet, the French Blue, and the Hope.

maximum. This was too thin to form a satellite stone. The researchers concluded that the French Blue was ground down, not cleaved, to form the Hope, and that the excess was mere diamond dust, with no satellite stone possible. A similar exercise with the French Blue model and the mold cavity of the Tavernier produced a similar conclusion: the diamond had been ground down, not cleaved, and no satellite stone was formed.

Sitting with Post and inspecting the wax remnants, I am inclined to agree, though here there is a bit more doubt.

The computer model of the Tavernier is based on rough drawings of the gemstone, which make it impossible to determine all the facets and their angles. The simulation relied on reasonable manipulation and interpretation, using the carat weight recorded by Tavernier and the specific gravity as measured by Brisson as parameters. But small errors are a certainty.

For the French Blue, the measures used in the simulation are derived from Morel, who relied on good, but technically imprecise, drawings made by Hirtz, for Bapst's study of the French Crown Jewels. Hirtz, in turn, made those drawings not from the actual diamond, but from the molds made for the Order of the Golden Fleece back in the mid-1700s. Thus, while as accurate as they could be, the measures also relied on manipulation and are virtually certain to exhibit some error.

Very small errors in the angles of the simulated gems and the cubic zirconia replicas could, if in the right places, magnify the distribution of the wax remnants representing the diamond cut away from first the Tavernier and then the French Blue. In fact, the illustration of the Golden Fleece drawn by its fabricator Pierre-André Jacquemin and provided by Herbert Horovitz, shows a French Blue with a more elongated tip than in Hirtz's drawing and more in keeping with Streeter's rougher representation. That is, there could be thicker material than revealed by this particular experiment. A diamond of perhaps a carat, maybe two or even three might be possible.

The finding that no satellite stone could be produced is probably correct, but not definitive. Certainly no satellite stone the size of the reputed 13¾-carat Brunswick Blue would have been possible. Given the risky nature of cleaving a diamond, one would have to ask whether it could possibly be worth destroying the whole mother stone—i.e., the French Blue, in order to create two pieces, one very large and the other quite small. Grinding the French Blue down to the Hope rather than cleaving it would be the more rational course of action. Still, it would be of immense interest to examine the Brunswick Blue and Pirie, check their facets, and see if they phosphoresce red—if one could find them.

Given the status of the Hope diamond as a famous gem and national treasure, other owners of blue diamonds like to claim kinship for their gems. Less than a month after the McLeans agreed to buy the Hope they received a letter from one Chas. A. Horne:

> I am informed you are the owner of a rare gem supposed to
> have been taken from a large blue diamond weighing in
> the rough 112¼ karats, sold by Tavernier to Louis XIV. I
> have a small diamond weighing 1½ karat supposed to have
> been cut from the same stone, and guess it must be true for
> I have tried to match it in my travels west north east and
> here, and have not found a jeweler that can match it. I am
> very anxious to see your stone and compare this one of
> mine with it. This little stone of mine is a sapphire blue and

a beauty. I would like to make an engagement to see you some time that would suit you.[2]

There is no record of any follow-up.

Some gemologists have speculated that a gem set in a necklace worn by Queen Maria Luisa and visible in the famous Francisco Goya painting *The Family of Charles IV,* the King of Spain, done in 1800–1801, is the blue diamond. The original painting is some 11 feet wide and hangs in the Prado in Madrid. In the painting, the King wears a sash and the insignia of a number of chivalric orders, including the Golden Fleece.

The hypothesis is that the Queen obtained the diamond from her lover, fled Spain, avoided Napoleon's efforts to get it and ended up pawning it. An inventive story indeed! The gem is nothing like the shape of the Hope or the French Blue, and the chain of supposed possession without plausibility. So, where does this claim come from? The first report is found in the *New York Sunday Mirror Magazine,* April 8, 1951. Apparently, a child visitor to the Taft Museum in Cincinnati noticed that the gem in the painting was like the Hope diamond exhibited for a Court of Jewels display in the same museum. Staff were informed and the supposed connection story spread.[3]

Yet another claim for diamond kinship was made more recently by curators of the famed Hermitage museum in St. Petersburg. Their presumption concerns a 7.6-carat blue diamond that came to the Corcoran Gallery of Art in Washington in 1997 as part of an outstanding and unprecedented exhibition of *Jewels of the Romanovs: Treasures of the Russian Imperial Court.* "Is it—or isn't it—a chip off the old block?" asked the *Washington Post.*[4]

The diamond in question is from the Russian State Diamond Fund and formerly owned by the Empress Maria Feodorovna who left it to her daughter-in-law in 1827.

Given its provenance, the diamond had to have come either from India or Brazil. The diamond is light blue in appearance and has an irregular rhomboidal shape, with its table and pavilion cut

Queen Maria Luisa wearing a blue gemstone.

into steps. Hermitage curator Olga Gorewa and her colleagues had written of the connection to the Hope in *Joyaux du Trésor de Russie,* and summed it up in their Corcoran brochure:

> Believed to have been cut from the famous stone as "Le Tavernier," this blue diamond and the Hope diamond may have been one.[5]

One of the proponents of the connection was Hermitage gemologist Lili Konstantinovna Kuznetsova. Kuznetsova claimed that based on its color and size, the Russian blue diamond may have been cut from the Tavernier Violet, not the French Blue. When the Russian exhibit was in Washington, Smithsonian staff expressed their interests in and their doubts about the diamond, and even offered to test it for

The Russian blue diamond set in a pin.

phosphorescence. The offer went unanswered—even though the two diamonds were less than a mile apart for some 2½ months.

When the exhibition was ready to leave Washington for a year-long tour across the United States, controversy erupted. The trucks transporting the gems were blockaded by Russian government personnel. The Russians had a problem with the split of exhibition proceeds with the American-Russian Cultural Cooperation Foundation that had organized the tour. What had been promoted as an American-Russian "goodwill mission" turned sour. The Russians felt they'd been ripped off. The idea of having millions of dollars of jewels literally held hostage on the street excited Washingtonians for some days until the revenue sharing was renegotiated, and the matter resolved.

I went to visit Kuznetsova in St. Petersburg in 1999 to see what evidence the Hermitage actually had for the purported link between their diamond and the Tavernier Violet. It turns out not much at all.[6] There is a record of the Feodorovna will. In the Russian records, the diamond is alternately described as *"goloovoiy,"* or light blue, and *siniy,* or dark blue, indicating the changing appearance depending upon the viewing angle. The diamond was thought to have been set in a ring in the early 1800s, purchased from Louis David Duval.

There was no evidentiary connection to Tavernier or the French Blue. Later, I was able to track down some coincidences. The Duvals were a family of jewelers who did business both in St. Petersburg and in London. A John Duval served as jeweler to King George III and sold his business to Rundell and Bridge. This Duval knew John Françillon—the first documenter of the Eliason Blue, serving with him on the commission examining the diamond necklace suit against Prince George. But we don't know if he was related to the

St. Petersburg Duvals. Another intriguing item is a Brunswick connection. Maria Feodorovna had married Catherine the Great's son Paul in 1776. Maria's brother's wife was Augusta, the daughter of the Duke of Brunswick, Carl Wilhelm Ferdinand and elder sister of Caroline of Brunswick. Augusta took up residence in the St. Petersburg court, and supposedly had an affair with Paul that so angered the Russian Empress that she had Augusta banished and imprisoned. If the blue diamond had been given to Augusta by her father and then confiscated by Maria Feodorovna it would provide a link to the French Blue, but such is sheer speculation, and given the results of the digital modeling exercise, unlikely.[7]

Indeed, the recent simulation project might now discourage future claimants from seeking to connect their diamond to the Hope diamond inheritance.

30

POP ICON

The *Hope diamond continues to draw* crowds and public attention. It is indeed the most sought-out object in the Smithsonian. Annual attendance to the National Museum of Natural History
has varied between 6 and 10 million visitors over the last decade.
That's a lot of people to peer at the Hope diamond.

Ironically, even though it is in a science museum, the Smithsonian nevertheless exploits the diamond's curse and its fame to gain
attention and attendance. Directional and informational signs in the
museum play this up—"and of course, the famous Hope diamond"—
they read. Many come to see the Hope diamond because they have
heard of it, even if they don't quite know why. They often describe
the diamond they intend to see as the biggest in the world—about
the size of a baseball—though in actuality it is far from it, more
like a walnut, and some twelve times smaller than the largest cut
diamond—the 545-carat Golden Jubilee, and tiny when compared
to the largest raw diamond ever found, the 3,106-carat Cullinan.
As they make their way to the Winston Gallery, visitors are aware
that there is a story attached to the Hope, "Isn't it supposed to be
cursed or something?" is a pretty common refrain.

The Hope diamond has become famous in its own right—an
icon of itself firmly enmeshed in popular American culture. A fast
Internet google.com search produces tens of thousands of Web page
mentions. Most of these repeat a standard story emphasizing the
legendary curse. But some go overboard. One Web site features a

lesson for children in grades 7–12 that is corre-
lated with national science education standards.
In this case, the author does not merely restate
the Hope diamond legend, but construes her
own rather elaborate version. In her tale, "in
the mysterious interior of India" live followers
of the great and powerful god Ramasutra who
worship a great idol with "one, huge, fiery, blue
eye."[1] Tavernier emerges as a thieving, ignorant
trader who steals the blue diamond, arrogantly
refusing to believe in its curse. Given these
"data," students are then asked to conduct research!

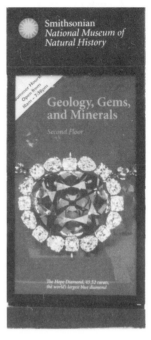

As a popular icon, the Hope is referenced in
numerous television comedy series—from *Sein-
field* to *Friends* to *Sex and the City*. The latter offers
one of the cleverer uses. The series' central figure and narrator, Carrie Bradshaw, played by
Sarah Jessica Parker, notices her sexpot friend

Hope diamond museum sign.

Samantha wearing a very large diamond. She asks where it came
from. Samantha explains that it is a make-up gift from her boy-
friend Richard, who had been cheating on her. Carrie asks: "What
do you get if he cheats on you again, the Hope diamond?" Actress
Kim Cattrall brilliantly responds in character, "Well, that's what
this is, the I *hope*—that f__ker doesn't ever break my heart again—
diamond!"[2]

A younger generation has become exposed to the diamond's fame
through the movies. The most recent major film to do so was *Titanic*.
The "Heart of the Ocean" blue diamond figures prominently in the
plot. Indeed, the fictional expedition is motivated by the attempt to
discover the heart-shaped blue diamond that is falsely assumed to be
at the bottom of the ocean. In the film, the blue diamond is the "other"
half of the French Blue stolen during the French Revolution in 1792.
On film, the diamond is easily confused with the famous Hope, though
it is actually more similar in style to the Blue Heart diamond, which

was owned by Cartier and Harry Winston before coming to the Smithsonian thanks to Marjorie Merriweather Post. In the wake of the film's popular success, Harry Winston, Inc. fabricated a sapphire version of the fictional gem worn by Celine Dion at the Academy Award ceremony in 1998 when she sang her award-winning hit, "My Heart Will Go On." A replica was mass-produced for public sale.

The Hope has been the subject of numerous documentaries, most with similar titles, playing upon the curse, and offering much of the same stock footage; they are typically inaccurate. In 1975, Rod Serling of *Twilight Zone* fame, narrated a made-for-television film special on CBS, *The Legendary Curse of the Hope.* Six months later, Serling was dead at age 50, convincing some of the curse's validity. In 1997, Diana Rigg hosted *The Curse of the Hope Diamond. Treasures! Secrets of the Hope Diamond,* and *The Deadly Diamond* aired in subsequent years.

The Hope diamond has become a popular literary metaphor. Consider the use by Carl Hiaasen in *Stormy Weather.* A character "Skink, had removed his glass eye and pressed it, for safekeeping, into the palm of Max's right hand. Max had clenched it as if it were the Hope diamond."[3] The Hope diamond stands for something both valuable and loathsome. In another novel, *Cadillac Jack,* Larry McMurtry's character unpacks a truncheon, "I unfolded the felt carefully, as if I were about to display the Hope diamond."[4] Richard Klein's fanciful novel *Jewelry Talks* cleverly opined that the Hope causes "unknown, untold trouble to the city of Washington (which hardly needs any more)."[5] And when Tony Kornheiser, a sports writer for the *Washington Post,* called Red Sox hurler Pedro Martinez "a Hope diamond of a pitcher," it certainly meant he was valuable—though whether cursed or blessed surely depended upon whether or not the reader was a Yankees fan.[6]

The Hope diamond metaphor was extended to a public art project in Los Angeles in the wake of the 1992 riots there. Artist Richard Posner had volunteers move earth, draw lines, and create a Hope "baseball diamond" landscape painting—an exercise in what he called "visual alchemy" to turn a cursed situation into a blessed one.[7] The Hope has also been exploited in seedier ways. In the

Smithsonian's official files is a newspaper advertisement for the Gayety Theatre Burlesk featuring a performer named "Hope Diamond," the so-called gem of the exotics.[8]

The diamond's flashiness has been used for various good purposes—replicas were worn annually for the charitable Project HOPE ball in Washington. The Smithsonian has used the real diamond for fund-raising, as when in 1991, the museum received $1 million from the Harry Winston Research Foundation toward the renovation of the Gem Hall. The museum orchestrated an event to bring attention to the gift to other possible donors, and draped the Hope diamond around the neck of wealthy Georgette Mosbacher.

For those who cannot wear the real diamond, the Smithsonian sells replicas in its shops. The Hope is good for business, with visitors buying postcards, books, costume jewelry, and other paraphernalia.

Rather than standing primarily for wealth and its resentment—or history, social or natural—the Hope diamond is now more an icon of its own fame. Seeing it up close, holding it, wearing it, are all ways people can share in its celebrity. Behind this is the idea that the diamond's fame is "contagious" and can somehow "rub off" on the people and things in its presence. That proximity carries its own fame is illustrated by the treatment accorded the original packaging that brought the Hope diamond to the Smithsonian in 1958. It was saved and put on exhibit at the Smithsonian's Museum of History and Technology (later, the National Museum of American History), and decades later, transferred to the National Postal Museum—established in the very same city post office building through which it had passed decades earlier in the hands of postman James Todd.

As a famous object, powered by its biography, sustained by its venerable setting, with rich, powerful and famous friends, the Hope diamond does not now need to stand for anything else, save itself. It is its own symbol, its own icon. Its fame must merely be renewed, so that it stays in the public eye. Hence, photographs of the Hope diamond sported by glamorous contemporary Hollywood actresses like Michelle Pfeiffer lend additional credence to its fame, and promote it to another generation. After all, icons tend to get along famously with one another.

This is why if it were to be placed next to any other object in the Smithsonian, the Hope diamond should probably be in the American History Museum, next to the ruby slippers from *The Wizard of Oz*. Those slippers, it will be remembered, were also thought to be magical and contain great power. The slippers were endowed by Hollywood writers—modern mythmakers—and helped tell a powerful tale about a child's quest, and indeed a nation's quest, to find its home. Taken together, the Hope diamond and the ruby slippers offer a nice structural parody on reality and illusion, mythmaking and history making, the valuing of museums and the museuming of value.

EPILOGUE

31

EXORCISING THE CURSE

I s the curse of the Hope diamond real?" friends, relatives, and even Smithsonian colleagues ask.

If by the curse we mean a supernatural causal agent or factor that somehow brings misfortune to the possessors of the stone, then there is no curse.

First, no such agents or factors have been proven to exist in particular empirical circumstances in ways that can be demonstrated to skeptical others.

Second, even if there were such a supernatural entity— presumably a Hindu deity in this case, why would he get involved in a curse manufactured by a Frenchman to sell a diamond to a rich American? The Hope diamond is not well known in India. It was not associated with a ruler or temple and there is no indigenous evidence of an Indian origin of the curse. Most Brahmins who I spoke to about the curse discuss it in terms of *nau ratna* theory. One, Bhavani Shankar, an erudite adviser to many of the jewelers of Hyderabad, answered in a typical way. When I asked him about the blue diamond and its effect upon the Smithsonian and the United States, he responded, "Well, how have you done since you acquired it?"

I f there were a curse, one would expect premature death and short life spans for those associated with the diamond.

Included below is a list of those who have definitely owned the

Life Spans of Hope Diamond Owners, Agents, Possible Owners, Stewards, and Immediate Family Members

Definite Owners

84	Jean-Baptiste Tavernier	75	Lord Francis Hope
77	King Louis XIV	82	Simon Frankel
64	King Louis XV	NA	S. Habib
39	King Louis XVI	NA	Simon Rosenau
71	Daniel Eliason	86	Pierre Cartier
68	King George IV	52	Edward McLean
65	Henry Philip Hope	60	Evalyn Walsh McLean
54	Henry Thomas Hope	82	Harry Winston
64	Anne Adéle Bichat Hope		

Possible Owners, Agents, Stewards, Cutters

NA	Sieur Pitau	69	Carl II Duke of Brunswick
NA	André Jacquemin	76+	Edwin Streeter
86	Jules Guay	NA	Adolph Weil
NA	Cadet Guillot	75	Sultan Abdul Hamid
NA	Paul Miette	NA	Louis Aucoc
51	Jean-Louis Carra	75	Leonard Carmichael
71	Carl W. F., Duke of Brunswick	86	George Switzer
		87	S. Dillon Ripley
53	Caroline of Brunswick	71	Paul Desautels
72	John Françillon	73*	John Sampson White
80	Phillip Rundell	80*	Robert McC. Adams
79	John Bridge	75*	I. Michael Heyman
44	William Duke of Brunswick	51*	Jeff Post
		64*	Lawrence Small

Close Family Members Associated with the Diamond

NA	Goisse Tavernier	72	May Yohe
45	Queen Marie Thérèse	58	Jacques Cartier
49	Louis Le Grand Dauphin	67	Louis Cartier

30	Louis Duke of Bourgogne	9	Vinson McLean
63	King Philippe	59	Jock McLean
65	Queen Marie Leszczinska	69	Edward McLean, Jr.
36	Louis Dauphin	25	Emily (Evie) McL. Reynolds
37	Queen Marie Antoinette	80	Edna Winston
10	Louis XVII	64*	Ronald Winston
21	Princess Charlotte	61*	Bruce Winston
70	Henrietta Adele Hope		

An "NA" indicates not available in those cases where the age is unknown.

An * indicates still living as of 2005.

Hope diamond as well as a category of people of possible owners, agents, handlers, and stewards—such as Smithsonian curators of the gem and secretaries of the institution, and a third category that includes those spouses and children who had a share or stake in the diamond, that is, those who might have inherited it, to the extent we can identify them. For each, the age at death is indicated, except in cases where the person is still living, in which case their current age is indicated with an asterisk.

For definite owners the average life span is a bit more than 68 years. For agents, possible owners, and stewards it is almost 72 years. Even the hapless postman, James Todd, though not included above, lived to the age of 68. For immediate family members, counting those still living, it is considerably lower—50 years—owing to the premature deaths of the McLean children, Louis XVII, and Princess Charlotte. Overall, life spans average about 63 years, a lengthy average considering many lived in past centuries. Premature death is not, on the whole, associated with the diamond.

The curse, while untrue, is nonetheless a real *story*. It is the genuine folklore of a modern society, a cultural creation for our times. Folklore is never a lie. For in its very construction it builds upon the culture of the tellers and those who hear it. Above all, *it must make sense*. It must resonate with an audience. It must be worth retelling because somehow, someway, though it may be fictional in fact, it nonetheless reveals a larger truth—a legitimate philosophical speculation about the nature of the universe, a moral aphorism, an insight into human behavior, a cutting critique of society and authority, a sad "fact" of life.

The curse of the Hope diamond as a story or interpretation of events captures a sense of an era, a moral conundrum about values, and a way of symbolizing a cultural encounter between civilizations. The era is modernity, the moral issue the role of wealth, and the relationship between civilizations West and East. The curse can be seen as a cautionary tale. It feeds upon uncertainty, ambiguity and the limitations of knowledge—is it true or not? It is humbling, and like other cautionary tales, it offers a lesson. There is a moral to the story. The curse of the Hope diamond suggests a proper course of action: our enthusiasm for progress should be tempered by an understanding of tradition; our wealth should be used wisely for broad benefit; our encounters with other people and cultures should be respectful. If not, we may get our just punishment. Who would disagree?

As useful or intriguing as the curse legend might be, it has crowded out other aspects of the Hope diamond's history. Rather than just imagining vengeful Hindu deities, that history is one of a long-term mutual engagement of Indian and European ways of thinking about diamonds, gemstones, nature, and divinity. Rather than imagining the blue diamond as an evil force hanging over the heads of the French monarchy, that history shows the diamond to have been an important symbol in the manipulation of class and factional interests—both royal and revolutionary. And if the blue diamond played a role at Valmy, that would be a much bigger story than any legendary curse.

Exploring the history of the blue diamond possibly with Caroline and certainly with George IV reveals conflicts over gender and national status, and strategies to resolve them. Throughout its 19th-century career—when no curse was ever mentioned—the diamond's history is intimately tied to the major social transformations and aesthetic accommodations arising from a new economic order in the West, and colonialism in the East. In the 20th century, it is no surprise that the Hope diamond's story is centered in the United States, where new wealth invited its presence. It becomes a center-piece in a mass media society, where money, power, and culture mix through the life of Evalyn Walsh McLean and her cohorts. That she and her family are "brought down," so to speak, resonated with the populist, democratic spirit of a country wracked first by the excesses of the Gilded Age and later by the severity of the Depression. With Winston, the aspirations of the United States, emerging more pow-erful after World War II are clear. Freedom and money buy dia-monds. The desire for the big, national, cultural correlates of American wealth and power in the face of a traditional insecurity leads Harry Winston to endow the nation with a world-class set of jewels, while at the same time protecting his business interests.

With the Hope diamond at the Smithsonian, the life of the gem reflects the same rationalization and institutionalization of historical treasures, icons, works of art, specimens, and artifacts that come into the museum. But, as is clearly the case with the Hope, its cultural life does not stop; it just becomes different, subject to governmental, pro-fessional, and bureaucratic norms, sensibilities, and aspirations. Fi-nally, as the gem's recent history suggests, it is incarnated as an object of popular mass culture—used, exploited, and viewed as a celebrity in itself.

In this way, then, the history of the Hope diamond over the past centuries provides a rich social commentary on the culture of the times. Taking on one role or another—treasure, trophy, heirloom, or even specimen number 217868—it becomes a powerful sign of the times, a means to engage the true forces of history well beyond the legend of the curse.

There are missing treasures of Hope diamond history—things I've looked for over the course of a decade that are still to be found. I expect that as archival and historical materials are increasingly digitized and translated they will become more broadly available. Discovery of these items is quite important in either corroborating findings offered in this book, revising and even upending them, or leading us in new directions. The major items in the Hope diamond treasure hunt are:

1. The missing page of annotations that was to accompany Tavernier's plate illustrating the diamonds he sold to King Louis XIV in his "Voyages to the East." This would give us a better idea of exactly where and how Tavernier acquired the diamond.

2. Specific records of diamonds found at the Kollur, as well any of those pertaining to the diamond gathering activities of Mir Jumla. Such could include the blue diamond.

3. Any diagrams or calculations or other records that might have been kept by Pitau, who reduced and faceted the big $112\frac{3}{16}$-carat stone down to the $67\frac{1}{8}$-carat French Blue. It would reveal his fashioning method and help solve any lurking doubts about the creation of satellite stones.

4. A test subjecting the Russian Blue to ultraviolet light to see if it phosphoresces red, and thus is possibly related to the original blue diamond.

5. Written documentation on the role of the key thieves or conspirators involved in the theft of the French Crown Jewels from the Garde Meuble. This could either confirm or deny the theory that the theft provided a bribe for Brunswick to "throw" the French Revolution.

6. Any documentation on any of the thieves who may have possessed gems after the theft.

7. The location, examination, and testing of the Brunswick Blue to see if it matches up with the Hope. It could either put to rest any speculation of the French Blue being cleaved or force us to revise assumptions in our latest gemological models and simulations of the blue diamond's development.

8. More documentation on the jewels of Carl Wilhelm

Ferdinand, the Duke of Brunswick, who cut them, and who received them when—specifically those given to Caroline upon her marriage in 1795 or transferred to her during the years of Napoleonic conflict. This could either reveal more evidence of her possession of the blue diamond, or rule it out.

9. Any receipt or written evidence concerning Eliason's purchase of the blue diamond, and its sale to George IV could reveal the time, price, and terms of the transfer of the diamond.

10. Any receipts or documents for the setting of the blue diamond within George's Golden Fleece. These could help determine the diamond's acquisition date and also its use in this gem and enable a better understanding of how it signaled relationships with Caroline and Napoleon.

11. The list of the deceased George IV's diamonds drawn up by Rundell and Bridge in 1830 and presumably turned over to the Duke of Wellington. If the Blue were on the list, it would provide definitive evidence of George's possession and help confirm the means of its resale.

12. A list or written record of the items in George's estate made by or for the Duke of Wellington that would not be inherited through the Crown. The Blue could be on that list, and some notation might indicate how it was disposed.

13. Documentation of Henry Philip Hope's acquisition of the blue diamond would reveal the time, amount, and terms of purchase. Records of the setting of the diamond in a medallion may also be helpful in this regard.

14. Records that Bram Hertz may have kept concerning his cataloging of the Hope diamond. This might explain his apparent desire to avoid mention of a provenance and its possible connection to the French Blue.

15. A letter, if it exists, written by Charles II, Duke of Brunswick that might discuss his reactions to seeing the blue diamond at the home of Henry Thomas Hope. This would provide insight as to what he thought about the acquisition of the Brunswick Blue.

16. Any record, whether in writing or preferably photo-graph or sketch that shows May Yohe actually wearing the Hope diamond. She says she did; Lord Francis said she never did. It would be nice to settle the matter. It would also help in judging Yohe's veracity on other matters of the diamond's life while she was Lady Francis.

17. Information about Habib, who he was, what he did, and the movement of the Hope while he owned it. Such could firmly rule out the supposition that the Hope may have gone to Turkey in 1908 or 1909. Alternatively, any documentation proving the diamond did go to Turkey would contradict current evidence and open up a whole new chapter in the diamond's history.

18. A list of books in the Cartiers' library near the time they sold the Hope to the McLeans. Did they have a copy of *The Moonstone* or John Mawe's *Treatise* or Edwin Streeter's gem books, or Louis Finot's work on Indian gemology? This would be useful in more precisely determining what elements Cartier used in spinning the curse story—and what he left out.

19. Documents that may have been prepared for the McLeans concerning the valuation of the Hope diamond. This would provide insight as to their strategy of at first refusing to pay Cartier for the blue diamond.

20. Internal memos or documents prepared for Harry Winston concerning valuation of the Hope for tax deduction purposes. Letters or other documentation specifically address-ing for Winston the issues raised by the creation of synthetic diamonds and any role the Hope might play in obviating them.

21. Internal documents from the Louvre concerning the exhibit of the Hope diamond and particularly any legal opin-ions generated at the time concerning the legal status of the Hope. This would reveal whether or not there was a debate about reclaiming the Hope as part of the missing Crown Jewels when it came to France.

Besides documents, other investigations, such as more advanced digital simulations, may help refine conclusions related to the cutting of the blue diamond. Certainly physical tests will continue to answer questions about the blue diamond's atomic structure: just why does it phosphoresce a deep red for so long? Knowledge about the diamond might also be gained by examining the question of any French claims on the Hope given the Napoleonic Code, laws in effect at the time, and international law subsequently regarding the return of cultural property; a legal brief or mock court is in order, and could make for interesting, revealing argument.

In all, then, there are still discoveries to be made. Additional knowledge should enable us to arrive at better, fuller, and more truthful interpretations of the Hope diamond's rich and amazing, and certainly legendary, cultural history.

We can also rest assured that the Hope's life at the Smithsonian will continue to be a vital one, replete with new chapters and new stories. One of the lessons the Hope teaches us is nothing that comes up from the earth or down from the sky remains a fixed and finished thing forever. Physically, the blue diamond has changed dramatically over time—refashioned, reset, and redisplayed. But while it has lost weight in carats, it has acquired ever more meaning. This is a stone that has been a sign of the times over a very long while, conveying a broad range of sentiments, relationships, and circumstances. No doubt new times will bring new meanings—and the Hope, more than the rest of us, will likely be here forever.

APPENDIX A
HOPE DIAMOND TIMELINE

1653	Gem merchant Jean-Baptiste Tavernier acquires a roughly cut 112³⁄₁₆-carat violet diamond in India.
1668	Tavernier sells the diamond to Louis XIV, King of France.
1673	The diamond is faceted and cut to 67⅛ carats and is called the French Blue.
1751	The French Blue is set into the insignia of the Order of the Golden Fleece for Louis XV.
1792	The French Blue and Crown Jewels are stolen from the Royal Warehouse in Paris during the French Revolutionary reign of Louis XVI.
1792–1806	Stories circulate that the French Blue was used to bribe the Duke of Brunswick from invading Paris and forestalling the Revolution; the Duke's daughter, Caroline, may have inherited the cut-down diamond.
1812	A 44¼-carat blue diamond is in the possession of London diamond merchant Daniel Eliason.
1820?–1830	George IV, Prince Regent, then King of Great Britain and husband of Caroline of Brunswick, owns the diamond.
1839	The diamond, owned by London banking heir Henry Philip Hope, is documented in the catalog of his collection.

1851	Henry Thomas Hope, having inherited the diamond from his uncle, displays it at the Crystal Palace for the Great London Exhibition.
1874	A 13¾-carat blue diamond sold at the Geneva auction of the estate of Charles of Brunswick is supposed to be a remnant stone from the cutting of the French Blue.
1901	Lord Francis Hope, the last of a line of Hope family owners of the diamond, sells it to the New York jewelry firm of Joseph Frankel's Sons & Co. via London jeweler Adolf Weil.
1908	Newspaper articles begin to call the Hope diamond unlucky. Frankel's sells the Hope diamond to S. Habib in Paris.
1909	Habib sells the diamond to Parisian jeweler Simon Rosenau via Louis Aucoc.
1910	Rosenau sells the Hope diamond to the Cartier Bros. in Paris. Pierre Cartier tells the Hope diamond curse story to Ned and Evalyn Walsh McLean in Paris.
1911	Cartier Bros. sells the Hope diamond to the McLeans in Washington, D.C.
1921	May Yohe, the former Lady Hope, develops a book and a silent film hyping the curse.
1932	Evalyn Walsh McLean temporarily pawns the Hope diamond for ransom in the Lindbergh kidnapping.
1947	Evalyn Walsh McLean dies.
1949	The McLean jewels, including the Hope diamond, are sold by her estate to Harry Winston of New York.
1949	Winston displays the Hope diamond publicly as part of the Court of Jewels, which goes on to tour across the United States, to Canada and Cuba. While in Winston's possession, the Hope's culet is slightly altered.

1958	Harry Winston donates the Hope diamond to the Smithsonian where it is exhibited in the new Gem Hall.
1962	With the intercession of First Lady Jackie Kennedy, the Hope diamond is loaned to the Louvre for the exhibition "Ten Centuries of French Jewels."
1965	The Hope diamond goes to South Africa for the Rand Easter Show in Johannesburg.
1982	The Hope diamond is displayed at the Metropolitan Museum of Art in New York for the 50th anniversary of Harry Winston, Inc.
1997	The Hope diamond is placed in the Harry Winston Gallery of the remodeled Janet Annenberg Hooker Hall of Gems in the Smithsonian's National Museum of Natural History.
2005	Experiments with computer-generated models of the Tavernier, French Blue, and Hope diamonds prove their long suspected relationship.

APPENDIX B
PRICES FOR THE BLUE DIAMOND

Year	Seller/ Appraiser	Buyer/ Owner	Currency Amount Then	2006 $ Equivalent
		Tavernier Violet		
1668	Tavernier	Louis XIV	*Livres* 220,000	$ 1.8 million
		French Blue		
1691	Inventory	Louis XIV	*Livres* 400,000	$ 3.6 million
1774	Inventory	Louis XVI	*Livres* 1 million	$ 5.5 million
1791	Inventory	Louis XVI	*Livres* 3 million	$18.3 million
1813	Mawe Treatise		*Livres* 3 million	$ 9.5 million
1823	Mawe Treatise		£100,000	$11.3 million
		Hope		
1823	Eliason/Mawe	George IV	£ 30,000	$ 3.0 million
1830	Estate	H. P. Hope	£ 18,000	$ 2.0 million
1901	F. Hope	Weil	£ 16,000	$ 1.9 million
1901	Weil	Frankel	$141,000	$ 2.9 million
1908	Frankel	Habib	$200,000	$ 4.4 million
1909	Habib	Rosenau	400,000 francs	$ 1.7 million
1910	Rosenau	Cartier	$110,000	$ 2.1 million
1911	Cartier	McLean	$180,000	$ 3.9 million

Year	Seller/ Appraiser	Buyer/ Owner	Currency Amount Then	2006 $ Equivalent
1947	McLean	Winston	$177,000	$ 1.6 million
1958	Winston	Smithsonian	$1 million	$ 6.8 million

ACKNOWLEDGMENTS

This book grows directly from participation in a Material Culture Forum panel, "Gem, Jewel and Icon: Looking at the Hope Diamond" held at the Smithsonian in 1993. The forum is a cross-disciplinary group of curators and museum professionals who periodically gather to discuss issues of representation in art, science, history, and culture. For the panel, chair Adrian Kaeppler asked me to look into the little-researched cultural history of the Hope diamond, particularly its curse. Other panelists, Jeff Post, the curator of the Hope diamond at the National Museum of Natural History, and David McFadden, then the chief curator for design at the Cooper-Hewitt Museum, offered presentations on the diamond's physical history and design aspects, respectively. While my revised paper was turned into a chapter in the book *Exhibiting Dilemmas,* published by the Smithsonian Press, questions raised by co-panelists and forum colleagues Amy Henderson, Sally Hoffmann, Bill Sturtevant, Mary Jo Arnoldi, and Francine Berkowitz stimulated me to learn more. The result has been more than a decade of research following the trail of the Hope diamond from India to France, Germany, Russia, Switzerland, England, Washington, New York, and back to the Smithsonian.

I have had much help from my wife, Allyn, and my two daughters, Danielle and Jaclyn, who have accompanied me on this physical and intellectual journey. We have explored caves, museums, and temples, searched archives, translated historical documents, produced maps and drawings, and worked in some of the greatest libraries in the world: the British Library, the New York Public Library, the Library of Congress, and the Bibliothèque Nationale de France.

I thank my Smithsonian colleagues, most sincerely the very gracious Jeff Post, and former Gem Hall docent Susanne Steinem Patch, whose own long-term researches on the Hope diamond have been exemplary. Post has studied the physical characteristics of the gem and overseen the transformation of its public presentation. Susanne Steinem Patch had done a fine job tracing the history of the diamond's possession in her book *Blue Mystery: The Story of the Hope Diamond,* first published in 1976 and revised in 1999. Both have read this book in manuscript form and offered comments, corrections and directions. I am also grateful to other readers, my editor Elisabeth Dyssegaard of Smithsonian Books, Pamela Henson of the Smithsonian Archives, David Shayt of the National Museum of American History, Caroline Newman of the Smithsonian Press, Diana Parker, Director of the Smithsonian Folklife Festival, Bruce Falk of the Office of Contracting, Judy and Robert Huret, members of the Smithsonian National Board. Ronald Winston, of Harry Winston, Inc., John Hope Franklin of Duke University, Ivan Karp of Emory University, Barbara Kirshenblatt-Gimblett of New York University, Ralph Nicholas of the University of Chicago, Steven Lubar of Brown University, Rubie Watson of Harvard University, Tony Hillerman, and long-term colleague and sceneographer Rajeev Sethi kindly offered wise suggestions and useful comments.

Research in India was supported in part by a grant from the Smithsonian Foreign Currency Program, and in Europe in part by the Smithsonian Center for Folklife and Cultural Heritage. The Center also helped to garner and process rights and permissions for illustrations used in this book. I am grateful to Barbara Strickland, Denise Arnot, and Rebecca Smerling for their work with these arrangements. I also thank Chip Clark and Dane Penland in the Office of Photographic Services, Rachelle Browne in the Office of General Counsel, and Jennifer Nichols in the Smithsonian Archives for their help.

Many others lent a hand along the way—Kousar Azam at the American Studies Research Centre in Hyderabad, I. K. Sharma at the Salar Jung Museum, Radhakrishna Sharma, Bhavani Shankar, Govindas Mukendas and Satish Shah in India, Sir Valentine Abdy in France, Daniel Alcouffe at the Louvre and Eric Nussbaum with the Cartier archives, Frau Strauss at the Niedersächsisches Staatsarchiv in Wolfenbüttel, Germany, Lili Kostantinovna Kuznetsova at the Hermitage in St. Petersburg, Romei Olivier with the Geneva City and University Library, Harish Kapur in Aubonne, Switzerland, Allison Derret of the Royal Archive at Windsor Castle, Andrew Cockburn, Regina and John Bendix, Andrea Meditch, and my French-speaking in-laws Merton and Janine Bland. I am also grateful for a succession of talented research assistants: Matt Hirsh, Susan Mazur, Ynske and Kotrien, Nahee Kim, Musthapha Osh, Nathaniel Gleicher, and Partrick Bergemann, who tracked down all sorts of leads and historical documents, and Katie Gualtieri, who helped research permissions needed for the book. In this regard the following individuals were both considerate and professional in arranging for images and text extracts: Russell James of the *Washington Post*, Eva Tucholka of Culver Pictures, Inc., Ed Kelley of the *Oklahoman*, Jennifer Belt of Art Resource, Angela Weihe of the Herzog Anton Ulrich-Museum, Bruno Piazza, Herbert Horovitz, Wulf Otte of the Braunschweig Landesmuseum, Bob Bier of the U.S. Geological Survey Library, Joseph Byrne of the University of Maryland, Frances Dimond and Lisa Heighway of the Royal Photograph Collection and Lucy Whitaker and Karen Lawson of the Royal Collection in the United Kingdom, Melanie Oelgeshläger of the Wallace Collection, James Kilvington of the National Portrait Gallery and Margaret Daly of the National Gallery in London, Amanda Wilson of the Royal Pavilion in Brighton, Carol Butler of Brown Brothers, Bonnie Selfe of Cartier, Faye Haskins of the Martin Luther King Jr. Memorial Library, Wendy Valle of RMS, Zoe Arey of Columbia University Press, Aida Garcia-Cole of Music Sales Corporation, Janis Elliott and Alex Harrison of Metal Bulletin plc, Vladimir Rybkin of Gokhran, Kristine Ballard of Getty Images, John Hatleberg, Melody Newberry and Sara Cole of Harry Winston, Inc., Sandy Green of Time, Inc., David Seitz of the *New York Times,* Andrei Andreyev, Maureen Kaiser, Daniel Niblock, Bala Subramaniyam, and Paul Taylor. I am especially grateful to Joseph Charles McLean Gregory, great grandson of Evalyn Walsh McLean and Hope Diamond Collection, Inc., Carol Ann Rapp, historian, and Hillsboro Press, for permission to use extensive quotations. I appreciate their good work in understanding the legacy of Evalyn Walsh McLean.

Colleagues at a meeting of the American Folklore Society, members of Delta Kappa Gamma, the sisterhood of Temple Rodef Shalom, and professors and students at Randolph-Macon Woman's College listened to my presentations on the Hope diamond, asked good questions, and made excellent suggestions.

As a cultural anthropologist, I benefited beyond measure from lessons and perspectives learned from a stellar group of scholars at the University of Chicago: Barney Cohn, Mircea Eliade, Clifford Geertz, Ron Inden, McKim Marriott, C. M. Naim, Ralph Nicholas, Talcott Parsons, A. K. Ramanujan, Frank Reynolds, Susanne Rudolph, Marshall Sahlins, David Schneider, Edward Shils, Milton Singer, Stanley Tambiah, and Victor Turner. Finally, I thank my colleagues at the Smithsonian Institution Center for Folklife and Cultural Heritage who daily engage in the good work of understanding and representing the intriguing, valuable, and often beautiful expressions of the world's peoples.

CREDITS AND SOURCES: PHOTOGRAPHS AND ILLUSTRATIONS

Frontispiece: Hope diamond in current setting, about three times actual size. Smithsonian Institution. Photograph by Dane Penland.

Section Part dividers: Hope diamond unset. Photograph © Tino Hammid.

CREDITS AND SOURCES: TEXT EXCERPTS AND LYRICS

Permission to quote extended text or lyrics from the following sources:

6   "U.S. to Get Hope Diamond," November 7, 1958. Used
           with permission of the Associated Press. Copyright ©
           2005. All rights reserved.

10   "The Legendary Hope Diamond." *Life,* March 1, 1995:
           72.

12–14;   Joseph Charles McLean Gregory, Great Grandson of
205–207;   Evalyn Walsh McLean and Hope Diamond Collection,
213; 231. Inc., and Carol Ann Rapp, Historian. *Queen of Diamonds:
           The Fabled Legacy of Evalyn Walsh McLean,* A Commemorative
           Edition of *Father Struck It Rich* by Evalyn Walsh McLean.
           Franklin, TN: Hillsboro Press, Providence Publishing
           Corp., 2000, 169–176, 246. (Orig. *Father Struck It Rich,* by
           McLean, Evalyn Walsh, with Boyden Sparkes. Boston:
           Little, Brown and Co., 1936).

218   Lyrics of "God Moves on the Water," song text from
           Negro Folk Music U.S.A., by Harold Courlander. Copy-
           right © 1963 Columbia University Press. Reprinted
           with permission of the publisher.

242   "Diamonds Are a Girl's Best Friend." Words by Leo
           Robin and music by Jule Styne. Copyright © 1949
           (renewed) by Music Sales Corporation (ASCAP).
           International copyright secured. Used by permission.

244   Edward Wharton-Tigar, *Burning Bright,* Metal Bulletin
Books, 1987. Reproduced by kind permission of Metal
Bulletin plc.

ENDNOTES AND REFERENCES

Unpublished sources are referenced by the abbreviations below to indicate the institution where they are held.

MANUSCRIPT AND DOCUMENTARY COLLECTIONS

BG   Charles, Duke of Brunswick Collection. Bibliothèque publique et universitaire de Genève

BL   Manuscript Collections, British Library, London

BNF   Bibliothèque nationale de France, Paris

CAG   Cartier Archives, Geneva

GMSS   Govindas Mukendas and Satish Shah, private holdings, Hyderabad

HSP   Hermitage. St. Petersburg

JFK   John F. Kennedy Presidential Library, Boston

LOC   Evalyn Walsh McLean Manuscript Collection. Library of Congress, Washington

NMNH   Collection item records of the National Museum of Natural History, Smithsonian Institution, Washington

NSW   Duke of Brunswick Collection. Niedersachsisches Staatsarchive, Wolfenbüttel

RA   Royal Archive, Windsor Castle

SI   Hope Diamond files. Smithsonian Institution Archives, Record Unit 192, United States National Museum,

Permanent Administrative Files, 1877–1975, box 667, folder
number 225042
V&A   Victoria & Albert Museum, London

NEWSPAPERS

NYT   *New York Times*
TL   *Times* of London
WP   The *Washington Post*

OVERALL SOURCES ON THE HOPE DIAMOND

Balfour, Ian. *Famous Diamonds.* London: William Collins, 1987.

Bruton, Eric. *Legendary Gems or Gems That Made History.* Radnor:
Chilton Book Co., 1986.

Fowler, Marian. *Hope : Adventures of a Diamond.* New York : Ballantine Books, 2002.

Morel, Bernard. *Les Joyaux de la Couronne de France.* Antwerp: Fonds
Mercator, 1988.

Krashes, Laurence. *Harry Winston: The Ultimate Jeweler.* Ronald
Winston, ed. New York and Santa Monica: Harry Winston Inc. and
the Gemological Institute of America, 1984.

Kurin, Richard. "The Hope Diamond: Jewel, Gem, and Icon,"
Exhibiting Dilemmas. Amy Henderson and Adrienne Kaeppler, eds.
Washington: Smithsonian Institution Press, 1997.

McGlashan, Ian. "The Story of the Hope Diamond," *Lapidary
Journal,* January 1980.

Patch, Susanne Steinem. *Blue Mystery: The Story of the Hope Diamond.*
Washington: Smithsonian Institution Press, 1976; 2nd edition with
New York: Harry Abrams, Inc., 1999.

Post, Jeffrey. *The National Gem Collection.* New York: Harry N.
Abrams, 1997.

Streeter, Edwin W. *Precious Stones and Gems.* London: Chapman
and Hall. 1st edition, 1877; 3rd edition, 1882; 5th edition, 1892; 6th
edition, 1898.

Streeter, Edwin W. *The Great Gems of the World*. London: George Bell and Sons. 1st edition, 1882; 2nd edition, 1898.

1 GIFT TO THE NATION

1. Michael Briglia, a 12-year veteran registry clerk, computed the cost at $2.44 for first class postage, $3.35 for registry fee, and $139.50 in a carrying surcharge. Later in the evening, the Post Office determined the surcharge should have been $151.85. Thus, Harry Winston owed $12.35. *cf.* Bracker, Milton. "The Hope Diamond Is Off in the Mail," *NYT,* November 9, 1958, 56.

2. Sampson, Paul. "Hope Diamond Show Opens Here Monday," *WP,* November 8, 1958, AI.

3. Bradley, Wendall P. "Hope Diamond, Insured for Million, Delivered to Museum by Postman," *WP,* November 11, 1958.

4. Furman, Bess. "Hope Diamond Put on Public Display," *NYT,* November 11, 1958, 60.

5. The weight given on the sign was off by a carat. The Smithsonian Press Release contains many mistakes and inaccuracies. Its substantive section is reproduced below:

Speculation ties the Hope to the famous "French Blue," once the eye of an idol in India, later part of the Royal Jewels of Louis XIV of France. Mr. Winston acquired the Hope from the estate of the late Mrs. Evalyn Walsh McLean of Washington in 1949. It was presented to Mrs. McLean by her late husband, Edward B. McLean, in 1911. Its known history, prior to the McLean purchase, dates from 1830 when David Eliason, a noted gem dealer, sold the stone to Henry Thomas Hope, an Irish squire and banker, whereupon it became known as the "Hope Diamond." The stone was shown at the London Exposition in 1851. In 1867 it was sold at Christie's in London along with other gems from the Hope collection. It was acquired in 1908 by the Sultan Habib Bey, but after the Young Turks revolt it again was placed on the market, and purchased by Mr. McLean in 1911.

6. "U.S. to Get Hope Diamond," Associated Press, November 7, 1958.

7. Furman, *op. cit.*

8. Carmichael, Leonard. Letter responding to John Edward Acker, November 18, 1958, SI.

9. The first member of the public to visit the Hope diamond was E. H. Walker, a student at the University of Maryland. Attendance at the museum just about doubled to 9,504 in the first three days compared to 5,519 the week before.

10. Fowler, *op. cit.*, 318.

11. One writer attributes this quote to Art Buchwald, but I could not confirm that. cf. Goodavage, Joseph, "The Curse of the Hope Diamond," n.d., n.p., NMNH.

12. The reaction to Winston's gift to the nation is consistent with the theory of the distinguished French ethnologist Marcel Mauss. Mauss noted that the English term "gift," derived from the German, and literally meant "poison." The linguistic root was a clue to the sociology of donation. Things thought to be good and valuable, could, even if generously given, cause great harm if accepted. Gifts could occasion unforgiving reciprocity, and turn out to be a curse, not a blessing. *cf.* Mauss, Marcel. *The Gift*. Ian Cunnison, trans. New York: W. W. Norton, 1967.

13. Letter to the Smithsonian, NMNH.

14. Kendrick, Thomas R. "Hope Diamond's Postman-Deliverer Beset by Tragedy, Accident and Fire," *WP,* August 21, 1959, A1.

15. Rolanders, L. Letter, November 28, 1958, SI.

16. Nestler, John W. Letter from the Chair, Tampa Free Port Committee to President Eisenhower, May 1, 1958, SI.

17. Letter to the Smithsonian, NMNH.

18. Caton, Barbara. Letter, April 25, 1983, NMNH.

19. Schindler, Mrs. John. Letter, April 18, 1964, SI. Todd was born in Pennsylvania, but as an adopted child was raised in Gridley, Kansas.

20. "The Legendary Hope Diamond." *Life.* March 1, 1995.

21. Post, Jeffrey. *The National Gem Collection*. New York: Harry N. Abrams, 1997, 27.

Additional references for the chapter include:

Bracker, Milton. "Winston Gives Hope Diamond to Smithsonian for Gem Hall," *NYT,* November 8, 1958.

"Curse of the Diamond," *Newsweek,* November 17, 1958.

"Gem 'Ferhexed' Bethlehem Girl," *Sunday Call-Chronicle,* November 9, 1958.

Greenberg, Daniel. "Hope Diamond Draws Crowds, but Spectators' Interest Is Varied," *WP,* November 13, 1958.

"Hope Diamond Shown in Color," *WP,* November 9, 1958.

Lange, Jim. "Bad Luck Hope Diamond Given to US," illustration, *Daily Oklahoman,* November 11, 1958.

Liebowitz, Meyer. "Dealer in the Fabulous," *NYT,* November 8, 1958.

Pearson, Drew. "Hope Diamond for the Smithsonian," *WP* and *Times Herald,* May 1, 1958.

Smithsonian Institution News Release, November 9, 1968, NMNH.

2 Legend Delivered

1. McLean, Evalyn Walsh, with Boyden Sparkes. *Father Struck It Rich.* Boston: Little, Brown and Co., 1936, 171. Evalyn McLean kept notes about daily occurrences and records of other matters throughout her life. With help from a Washington writer, these were turned into an autobiography. Evalyn McLean's papers and memorabilia were donated to the LOC after her death. Gary Cohen "The Lady and the Diamond." *Vanity Fair.* August 1997: 138–146, reports that he found Boyden Sparkes's notes.

2. McLean, *ibid.,* 172.

3. *ibid.* Cartier insisted that Evalyn saw the blue diamond in the Turkish harem. Evalyn noted that "it was too early to argue"

with Cartier about it. As reported by Gary Cohen, Evalyn later recalled this particular incident to Sparkes and her conclusion was that she could not recall actually having seen the blue diamond in Turkey.

4. McLean, *ibid.*, 172.

5. *ibid.*, 172.

6. *ibid.*, 172.

7. *ibid.*, 174.

8. *ibid.*, 175.

9. "Ein Unglüctsdiamant," *Braunschweiger Neuste Nachrichten,* February 7, 1911, NSW.

10. "J. R. M'Lean's Son Buys Hope Diamond," *NYT,* January 29, 1911.

Additional references for the chapter include:

McLean, Evalyn Walsh, with Boyden Sparkes. *Father Struck It Rich.* Republished as *Queen of Diamonds: The Fabled Legacy of Evalyn Walsh McLean,* with a foreword by Joseph Gregory and an epilogue by Carol Ann Rapp. Franklin, Tennessee: Hillsboro Press, 2000.

3 TAVERNIER'S QUEST

1. Polo, Marco. *The Travels of Marco Polo.* Ronald Lathem, trans. Harmondsworth, 1958, 273–74.

2. Methold, William. "Relations of the Kingdome of Golconda," *Relations of Golconda,* William H. Moreland, ed. London: Hakluyt Society, 1910, 8–9.

3. Tavernier also called the Kollur mine "Gani."

4. Tavernier, Jean-Baptiste. *Les six voyages de Jean-Baptiste Tavernier.* Paris: G. Clouzier, 1676, 1679, 1681, 1682; Amsterdam: J. van Someren, 1678; Paris: les Elzevier 1679; Rouen: P. Ribou, 1713. The most comprehensive work on Tavernier is Joret, Charles. *Jean-Baptiste Tavernier.* Paris: Librarie Plon, 1886. Tavernier's publications came out over several years and were repackaged into various compendia. The most accessible English works are Tavernier, Jean-Baptiste.

Travels in India. Valentine Ball, trans. [1889], 2nd Edition, William Crooke, ed. London: Humphrey Milford, Oxford University Press, 1925.

5. Mir Jumla had multifaceted relationships with other Frenchmen which smoothed his way in diamond dealing with Tavernier. Jumla had Claude Maile make a cannon for his military assaults. Jumla was friends with Father Ephraim, a former French noble priest, who resided in Golconda city and sparked his intellectual curiosity in European knowledge. Jumla freed Father Ephraim from a Portuguese jail after he'd been imprisoned by the Inquisition, gaining Tavernier's admiration and praise.

6. Upon my return to Washington, Bruce Tapper was gracious enough to make me copies of some of the historical maps of the Deccan in his fine collection. Many designate Kollur or Gani, but none close to the scale of the Mukendas and Shah map.

7. From Tavernier, *op. cit.,* book III, 73. When computed, this actually comes out to 15¼ *gos.* Tavernier also gives another route to the Kollur diamond fields in Indian *cos.* This route, with modern names in brackets, goes from Golconda to Tenara [Sarurnagar], Iatenagar [Hayatnagar], Patengy [Patangi], Penegeul [Pangal], Nagelpur [Nagelpad], Lakabaron [Lacuaron], to Colour, *ibid.,* 140.

8. Gandabherunda could be the local mythic equivalent of Alexander's vultures, Sinbad's roc, and Polo's white eagles. The earliest depiction of a two-headed eagle figure is dated to the third millennia B.C. in the city of Lagash in ancient Sumeria, now Iraq. The symbol served as a crest and was adopted by Akkadians and later the Hittites. The double-headed eagle became a symbol of Imperial Rome in 102 B.C. It was used in Byzantium, and came to symbolize the eastern and western parts of the Roman Empire. In the West, Charlemagne used the double-headed eagle in the 9th century to symbolize his Holy Roman Empire; its use persisted during the Crusades and among the nobility. It was

adopted by Russia in the 15th century, and has been used widely in Central and Eastern Europe. Freemasons adopted the symbol in the 18th century, as did Jewish folk artists in Poland. It was also used by Hitler's Germany. Eastward, the two-headed eagle journeyed to Central Asia along the Silk Road, and is found in excavations of the Greco-Buddhist Gandharan site at Taxila, presumably brought to the region by Scythians in the first century A.D. It is evidenced in South India by about 1047 A.D., incorporated into the iconography of several regional kingdoms including Vijayanagar. On coins minted under the rule of Achuyta Raya (1515–40?) the two-headed eagle is depicted as miraculously carrying four elephants, one in each beak and in each talon. The elephants could be a substitute for the sheep, goats, water buffalo and other meat mentioned in the legends. *cf.* Nagar, Shanti Lal. *Garuda: The Celestial Bird.* [Original 1927]. New Delhi: Book India Publishing, 1992.

Additional references for the chapter include:

"A History of the Golconda Diamond Mines with a reprint from the Transactions of the Royal Society of a paper read in 1677 by Earl Marshall." GMSS.

A Manual of the Kistna District in the Presidency of Madras. Andhra Pradesh District Gazetteers. Originally by Gordon MacKenzie [1883]. Hyderabad: Government of Andhra Pradesh, 1992.

"Annual Report of Hyderabad Geological Survey." Hyderabad: Government Central Press, 1929. GMSS.

Ball, Valentine. *The Diamonds, Coal, and Gold of India.* London: Trubner & Co., 1881.

Bernier, François. *Travels in the Mogul Empire.* 1668. Irving Block, trans. London: William Pickering, 1826.

Biswas, Arun Kumar and Suleka Biswas. *Minerals and Metals in Ancient India.* New Delhi: D. K. Printworld, 1996.

Carré, Abbé. *The Travels of Abbé Carré.* [Orig. 1672–74]. London: Hakluyt Society, 1947.

Chandra, Ramesh. "Diamond Mines of the Deccan," *Proceedings of the Indian History Congress,* 44th Session, Kurdwan, 1983.

Dickinson, Joan Younger. *The Book of Diamonds: Their History and Romance from Ancient India to Modern Times.* New York: Bonanza Books, 1965.

Gros, François, *Passeurs d'Orient/Encounters between India and France.* Published by the French Foreign Ministry's Secretariat for International Cultural Relations.

Heyne, Benjamin. "Account of the Diamond Mines in India." GMSS.

Lane, E.W, trans., *Stories from Thousand and one nights.* New York: P.F. Collier & Son, 1909.

Lenzen, Godehard. *The History of Diamond Production and the Diamond Trade.* F. Bradley, trans. London: Barrie and Jenkins, 1970.

Neubecker, Ottfried. *Heraldry: Sources, Symbols and Meanings.* New York: McGraw-Hill, 1976.

Peltzman, Ronne and Neil Grant, ed. *Diamonds: Myth, Magic, and Reality.* New York: Crown Publishers, Inc., 1980.

Ramesan, Thiru N. *Catalogue of Vijayanagar Coins in the Andhra Pradesh Government Museum.*

Sakuntala, S. "Diamond Mining in the Golconda and Bijapur Kingdoms During the 17th Century," *Proceedings of the Indian History Congress,* 44th Session, Kurdwan, 1983.

Sharma, Shalini. "Where Are the Diamonds?" *Society,* December 1997.

Stephen, S. Jeyaseela. "Emerging Trends of Diamond Mining Enterprise and Industrial Development in Pre-Modern Andhra," *Proceedings of the Indian History Congress,* 44th Session, Kurdwan, 1983.

"The Golconda Diamond Mines." GMSS.

"Under The Double Eagle." www.srmason-sj.org/reilly.htm.

Vincent, Rose. *The French in India: From Diamond Traders to Sanskrit Scholars.* Latika Padgaonkar, trans. Bombay: Popular Prakashan, 1990.

4 GOLCONDA'S WEALTH

1. Word about Golconda got to America. Several towns—in Illinois, Arizona, and Nevada—eventually took the name in the hope that they too would generate riches for their inhabitants.

2. Vijayanagar, while a Hindu kingdom, nonetheless established many of the precedents for Golconda exploiting the alluvial fields, establishing a diamond market and European trade—through Goa, and reserving large gemstones for the ruler. Vijayanagar's wealth and civic amenities astounded Italian and Portuguese visitors. The King supported great lapidaries that cut and polished diamonds. Adornment was official and personal. "Idols" in temples and the King were ornamented in diamond and gold jewelry. Jewelry use in the court was extensive, worn by men and women, even dancing girls. For one annual festival, hundreds of buffalo and sheep were sacrificed and powder, made from various gems, was thrown into the fire. cf. *The Vijayanagar Empire: Chronicles of Paes and Nuniz.* [Original 1520–22 and 1535–37]. New Delhi and Madras: Asian Educational Services, 1991 and Mitchell, George and Vasundhara Filliozat, eds. *Splendours of the Vijayanagara Empire, Hampi.* Bombay: Marg Publications, 1981.

3. Poem, quoted in Khalidi, Omar. *Golconda Diamonds and Mines in Legend and History.* Ahmedabad: Mapin Publishing Ltd., 1997.

Additional references for the chapter include:

Ahmed, Afzal. *Indo-Portuguese Trade in the Seventeenth Century.* New Delhi: Gian Publishing House, 1991.

Allen, Charles and Sharada Dwivadi. *Lives of the Indian Princes.* London: Century Publishing, 1984.

Harle, J. C., and Smith, Nima, and Stronge, Susan. *A Golden Treasury: Jewellery from the Indian Subcontinent.* Ahmedabad: Mapin Publishing Ltd, 1995.

Lach, Donald. *India in the Eyes of Europe.* Chicago and London: University of Chicago Press, 1968.

Mathew, K. S. *Portuguese Trade with India in the Sixteenth Century*. New Delhi: Manohar, 1983.

Murti, K. V. Suryanarayana. "Hyderabad in the Poetry of Sarojini Naidu." *Kohinoor in the Crown*. New Delhi: Sterling Publishers, 1987.

Nigam, M. L. "The Glittering Diamonds of World are from Golkonda," *Deccan Chronicle, 1996.*

Parthasarthy, R. *Places of Interest in Andhra Pradesh*. Hyderabad: Government of Andhra Pradesh, 1984.

Qadeer, Mrs. Iqbal Jahan. "The Jewelry of Hyderabad." *Salar Jung Museum Bi-annual Research Journal, 1988–89.*

Rao, M. Basava. "Qutb Shahis and Eastern Trade." *Salar Jung Museum Bi-annual Research Journal, 1983-84.*

Stronge, Susan, ed. *The Jewels of India*. Bombay: Marg Publications, 1995.

Wolpert, Stanley. *A New History of India*. New York: Oxford University Press, 1993.

5 Cosmic Gem

1. Most other diamonds are made from organic carbon and formed from the sea algae of the ocean floor subducted under continental tectonic plates for hundreds of millions of years, and also subjected to tremendous pressure and temperature. Another rare type of diamond is formed when a meteor impacts the earth. If it contains carbon, it may metamorphose into diamond. There are also rare diamonds, microscopic in size, thought to be formed of carbon-based gases from dying stars and supernovas. These celestial nano-diamonds are carried to earth on meteorites, and have the almost unbelievable property of "melting" and forming a diamond gel when placed in water. *cf.* Harlow, George E., ed. *The Nature of Diamonds*. United Kingdom: Cambridge University Press, 1998, 53–68.

2. Polo, *op. cit,* 273.

3. Kunz, George Frederick. "Six Famous Diamonds," *The Mentor,* v. 13, n. 11, December 1925.

4. Quoted in Patch, *op. cit.,* 15.

5. Miners' practices reflect this widespread belief. They generally return to previously dug pits to see if any new diamonds grew. If a new technique or technology comes along that allows finer inspection for and extraction of extant diamonds this can be especially advantageous. Miners also have a practical knowledge of where to dig for diamonds. Telegu miners of the Kondaganikaandlu caste figured they'd find diamonds associated with various rock and mineral correlates—gray calc flag, quartz, coarse-grained ferruginous sand, corundum, sandstone, red ochre, banded ferruginous quartzite, massive limestone, yellow ochre, brown jasper, flint, conglomerate with rounded pebbles, and galena.

6. The legend of the diamond valley might represent a refracted account of animal sacrifice as part of miners' *puja* or worship ceremonies to appease the snakes. Miners understood that what they found was not theirs, but rather belonged to Yama, the god of the dead and the underworld. The meat is a payoff for the snakes and other vermin that help guard the subterranean treasures of Yama's domain.

British folklorists in 19th century India reported a belief that snakes are actually the reincarnated ghosts of former owners, watching over and protecting their gems even after death.

7. For example, an Indian archaeologist told me that the temple of Kalahasti is located at the mouth, Tirupati at the back of the hood, Ahobilam at the trunk, and Srisailam at the tail of a serpentine river.

8. Interview with a Hyderabadi gemologist and jewelry store owner.

9. *cf.* Dickinson, *op. cit.,* 9.

10. Cognate terms for *adamas* include such words as "adamant," "dominant," and "dame." Scientifically, hardness is the ability of one substance to scratch and thus cut another. Nothing in nature

or yet made by man is harder than a diamond. Diamonds are rated 10 on a scale invented by Austrian mineralogist Friedrick Mohs in 1822. So hard is diamond that it is four times harder than the next hardest element on the scale, corundum (ruby and sapphire), and eight times harder than number 8 on the scale, topaz.

11. Heyne, a British officer serving in the Deccan in the early 19th century, found diamond merchants using the caste system for gems in their pricing. For example, a rough two-carat *brahmīn* diamond was 10 Madras *pagodas* while a low caste *śudra* diamond was half the price.

12. Tagore, Sourindro Mohun. *Mani-Mala, or A Treatise on Gems.* Calcutta, 1879–81.

13. Mookerji, B. *Rasa-Jala Nidhi or Ocean of Indian Chemistry and Alchemy.* New Delhi: Avari Prakashan, 1984, 168.

Additional references for the chapter include:

Adigal, Prince Ilango. *Shilappadikaram.* Alain Daniélou, trans. A New Directions Book, 1965.

Alberuni. *Alberuni's India.* Ainslie Embree, ed., Edward Sachau, trans. New York: W. W. Norton & Co., 1971.

Babu, T. M. *Diamonds in India.* Bangalore: Geological Society of India, 1998.

Ball, Sydney. *Roman Book on Precious Stones.* Los Angeles: Gemological Institute of America, 1950.

Banerjee, Jitendra Nath. *Development of Hindu Iconography.* Calcutta: Calcutta University Press, 1956.

Basham, A. L. *The Wonder That Was India.* London: Sidgwick and Jackson, 1954.

Bechert, Heinz and Richard Gombrich, eds. *The World of Buddhism.* London: Thames and Hudson, 1984.

Beer, Robert. *Encyclopedia of Tibetan Symbols and Motifs.* London: Serindia Publications, 1999.

Blakey, George. *The Diamond.* New York: Paddington Press, 1977.

Clark, Grahame. *Symbols of Excellence.* Cambridge and New York, Cambridge University Press, 1980.

Craven, Roy. *Indian Art*. New York: Thames and Hudson, 1997.

Crooke, William. *The Popular Religion and Folklore of Northern India*. [Original 1896]. Delhi: Munshiram Manoharlal, 1968.

Finot, Louis. *Les Lapidaires Indiens*. Paris, Librairie Émile Bouillon, 1896.

Garuda Purana. GMSS.

Kautalya. *Arthasastra*. R. Shamasastry, trans. Mysore: Sri Raghuveer Print Press, 1951.

King, C. W. *The Natural History of Gems or Decorative Stones*. London: Bell & Daldy, 1867.

Kozminsky, Isidore. *Magic and Science of Jewels and Stones*. New York: G. P. Putnam's Sons, 1922.

Kunz, George F. *Natal Stones: Birthstones, Sentiments and Superstitions with Precious Stones*. New York: Tiffany, 1906.

Kunz, George F. *The Curious Lore of Precious Stones*. Philadelphia: J. B. Lippincott, 1913.

Mueller, F. Max, ed. *Sacred Books of the East*, vol. 10, Dhammapada; vol. 36, Satapatha-Brahmana; vol. 49, Amitayur Dhyana Sutra.

Parthasarthy, R. *Andhra Culture: A Petal in Indian Lotus*. Hyderabad: Government of Andhra Pradesh, 1984.

Pliny, The Elder. *Natural History*, vol. 7. H. Rackham, trans. Cambridge: Harvard University Press, 1963.

Santini de Riols, Emmanuel Napoleon. *Dictionnaire des pierres et des parfums magiques. Historique, symbolique, vertus, therapeutiques, et occultes*. Paris: P. Belfond, 1981.

Temple, R. C. *The Legends of Punjab*. Patiala: Language Department, Punjab, 1962.

Temple, R. C. *Panjab Notes & Queries*, September 1884 and December 1884.

Tolansky, Samuel. *The History and Use of Diamonds*. London: Methuen, 1962.

Untracht, Oppi. *Traditional Jewelry of India*. New York: Harry N. Abrams, 1997.

Zimmer, Heinrich. *Myths and Symbols in Indian Art and Civilization*. Princeton: Princeton University Press, 1972.

6 THE FRENCH BLUE

1. Translation by Allyn Kurin of Boileau poem on frontispiece, Tavernier [Crooke], *op. cit.*

2. "A Note About Some Unusual Diamonds." *Philosophical Transactions,* May 25, 1674, 26.

3. In *La Bibliographie,* a Russian publication of 1885, M. T. Tokmakof claimed to have come upon Tavernier's grave while visiting the cemetery. *cf.* Tavernier [Crooke], *op. cit.* xxix.

4. Tavernier [Crooke], *ibid.,* book 3, 176.

5. *ibid.*

6. Tavernier reported that Indian diamond cutters at the Kollur mines knew how to ascertain grain.

7. Most gemological historians describe a slow evolution of diamond cutting techniques occurring in Europe over the course of about three centuries—new "cuts" evolving from very simple geometric patterns to more complex and elaborate ones and named after particular innovators. Others like Tillander argue for a quicker development of rather complex styles, difficult to attribute to particular inventors. They argue the history of diamond cutting is highly mythologized and replete with misinformation. One reason is that most diamond cutting was carried out by Jewish cutters, living and working in tightly knit communities, often marginalized by the societies in which they labored. Skill and knowledge were narrowly imparted through familial apprenticeships; hence cutting techniques and styles were not readily known by a broader artisanal class.

8. Although some attribute the design of the brilliant to Peruzzi, a Venetian diamond cutter, no such individual has been identified in the historical record, according to Tillander. In his view, the brilliant cut developed from other innovations and cut styles that converged at the time.

9. The rhyme is the first stanza of a poem, "The Star," by sisters Jane and Ann Taylor. More recently, astronomers at the Harvard-Smithsonian Center for Astrophysics announced that

a white dwarf star BPM37093, some 50 light-years from earth, was formed almost entirely of crystal carbon, making it a diamond in the sky. It was estimated to be 10 billion trillion trillion carats. *cf.* "White Dwarf Star Is Girl's Best Friend," *WP*, February, 14, 2004, A6.

Additional references for the chapter include:

Bapst, Germain. *Histoire des Joyaux de la Couronne.* Paris: Libraire Hachette et Cie, 1889.

Bauer, Max. *Precious Stones.* Rutland, Vermont: Charles E. Tuttle, 1969.

Berquem, Robert de. *Les merveilles des Indes orientales et occidentales.* Paris: C. Lambin, 1661.

Bordonore, George. *Louis XV le bien aime.* Paris: Pymalion, 1982.

Boyle, Robert. *Essay about the Origine and Virtue of Gems.* London: William Godbid, 1672.

Bruton, Eric. *Diamonds.* London: N. A. G. Press, 1979.

Cole, Charles. *A Century of French Mercantilism.* New York: Columbia University Press, 1939.

Dake, H. C. *The Art of Gem Cutting.* Mentone, California: Gem Books, 1963.

Durant, Will and Ariel. *The Age of Louis XIV.* New York: Simon and Schuster, 1963.

Evans, Joan. *Magical Gems of the Middle Ages and the Renaissance.* New York: Dover, 1976.

Ford, John. *The Lover's Melancholy.* [1629]. Manchester: Manchester University Press, 1985.

Le Temps: Versailles in the Age of Louis XIV. Paris: La Réunion des Musées Nationaux, 1993.

Ludel, Leonard. "How to Cut a Diamond." Nevada, 1985.

Mitford, Nancy. *The Sun King.* New York : Harper and Row, 1966.

Morel, Bernard. *Les Joyaux de la Couronne de France.* Antwerp: Fonds Mercator, 1988.

Nicols, Thomas. *A Lapidary, or The History of Precious Stones.* Cambridge: T. Buck, 1652.

Polak, Henri. *A Short History of the Diamond Cutting Industry.* 1948.

Smith, Marcell. *Diamonds, Pearls and Precious Stones.* Boston: Smith Patterson Company by Griffith-Sterling Press, 1913.

Tillander, Herbert. *Diamond Cuts in Historic Jewelry.* London: Art Books International, 1995.

Twining, Edward Francis. *A History of the Crown Jewels of Europe.* London: Bt. Batsford, 1960.

7 INSIGNIA OF THE GOLDEN FLEECE

1. The two orders, the Spanish and the Austrian, still exist today. The Austrian *Orden vom goldenen Vliess* was given out by Sovereign Otto Von Hapsburg, the former Crown Prince and son of Emperor Charles, who renounced his heir-apparency in the 1960s. Members of the Order include among others several Archdukes, the Duke and Princes of Bavaria, Albert II, King of the Belgians, the Dukes of Würtemberg and Saxony, and the Princes of Liechtenstein. The Spanish *Orden del Toisón de Oro* was given out by the Spanish government up until 1931, and then by the pretender and King of Spain. King Juan Carlos is the Grand Master of the Order; awardees have included King Baudouin of Belgium and King Constantine of Greece. In 1988, Queen Elizabeth of Great Britain was the first female to be knighted. The Order was recognized in the 20th century by Pope Pius X, who confirmed the spiritual privileges of the knights.

Additional references for the chapter include:

Azcárrage, Joaquín de. *La Insigne Orden del Toisón de Oro.* Madrid: Unversidad Nacional de Educación a Distancia, 2001.

Bapst, Germain. *Histoire des Joyaux de la Couronne.* Paris: Libraire Hachette et Cie, 1889.

Ceballos-Escalera y Gila, Alfonso. *La Insigne Orden del Toisón de Oro.* Madrid: Palafox & Pezuela, 2000.

Colum, Padriac. *The Golden Fleece.* New York: Scholastic, 1990.

Haggard, Andrew. *The Real Louis the Fifteenth.* London, Hutchinson, 1906.

Pinches, Rosemary and Anthony Wood. *A European Armorial: An Armorial of Knights of the Golden Fleece and 15th century Europe, from a contemporary manuscript.* Orig. compiled by Saint-Remy. London, 1971.

Prosser, Ronald. *The Order of the Golden Fleece.* Iowa City: Raven Press, 1981.

Pouget, Jean Henri Prosper. *Traité des Pierres Précieuses.* Paris: Librairie Centrale d'Architecture, 1762.

Sainty, Guy Stair. "The Most Illustrious Order of the Golden Fleece." www. Chivalricorders.org/chivalric/goldflee.htm.

Scott, Philippa. *The Book of Silk.* London: Thames & Hudson Ltd, 1993.

Segar, William. *Original Institutions of the Primary Orders of Collars.* Edinburgh: W. H. Lizars, 1823.

Twining, Edward Francis. *A History of the Crown Jewels of Europe.* London: Bt. Batsford, 1960.

Werlich, Robert. *Orders and Medals of All Nations.* Washington: Quaker Press, 1974.

8 STOLEN CROWN JEWEL

1. Twining, *op. cit.,* 253.

2. The specific gravity for the French Blue was 3.5254. He found rose and orange diamonds in the Crown Jewels to have a slightly higher specific gravity than the blue; yellow- and green-colored diamonds slightly less. *cf.* Brisson, Mathurin-Jacques. *Pesanteur specifique de corps,* 1787, 63–64.

3. Brunswick Manifesto. Sheehan, James. *German History.* Oxford: Clarendon Press, 1989.

4. Massenbach, as reported in Fitzmaurice, Lord Edmond. *Charles William Ferdinand, Duke of Brunswick.* London: Longmans, Green & Co., 1901, 57.

5. Lemny, Stefan. *Jean-Louis Carra: Parcours D'un Révolutionnaire.* Paris: L'Harmattan, 2000, 245.

6. Roland, Mme. *Mémoires de Mme. Roland.* Paris: Librairie de la Bibliothèque Nationale, 1884, v. 2, 140–41.

7. *ibid.,* 141.

Additional references for the chapter include:

Bapst, Germain. *Histoire des Joyaux de la Couronne.* Paris: Libraire Hachette et Cie, 1889.

Barbet de Jouy, H. *Les Gemmes et Joyaux de la Couronne au Louvre.* Paris: Musées Imperiaux, 1865.

Barbot, Charles. *Guide pratique du joaillier, ou traité complet des pierres précieuses.* 1st edition, 1858, Paris: Morris; 2nd edition. Paris: J. Hetzel et Cie, 1884.

Bion, Jean-Marie. *Inventaire des diamants de la Couronne.* Paris: National Assembly, 1791.

Christophe, Robert. *Danton.* Peter Green, trans. London: Arthur Baker Limited, 1967.

Drumont, Edouard. *Le vol des diamants de la couronne au garde meuble.* Paris: A. Sauton, 1885.

Loomis, Stanley. *The Fatal Friendship.* New York: Doubleday, 1972.

Mathiez, Albert. *Autour de Danton.* Paris: Payot, 1926.

9 REVOLUTIONARY BRIBE

1. Goethe, Johann Wolfgang von. *Miscellaneous Travels of J.W. Goethe.* L. Dora Schmitz, ed., Robert Farie, trans. London: G. Bell 1882, 113.

2. Bouliaguet, Léonce. *The Guns of Valmy.* John Buchanan-Brown, trans. London: Abelard-Schuman, 1968, 114.

3. Goethe, *op. cit.,* 116.

4. "A Short Journal of the Proceedings of the Austrian Army Commanded by General Clarsayt from the 11th September to the 10th October, 1792." Kings MS 237, BL.

5. "A Journal of the Proceedings of the Austrian and Prussian Combined Armies in France" in "A Narrative of the Operations of

the Combined Army under the Duke of Brunswick in France in 1792." King's MS 237, BL.

6. Goethe, *op. cit.*, 118.

7. Loomis, Stanley. *The Fatal Friendship*. New York: Doubleday, 1972, 244.

8. Bouliaguet, *op. cit.*, 122.

9. Christophe, Robert. *Danton*. Peter Green, trans. London: Arthur Barker Limited, 1967, 286.

10. Harris, James. *A Series of Letters of the First Earl of Malmesbury*. London: R. Bentley, 1870, 155.

Additional references for the chapter include:

Biegel, Gerd. *6. Februar 1794: Rückkehr von Herzog Carl Wilhelm Ferdinand aus Frankreich*. Braunschweig: Braunschweigisches Landesmuseum, 1994.

Boisantais, Bernard. *La Bataille de Valmy*. Paris: Editions France-Empire, 1967.

Goethe, J. W. *Campaign in France in the Year 1792*. Robert Farie, trans. London, Chapman and Hall, 1849.

Daudet, Ernest. *Coblentz 1789–1793*. Paris: Ernest Kolb.

Dumouriez, Charles. *La vie du Général Dumouriez*. Hamburg: B. G. Hoffman, 1795.

Fuller, J. F. C. *A Military History of the Western World*. New York: Funk & Wagnalls, 1954.

Hugo, Victor. *Ninety-three, A story of the French revolution*. New York: University Publishing Company, 1896.

Lemny, Stefan. *Jean-Louis Carra: Parcours D'un Révolutionnaire*. Paris: L'Harmattan, 2000.

Mathiez, Albert. *Danton et la Paix*. Paris: Renaissance du Livre, 1919.

Thiers, Adolphe. *The History of the French Revolution*. Philadelphia: Carey and Hart, 1844.

Wolfgang, Ulrich. "Valmy 1792: Eine Europäische Tragikomödie War Alles Ein 'Freimaurerischer Verrat?'," *Quatuor Coronati*, no. 37, 2000.

10 CAROLINE'S LEGACY

1. Some believe that it was Lady Jersey, Prince George's latest mistress, who initially came up with the idea to have the two cousins marry as part of her effort to lower the standing of George's illegal wife, Mrs. Fitzherbert, and thus raise her own profile. *cf.* Nightingale, Joseph. *Memoirs of the public and private life of Queen Caroline.* [1820]. Christopher Hibbert, ed. London: The Folio Society. 1978, 14.

2. Harris, James, *op. cit.,* 210–11.

3. Strauss, the archivist at the Staatsarchiv in Wolfenbüttel had helped me with my research, and I had left her a glass model of the Hope diamond as a gift. When she saw a copy of the lithograph in an exhibition catalog, Strauss thought she found a match, writing me, *"den Caroline hier trägt, deutlich zu erkennen—die Ähnlichkeit mit dem Hope ist m.E. ganz eindeutig!"* *cf.* Romer, Christopf. *Braunschweig-Bevern.* Braunschweig: Braunschweigisches Landesmuseum, 1997.

4. Barbot, Charles. *Traité Complet des Pierres Précieuses.* Paris: Morris, 1858, 249–50.

5. Nightingale, op. cit. 1820, 29.

6. Bury [Campbell], Charlotte. *Diary Illustrative of the times of George IV.* London: Henry Coburn, 1838.

7. Lofts, Norah. *Queens of England.* Garden City, NY: Doubleday, 1977, 154.

8. Letter from Princess Caroline to Lady Townsend, June 23, 1806. Richardson, Joanna. *The Disastrous Marriage: A Study of George IV vs. Caroline of Brunswick.* Westport, Conn.: Greenwood Press, 1975, 59.

9. Bury, *op. cit.,* John Galt, ed. 1839, v. 1, 218.

10. *ibid.,* v. 1, p. 67–68.

11. Lady Hamilton and Lord Nelson were social friends of Abraham Goldsmid. After Nelson's death in 1806, Abraham arranged for sale of Lady Hamilton's house to his brother Asher.

Abraham served on the board of the Jewish Hospital, as did Eliason. Both were regarded as mainstays in the Great Synagogue, and Duke Frederick visited there in 1809 at Abraham's invitation. Eliason was married to Abraham's sister Sarah, and Abraham was married to Eliason's sister Anna. *cf.* Hyamson, Albert M. "An Anglo-Jewish Family," *Transactions of the Jewish Historical Society of England,* 1953, 1–10.

Additional references for the chapter include:

Aspinall, A., ed. *The Correspondence of George, Prince of Wales 1770–1812.* London: Cassell, 1967.

Barlow, Andrew. *The Prince and His Pleasures: Satirical Images of George IV and His Circle.* Brighton: The Royal Pavilion, Libraries & Museums, 1997.

Bonaparte, Napoleon. *Mémorial de Sainte Hélène.*

Clerici, Graziano Paolo. *Queen of Indiscretions.* Frederic Chapman, trans. London: John Lane, 1907.

Doran, Dr. *Lives of the Queens of England of the House of Hanover.* London: R. Bentley & Son, 1875.

Edgington, Harry. *Prince Regent, The Scandalous Private Life of George IV.*

Fraser, Flora. *The Unruly Queen.* London: Macmillan, 1996.

Granville, Harriet. *Letters of Harriet, Countess of Granville.* London: Longmans, Green & Co., 1894.

Greville, Charles. *The Greville Diary.* London: W. Heinemann, 1927.

Hamilton, Lady Anne. *The Secret History of the Court of England.* London: W. H. Stevenson, 1832.

Hannibal, Evans Lloyd. *George IV: Memoirs of His Life and Reign.* London, 1830.

Huish, Robert. *Memoirs of Her Late Majesty Caroline Queen of Great Britain.* London: T. Kelley, 1821.

Melville, Lewis. *The First Gentleman of Europe.* London: Hutchinson & Co., 1906.

Parker, Michael St. John. *Britain's Kings & Queens.* Great Britain: Pitkin Unichrome Ltd, 2001.

Repton, Humphrey. *Designs for the Pavilion at Brighton.* London: J. C. Stadley, 1808.

II CONTRABAND

1. George Frederick Kunz discovered the Françillon memo inserted in a rare book by Pouget in a London bookstore. *cf.* Kunz, George Frederick. "The Gem Collector in Europe," *The Saturday Evening Post*, January 21, 1928, 34. Kunz donated the book and memo along with other material to the U.S. Geological Survey in whose archives collection it resides.

2. A copy of this document is in the archival files, NMNH. Susanne Patch, Bernard Morel, and Marian Fowler have all called attention to it. It also places the blue diamond in the possession of Eliason. Mary Winters and John Sampson White believe it is a sales prospectus; it reads:

Le sujet du Dessein ci-annéxé est un Diamant brillant, Oriental, unique et de très grande valeur. Il est considéré comme une des curiosités les plus rares de la nature en ce qu'il deploye le fond, la richesse et le bleu du Saphir et en même tems tout le brillant et la perfection qu'il est possible a un Diamant d'avoir. Il est tout-à-fait transparent, sans tache ni defaut et sans fletrissure quelconque. Il est à presumer de cette assemblage de qualities que l'univers entier n'en peut produire un semblable, vu que les Diamans' extraordinaires (soit qu'ils se trouvent dans les couronnes ou les cabinèts, sont mentionnes si publiquement qui'il est à peine possible qu'un tel Diamant existant dans l'endroit le plus reculé du monde et cut échappé à l'observation. Il est taillé et poli d'après les meilleurs principes, étant ni trop epais ni trop étendu mais parfaitement bien proportionne de manière à donner le plus grand lustre. Cet incomparable Diamant pese 177 Grains, ou 44¼ Carats, et se trouve actuellement en la possession de Mr. Daniel Eliason. Les dimensions de l'equisee ci-joint sont exactement celles du Diamant, et la couleur approche autant de l'original que le dessein le permet.

3. Mawe, John. *A Treatise on Diamonds and Precious Stones.* London: Longman, Hurst, Rees, Orme, and Browne, 1813, 17; 1815, 16; 1823: 44.

4. Mawe, *ibid.*, 1813, 35.

5. Fox, George. "History of Rundell, Bridge & Company," 33/17. V&A.

6. *ibid.*

7. *Memoirs of the Late Philip Rundell.* London: John Fairburn, 1827, 11. V& A.

8. *Chambers' Edinburgh Journal,* Saturday, February 20, 1836, 2.

9. Eliason paid for a Torah scroll and its various appurtenances for the Great Synagogue of London in 1818. The scroll cover acknowledges his good acts. Upon his death, Eliason left "some thousands of pounds" to the synagogue as a legacy fund for the perpetual upkeep of the scroll and cover. That money could very well have come from the sale of the blue diamond. *cf.* Will of Daniel Eliason. Catalog Reference: Prob 11/1693, Public Record Office.

Additional references for the chapter include:

Barbot, Charles. *Traité Complet des Pierres Précieuses.* Paris: Morris, 1858.

Code Penal du Fevrier 1810 (France).

Cope, Sydney. *The Goldsmids and the Development of the London Money Market during the Napoleonic Wars, 1942.*

"Deaths." *Gentleman's Magazine.* London, 1824.

"Died." *TL,* November 19, 1824.

French Civil Code. Book III. Of the Different Modes of Acquiring Property, Decreed the 19th of April, 1803. Promulgated the 29th of the same month; Title XX. Of Prescription, Decreed the 15th of March, 1804. Promulgated the 25th of the same month.

Fox, George. "History of Rundell, Bridge and Rundell," 1843. V&A.

Goldsmid. www.jewishencyclopedia.com/view. jsp?artid=322&letter=G.

Lovett, Robert. "Rundell, Bridge and Rundell—An Early Company History," *Bulletin of the Business Historical Society.*

Roth, Cecil. *The Great Synagogue London.* London: E. Goldston & Son, 1950.

Shire, Angela. *The Great Synagogue Marriage Records.* Devon: Frank J. Gent, 2001.

Will of Aaron Goldsmid. Catalog Reference: Prob 11/1093, Public Record Office.

Winters, Mary, and John Sampson White. "George IV's Blue Diamond," *Lapidary Journal,* December, 1991.

12 GEORGE'S TROPHY

1. Letters from William, Duke of Brunswick to HRH George III, RA/GEO/21287, 21342-3.

2. *TL*, April 22, 1814.

3. *TL*, June 10, 1814.

4. Hazlitt, William, "The Exhibition of the Royal Academy," *Champion,* May 7, 1815.

5. Portrait painters and their royal and military subjects were quite attuned to accurately representing their decorations. For example, Arthur Wellesley's victory in Spain was memorialized by Francisco Goya, who painted the then Earl of Wellington in full military regalia in Madrid in August 1813. A month or two later, Goya painted in the Order of the Golden Fleece, which had been awarded by the Spanish monarch. The next year, Goya added an additional military cross.

6. Mawe, *op. cit.,* dedication.

7. Fox, George, *op. cit.* 84/40.

8. Eliason may still be in possession of the blue diamond at this time. Sowerby, James. *Sowerby's Exotic Mineralogy.* London: Arding & Merrett. 1817, p. 40.

9. Mawe, 1823, *op. cit.,* 44.

10. Murray, John. *A Memoir on the Diamond.* London: Longman, Rees, Orme, Brown & Green, 1831, 44.

11. Mawe, 1823, *op. cit.,* 44.

12. *ibid.,* 46.

13. Walter Scott in a letter to James Ballantyne quoted by Richardson, *op. cit.,* 208.

14. Lord Stravordale, quoted in Fraser, *op.cit.,* 454–55.

15. Murray, *op. cit.,* 44. According to an entry in an English encyclopedia in India, "George IV of England purchased a magnificent brilliant of a blue colour, which formed the chief ornament of the crown at his coronation. It cost £20,000."

16. Fox, *op. cit.,* 137/67.

17. Hamilton, *op. cit.,* v. 2, 163.

Additional references for the chapter include:

Addington, Richard. *The Duke, being an account of the life and achievements of Arthur Wellesley, 1st Duke of Wellington.* New York: Viking Press, 1943.

An Account of the Last Moments and Death of H. M. King George IV.

Arbuthnot, Harriet. *The Journal of Mrs. Arbuthnot 1820–1832.* London: Macmillan & Co., 1950.

Aspinall, A., ed. *The Correspondence of George, Prince of Wales 1770–1812.* London: Cassell, 1967.

"Auction by Rundell and Bridge," *TL,* July 21, 1837.

British Regalities. London: T. Dolby, 1821.

Bury, Shirley. *Jewelry 1789–1910.* Woodbridge: Antique Collectors, 1991.

Chambers' Edinburgh Journal, February 20, 1836.

Claudio. *An Antidote to Poison.* London: W. Clowes for Mathews and Leigh, 1806.

Davenport, Cyril. *The English Regalia.* London: K. Paul, Trench, Trubner, 1897.

Edgington, Harry. *Prince Regent, The Scandalous Private Life of George IV.* London: Hamlyn, 1979.

Evans, Hilary and Mary. *The Life and Art of George Cruikshank 1792–1878.* New York: S. G. Phillips, 1978.

Garlick, Kenneth and Angus MacIntyre. *The Diary of Joseph Farrington.* New Haven: Yale University Press, 1978.

George IV and the Arts of France. Buckingham Palace: The Queen's Gallery, 1966.

Gilliland, Thomas. *Diamond Cut Diamond.* London: B. McMillan for C. Chapple, 1806.

Hamilton, Lady Anne. *The Secret History of the Court of England.* London: W. H. Stevenson, 1832.

Hannibal, Evans Lloyd. *George IV: Memoirs of his Life and Reign.* London, 1830.

Huish, Robert. *Memoirs of Her Late Majesty Caroline, Queen of Great Britain.* London: T. Kelley, 1821.

Huish, Robert. *Memoirs of George the Fourth.* London: T. Kelley, 1830.

Huish, Robert. *An Authentic History of the Coronation of His Majesty King George IV.* London: J. Robins, 1821.

Levy, M. J. *The Mistresses of King George IV.* London: Peter Owen, 1996.

Lloyd, H. E. *George IV: Memoirs of His Life and Reign.* London: Treuttel and Wurtz, 1830.

Melville, Lewis. *The First Gentleman of Europe.* London: Hutchinson & Co., 1906.

Memoirs. Bartolomeo Baron Pergami. Paris. Brissot-Thivars, Ponthieu, Leroy 1820.

Memoirs of the Late Philip Rundell. 1827. London: John Fairburn, Ludgate Hill, 1827. V&A.

Naylor, Sir George. *The Ceremonial of the Coronation of his most Sacred Majesty King George IV.* Henry George Bohn, 1823, 1837.

Official Inventory of the Crown Jewels of Britain's Royal Family. Shirley Bury, Stationery Office, 1999.

Parker, Michael St. John. *Britain's Kings & Queens.* Great Britain: Pitkin Unichrome Ltd, 2001.

Patterson, Stephen. *Royal Insignia: British and Foreign Orders of Chivalry from the Royal Collection.* London: Merrell Holberton, 1996.

Phillips, Samuel. *Memoir of the Duke of Wellington.*

Priestly, J. B. *The Prince of Pleasure and His Regency 1811–20.* London: Heinemann, 1969.

Rundell, Bridge, and Rundell. *An account of Sundry Crown Jewels received from His Majesty.* 1830. [missing].

Secrets of the Castle. The Life of the Marchioness of Conyngham.

Shramm, P. E. *History of English Coronation.*

Levey, Michael. *Sir Thomas Lawrence.* London: National Portrait Gallery.

Wellington, Arthur Wellesley Duke of. *The Duke of Wellington.* London: Longman, Brown, Green, and Longmans, 1852.

Wellington, Arthur Wellesley Duke of. *Wellington and His Friends.* London, Macmillan, 1965.

Williams, D. E. *The Life and Correspondence of Sir Thomas Lawrence.* London: Henry Colburn and Richard Bentley, 1831.

Winters, Mary, and John Sampson White. "George IV's Blue Diamond," *Lapidary Journal*, January, 1992.

Younghusband, G. *The Jewel House.* New York: George Doran, 1920.

13 HOPE'S COLLECTIBLE

1. Lord Byron sarcastically criticized Thomas Hope's early work on furniture, but said he cried upon reading *Anastasius* in 1819 because Hope had written it and he had not.

2. Hope, Henry Philip. *A Catalogue of a Collection of Pearls and Precious Stones.* Compiled by Bram Hertz. London, 1839, 25.

3. *ibid.*

4. *ibid.*

5. *ibid.*

6. *ibid., iv.*

7. *Gentleman's Magazine.*

8. Law, Henry and Irene. *The Book of the Beresford Hopes.* London: Heath Cranton, Limited, 1925, 114.

9. Disraeli, Benjamin. *Disraeli's Reminiscences.* Helen and Marvin Swartz, eds. London: Hamish Hamilton, 1975, 19–20.

10. Law, *op. cit.,* 116. Such an idea paralleled that of James Smithson's bequest a generation earlier.

11. Neither Henry Philip Hope, nor Henry Thomas Hope, appears to have actually used the term "Hope diamond." Instead, as in the catalog for the exhibition, it was usually referred to as Mr. Hope's blue diamond. *Catalogue,* "Diamonds," p. 625.

Additional references for the chapter include:

Arbuthnot, Harriet. The Journal of Mrs. Arbuthnot 1820–1832. London: Macmillan & Co., 1950.

Aspinall, A., ed. *The Correspondence of George, Prince of Wales 1770–1812.* London: Cassell, 1967.

Baumgarten, Sandor. *Le Crépuscule Néoclassique: Thomas Hope.* Paris: Didier, 1958.

Buist, Martin. *Atspes non fracta. Hope & Co. 1770–1815: Merchant Bankers and Diplomats at Work.* The Hague: Martinus Nijhoff, 1974.

"Henry Philip Hope Obituary," *TL,* 1840.

"Henry Thomas Hope Obituary," *TL,* December 5, 1862.

Niemeijer, J. W. "Die Kunsterzameling van John Hope (1737–1784)." Nederlands Kunsthistorisch Jaarboek, 1981.

Winters, Mary, and John Sampson White. "George IV's Blue Diamond," *Lapidary Journal,* December, 1991.

14 BRUNSWICK'S OBSESSION

1. Letter from Henry Thomas Hope to Charles, Duke of Brunswick, April 21, 1850. BG MS 36, folio 74.

2. Braun-Wiesbaden, Karl. *Der Diamanten Herzog.* Berlin: Berlag von Hofmann & Co., 1881.

3. Barbot, Charles. *Traité Complet des Pierres Précieuses.* Paris: Morris, 1858, 269.

4. Petition of Charles, Duke of Brunswick, BG MS 120, folio 229. Letter from Charles, Duke of Brunswick to King George IV, June 7, 1822. BG MS 3, folio 112. "Answer" from Charles, BG MS 125, folio 95. List of personal property, folio 37.

5. Braun-Wiesbaden, *op. cit.,* 102.

6. *ibid.,* 150.

7. *ibid.,* 149.

8. *ibid.,* 153.

9. *Journal de Genève,* April 24, 1874, 3.

10. Streeter, *Precious Stones and Gems,* 1877, *op. cit.,* 116.

11. *ibid.,* 118.

12. *ibid.*

13. Streeter, *The Great Gems of the World,* 1882, *op. cit.,* 294.

14. "In re Hope. De Cetto v. Hope," 1899 H. 660. *The Law Reports. Supreme Court of Judicature, Cases Determined in the Chancery Division.* London: William Clowes and Sons for the Council of Law Reporting, 1899, v. 2, 695.

15. The Ochs brothers were Alphonse and Louis, with offices at 106 boulevard Sebastopol, Paris. They had done business with Charles of Brunswick in 1856, if not before. They were also involved in the *Chambre syndicale de la bijouterie, joaillerie et orfèvrerie* with Alphonse chairing a conference in April 1890.

16. "The Brunswick Jewels," *NYT*, May 22, 1874.

Additional references for the chapter include:

Bose, Otto. *Karl II, Herzog du Braunshweig.* 1956.

Brunswick, Charles Duke. *A Catalogue of Diamonds and Precious Stones Belonging to His Honorable Duke of Brunswick.* BG MS 99.

Catalogue des Diamants. Genève: Vente aux Enchères, 1874.

Déne, Tibor. "En Contemplation Devant un Prestigieux Diamant," *Musées de Genève,* January 1977.

"Die Diamanten des Herzogs Karl II von Braunschweig," *Braunschweiger Allgemeiner,* February 14, 1912.

King, C. W. *Gems or Precious Stones.* 1870.

"Les Diamants de la Couronne." *L'Illustration, Journal Universel,* 1867.

Mainardi, Patricia. *Art and Politics of the Second Empire: The Universal Expositions of 1855 and 1867.* 1987.

Mesnard, Jules. *Les Merveilles de L'Exposition Universelle de 1867. Raport sur le exposition universelle de 1855.*

Stern, Selma. *Karl Wilhelm Ferdinand: Herzog zu Braunschweig u Luneburg.* Hildesheim and Leipzig: Uugust Lar, 1921.

15 FROM HEIRLOOM TO VALUABLE

1. Gates, H.L. *The Mystery of the Hope Diamond.* From the Personal Narrative of Lady Francis Hope [May Yohe]. New York: International Copyright Bureau, 1921, 75.

2. *ibid.*

3. Patch, *op. cit.,* 30.

4. Gates, *op. cit.,* 100.

5. "Hope Diamond Not Worn," *NYT,* February 5, 1911.

6. Bernard Shaw quoted in Fowler, *op. cit.*

7. Shaw, Bernard. *Our Theatres in the Nineties by Bernard Shaw.* London: Constable and Company, 1932, v. 2, 163.

8. *ibid.,* 164.

9. "In re Hope. De Cetto v. Hope," *op. cit.,* 682. Streeter's estimate for the value of the Hope was the lowest among several appraisals solicited. One authority, John B. Carrington, suggested £15,000, William Boore, of the Strand, put its value at £20,000. *cf.* "The Hope Diamond," *TL,* June 28, 1909.

10. *TL,* May 18, 1899, 11.

11. *ibid.*

12. "Law Report," *TL,* July 17, 1899, 3.

13. Gates, *op. cit.,* 211.

14. *ibid.,* 220.

15. *ibid.*

16. "Hope Diamond," *TL,* November 13, 1901. The *New York Times* reported the item the next day and added that the diamond had been sold by order of the Master in Chancery. *Cf.* "Hope Diamond Coming Here," *NYT,* November 14, 1901, 3.

Additional references for the chapter include:

Chancellor, E. Beresford. *Life in Regency and Early Victorian Times.* London: B. T. Batsford, 1927.

Mander, Raymond and Joe Mitchenson. *Theatres of London.* London: Rupert Hart-Davis, 1963.

Shaw, Bernard. *Our Theatres in the Nineties: His Weekly Criticisms for Saturday Review.* London: Constable & Co., 1954.

Wearing, J. P. *The London Stage 1890–1899.* Metuchen, New Jersey: Scarecrow Press, 1976.

16 ORNAMENT OF THE EAST

1. Singh, Bhai Narbar and Kirpal Singh. *History of the Koh-i-Noor, Darya-i-Noor and Taimur's Ruby.* New Delhi: Atlantic Publishers & Distributors, 1985, 34.

2. Mawe, *op. cit.*, 1813, 41–42.

3. Collins, Wilkie. *The Moonstone.* Anthea Trodd, ed. Oxford and New York: Oxford University Press, 1982, 2.

4. *ibid.*, 3.

5. *ibid.*, 5.

6. *ibid.*, 6.

7. Streeter, *Great Diamonds of the World, op. cit.*, ix.

8. *ibid.*, 213.

9. Crawford, Emily. *Victoria, Queen and Ruler.* London: Bristol Arrowsmith, 2nd edition, 1903, 26.

10. Shakespeare, William. *King Lear.* 1, ii., 131.

Additional references for the chapter include:

Annand, Sushila. *Indian Sahib: Queen Victoria's Dear Abdul.* London: Duckworth, 1996.

Collins, Wilkie. *The Moonstone.* Foreword by Alexander Woollcott. New York: The Press of the Readers Club, 1943.

"Colonialism and Morality in *The Moonstone* and *The Man Who Would Be King,*" www.qub.ac.uk/English/imperial/India/col-moral. htm, June 21, 1999.

Doyle, Arthur Conan. *The Sign of the Four.*

Finot, Louis. *Les Lapidaires Indiens.* Paris, Librairie Émile Bouillon, 1896.

Hibbert, Christopher. *Queen Victoria in Her Letters and Journals.* New York: Viking Penguin, Inc, 1985.

Kern, H. ed. *The Brhatsanhita or Complete System of Natural Astrology.* 1865.

Kunz, George. *Natal Stones: Birthstones, Sentiments and Superstitions with Precious Stones.* 1908.

Kunz, George. *The Magic of Jewels.* 1915.

Marshall, William. *Wilkie Collins.* New York: Twayne Publishers, Inc., 1970.

Ponsonby, Frederick. *Recollections of Three Reigns.* London: Eyre & Spottiswoode, 1951.

Tagore, Sourindro Mohun. *Mani-Mala, or A Treatise on Gems.* 1881.

Sen, Ram Das, ed. *Ratnarahasya: A Treatise on Diamonds and Precious Stones.* 1884.

17 LOVE COMMODITY

1. A. C. Roebuck. *Our Diamond Catalogue.* Minneapolis, 1892.

2. Unattributed article by Frank Carpenter, 1885.

3. The quote appears in the *Saturday Review of Literature,* Dec. 1, 1945.

Additional references for the chapter include:

Babe, J. L. *South African Diamond Fields.* New York: David Wesley & Co., 1872.

Cattelle, Wallis. *Precious Stones.* Philadelphia: J. B. Lippincott Co., 1903.

Chilvers, Hedley. *The Story of De Beers.* 1939.

Evans, Joan. *A History of Jewelry, 1100–1870.* Boston: Boston Book and Art, 1970.

Kunz, George Frederick. "Six Famous Diamonds," *The Mentor,* v. 13, n. 11, December 1925.

Levinson, Alfred. "Diamond Sources and Their Discovery." *The Nature of Diamonds.* George Harlow, ed. United Kingdom: Cambridge University Press, 1998, 72–104.

Scarisbrick, Diana. "The Diamond Love and Marriage Ring." *The Nature of Diamonds.* George Harlow, ed. United Kingdom: Cambridge University Press, 1998, 163–170.

Sears, Roebuck and Co. Watches, Diamonds, Jewelry and Silverware Catalog. Minneapolis, 1893.

Zapata, Janet. *The Jewelry and Enamels of Louis Tiffany.* New York: Harry N. Abrams, 1993.

18 UNLUCKY INVENTORY

1. "Personal and Otherwise." *NYT,* April 28, 1907, X4.

2. "Gossip of Society," *WP,* January 9, 1908, 9.

3. "Hope Diamond Has Brought Trouble to All Who Have Owned It," *WP* [credited to *New York Herald*], January 19, 1908.

4. *ibid.*

5. "How Gems are Prepared for the People Who Love Them," *NYT,* April 5, 1908.

6. "Hope Diamond Is Sold," *NYT,* May 6, 1908.

7. "Sale of the Hope Diamond," *TL,* June 25, 1909, 5.

8. *ibid.*

9. *ibid.*

10. *ibid.*

11. *ibid.*

12. "Hope Diamond's Owner Lost," *NYT,* November 17, 1909, 1.

13. *ibid.*

14. "Puzzle of Hope Diamond," *NYT,* November 18, 1909, 3.

15. "Hope Diamond in Paris," *NYT,* March 27, 1910, 3.

Additional references for the chapter include:

Aucoc, Louis. *Exposition Internationale d'Anvers.* Paris: Chamerot et Renouard, 1895.

Catalog de la vente Habib, Paris: 24 June 1909.

Brown, Charles. *Gems, Magic, Mysteries and Myths of Precious Stones.* Madison: State Historical Museum, 1932.

Burnham, S. M. *Precious Stones.* Boston: Bradlee Whidden, 1886.

Catelle, W. R. *The Diamond.* New York: John Lane Company, 1911.

Crookes, Sir William. *Diamonds.* 1909.

"Diamond Dealer Fails for $150,000," *NYT,* January 8, 1908, 2.

"Duty on the Hope Diamond," *NYT,* November 28, 1902.

"Famous Hope Blue Diamond Sold In Paris for the Joseph Frankel's Sons Co.," *The Jewelers' Circular-Weekly,* May 6, 1908, 67.

Fromanger, H. D. *Bijoux et Pierres Précieuses.* Paris: Hachette, 1970.

"Great Hope Diamond Here," *NYT,* November 27, 1901, 1.

"Hope Diamond Again Offered for Sale," *NYT,* October 29, 1910.

"Hope Diamond Goes Cheap," *NYT,* June 25, 1909.

"Hope Diamond in America," *The Jewelers' Circular-Weekly,* December 4, 1901, 19.

"Hope Diamond Not Lost," *NYT,* November 20, 1909.

"Joseph Frankel's Sons and Joseph Frankel's Sons Co. Pay Creditors in Full," *The Jewelers' Circular-Weekly,* June 9, 1909, 71.

"Noted Diamonds in America," *The Jewelers' Circular-Weekly,* February 5, 1902, 17.

Orpen, Adela Elizabeth Richards (Mrs. Goddard Orpen). *Stories about Famous Precious Stones.* Boston: D. Lothrop Company, 1901; 1890 edition not seen.

Rowe, John. "The Mystery of the Blue Hope Diamond." *The Wide World Magazine,* v. 26, October 1910–March 1911.

"The Hope Blue Diamond," *The Jewelers' Circular-Weekly,* November 20, 1901.

"Sale of the Habib Collection of Rare Diamonds Takes Place at Paris," *The Jewelers' Circular-Weekly,* June 30, 1909, 71.

"Sultan of Turkey Was Not the Purchaser of the Hope Blue Diamond," *The Jewelers' Circular-Weekly,* May 13, 1908, 49.

Wodiska, Julius. *A Book of Precious Stones.* New York: G. P. Putnam's Sons, 1909.

19 CARTIER'S STORY

1. Fornaro, Carlo de. *Prince Tissa: Legend of the Ruby.* New York: Marcus & Co., 1902, 7.

2. Fornaro, Carlo de. *Krishna's Gift: The Legend of the Diamond.* New York: Marcus & Co., 1901, 15.

3. Pierre Cartier gained knowledge of the American market and customer sensibilities by working closely with antiques dealer Jules Glaenzer, who ran the New York store.

Additional references for the chapter include:

Fornaro, Carlo de. *Tsvara' Ring: The Legend of the Jade; The Necklace of Untold Sighs: The Legend of the Coral; Shiva, The Destroyer: The Legend of the*

Moonstone; White Lotus: The Legend of the Cat's Eye. New York: Marcus & Co., 1902.

Loring, John. *Tiffany: 150 years.* 1987.

Nadelhoffer, Hans. *Cartier: Jewelers Extraordinary.* New York: Harry Abrams, 1984.

Rudoe, Judy. *Cartier: 1900–1939.* New York: Harry Abrams and the Metropolitan Museum of Art, 1997.

Schneirla, Peter. *Tiffany: 150 Years of Gems and Jewelry.* New York: Tiffany, 1987.

Scott, Sir Walter. *Anne of Geiérstein.* 1829.

Tiffany & Co., *Catalogue de la collection pierres précieuses.*

Tretiak, Philippe. *Cartier.* New York: Universe/Vendorne Pub., 1997.

Vever, H. *La bijouterie franaise au XIX siècle. 1908.*

Zapata, Janet. *The Jewelry and Enamels of Louis Tiffany.* New York: Harry N. Abrams, 1993.

20 McLean's Temptation

1. McLean, Evalyn Walsh with Boyden Sparkes. *Father Struck It Rich.* Boston: Little, Brown and Co., 1936.

2. *ibid.,* 38.

3. *ibid.,* 50.

4. Unattributed magazine article.

5. McLean *op cit.,* 142.

6. *ibid.,* 175.

7. *ibid.,* 176.

8. The contract memorandum is included in "Jewlers Who Sold Hope Diamond Bring Suit to Recover the Purchase Price," *Jewelers' Circular Weekly,* March 15, 1911, 71.

9. McLean *op. cit.,* 177.

10. *ibid.*

11. *ibid.*

12. *ibid.,* 178.

13. "J. R. M'Lean's Son Buys Hope Diamond," *NYT,* January 29, 1911, 1.

14. "Sues the M'Leans for Hope Diamond," *NYT,* March 9, 1911, 1.

15. Affidavit of Edward B. McLean; Affidavit of Evalyn W. McLean. Court Papers: Law No. 53,384. January 28, 1911. LOC Box 104.

16. Letter from Virginia Calhoun to Mrs. Ned McLean, March 13, 1911. LOC, Box 79.

17. "Big Diamonds Really Are Unlucky," *NYT,* February 3, 1912.

18. "M'Leans to Keep the Hope Diamond," *NYT,* February 2, 1912, 1; "Hope Diamond Worn at M'Lean Dinner," *NYT,* February 3, 1912, 3.

19, Letter from P. J. Byrne to Edward McLean, January 30, 1911. LOC, Box 16.

20. Wilson, T. Edgar. "The Hope Diamond," Letter to the Editor, *NYT,* November 9, 1911, 6.

21. *ibid.*

22. McLean, *op. cit.,* 179.

23. Cohen, Gary. "The Diamond," *Vanity Fair,* August 1997.

24. "M'Lean Heir Killed by an Automobile," *NYT,* May 19, 1919.

Additional references for the chapter include:

"A Historical Landmark," www. Washington.kbri.org/kbri.org/kbri/gedungkbri.htm.

"Court Decides Jury Must Hear Cartier's Suit to Recover Purchase Price of the Hope Diamond," *The Jewelers' Circular-Weekly,* May 10, 1911, 71.

"Famous Hope Diamond Reported to Have Been Sold to Edward McLean," *The Jewelers' Circular-Weekly,* February 1, 1911, 165.

"McLeans File Answer," *NYT,* April 2, 1911.

"Mr. and Mrs. E. B. McLean File Answer to Suit Over Purchase Price of the Hope Diamond," *The Jewelers' Circular-Weekly,* April 5, 1911, 73.

Roberts, Chalmers. *In the Shadow of Power: The Story of the Washington Post.* Cabin John, MD and Washington, DC: Seven Locks Press, 1989.

Sfrerrazza, Carl Anthony. *Florence Harding: The First Lady, the*

Jazz Age, and the Death of America's Most Scandalous President. New York: William Morrow and Co., 1998.

"The Walsh-McLean House," embassy.org/associates/Kelsey/ history004.html.

21 MODERNITY'S CURSE

1. "Ill-Luck and the Hope Diamond," *NYT,* March 10, 1911.

2. "Big Diamonds Really Are Unlucky," *NYT,* February 3, 1912.

3. "God Moves on the Water," song text from Courlander, Harold. *Negro Folk Music, U.S.A.,* New York, Columbia University Press, 1963.

4. Carnegie, Andrew. *The Gospel of Wealth.* [Original 1889]. Indianapolis: Indiana University Center on Philanthropy, 1993,

5. Quoted in Allen, Henry. "Starting From Zero," *WP,* September 20, 1991, C1.

Additional references for the chapter include:

Brademan, Arnold. *The Search for the Gold of Tutankhaman.* New York: Van Nostrand Reinhold Company, 1976.

Courlander, Harold. *A Treasury of Afro-American Folklore.* New York: Crown Publishers, Inc., 1976.

Hoving, Thomas. *Tutankhamen: The Untold Story.* New York: Simon and Schuster, 1978.

Howells, Richard. *The Myth of the Titanic.* New York: St. Martin's Press, 1999.

Hull, Dana. "The Toast of the Titanic," *WP,* December 20, 1997, F1.

Kamil, Fred. *The Diamond Curse.* London: Allen Lane, 1979.

Place, Jeff. "Supplemental Notes on the Selections," *Anthology of American Folk Music,* ed. Harry Smith, selection 22. Smithsonian Folkways Recordings, SFW40090.

Veblen, Thorstein. *The Theory of the Leisure Class.* [Original 1899]. New York: Penguin Books, 1967.

22 YOHE'S PROP

1. McLean, *op. cit.*, 178.
2. Gates, *op. cit.*, 253.
3. *ibid.*
4. *cf.* Sferrazza, Carl Anthony. "Bittersweet Friends," *WP*, C1, August 18, 1986; *Life, op. cit.*

Additional references for the chapter include:
"Diamond Legend Involves Late Bethlehem Woman," *The Morning Call*, December 3, 1971, 49.

"Gem Ferhexed Bethlehem Girl," *Sunday Morning Call-Chronicle*, November 9, 1958, 1.

Meyers, Richard. "Bethlehem Woman Once Owned Hope Diamond," *Sunday Morning Call-Chronicle*, May 30, 1965.

The Mystery of the Hope Diamond. Stuart Paton, director, May Yohe, writer, screen adaptation Charles Goddard and John B. Clymer. Kosmik Films, 1921.

23 HIGH SOCIETY TALISMAN

1. Wilson, Vylla Poe. "My Sister Pawned the Hope Diamond." *Sunday, The Star Magazine*, May 17, 1959.
2. Invitation for First and Only Public Showing of the Hope Diamond. LOC, Box 97.
3. Letter from Minnie Koontz to Evalyn Walsh McLean, January 1, 1945, LOC, Box 3.
4. McLean, *op. cit.*, 177.
5. *ibid.*, 179.
6. *ibid.*, 251.

Additional references for the chapter include:
Alexander, John. *Ghosts: Washington's Most Famous Ghost Stories.* Arlington: Washington Book Trading Company, 1988.

Arnold, Thurman. *Fair Fights and Foul: A Dissenting Lawyer's Life.*
New York: Harcourt, Brace and World, 1951.

Hogan, Bill. "Losing It," *Regardie's,* February/March 1982.

Kernan, Michael. "Around the Mall and Beyond," *Smithsonian*
magazine, May, 1995.

Monnickendam, A. *The Magic of Diamonds.* Harford Co., 1955.

Sferrazza, Carl Anthony. *Florence Harding: The First Lady, the Jazz
Age, and the Death of America's Most Scandalous President.* New York:
William Morrow and Co., 1998.

Shipley, R.M. *Famous Diamonds of the world.* Los Angeles:
Gemological Institute of America, 1939.

"The Gem and the Curse," *Newsweek,* April 18, 1949.

"Two Diamonds in Rough Meet the Hope," *Expose,* Washington,
D.C., Army War College, no. 3, January 8, 1942.

Wilcox, Marguerite. "The Hope Diamond," a poem. NMNH.

24 WINSTON'S BABY

1. *cf.* "Big Rocks," *Time,* April 18, 1949.

2. Runyon's attribution parallels the sports figures he covered.

3. Ross, Lillian. "Profiles: The Big Stone-1," *The New Yorker,* May
8, 1954, 58; also Krashes, *op. cit.*

4. Proddow, Penny and Marion Fasel. *Diamonds: A Century of
Spectacular Jewels.* New York: Harry N. Abrams, 1996, 99.

5. Loos, Anita. *Gentlemen Prefer Blondes.* New York: Boni &
Liveright, 1925, 100.

6. Boufflers, Stanislas-Jean de. *The Queen of Golconda and Other Tales.*
Eric Sutton, trans. London: Chapman & Hall, 1926, 20. The story
inspired a 19th century poem by Chandos Leigh and a musical
score by the famous Swedish composer Franz Berwald.

7. Tupper, Harmon and Elsie. "Harry Winston, King of
Diamonds." *Cosmopolitan.* April 1947, 110.

8. "Golconda on E. 51st." *Life,* March 17, 1952.

9. Tupper, *op. cit.*

10. "Diamonds Are a Girl's Best Friend," by Leo Robin and Jule Styne.

11. Wharton-Tigar, Edward. *Burning Bright.* Metal Bulletin Books, Ltd., 1987.

12. McLean, Evalyn Walsh. "My Say," LOC, Box 99.

13. Baerwald, Marcus. *The Story of Jewelry.* London: Abelard-Schuman, 1960, 41.

14. Chase, Ilke, 1960.

Additional references for the chapter include:

Gregory, Alexis. *Harry Winston: Rare Jewels of the World.* Paris: Assouline, 1998.

Ross, Lillian. "The Big Stone." *New Yorker,* May 15, 1954.

25 Tax Deduction

1. This and all subsequent documents, SI.

26 Museum Specimen 217868

1. Crowingshield, Robert. "Grading the Hope Diamond," *Gems and Gemology,* Summer 1989.

2. Westman, Burton. "The Enigmatic Hope," *Lapidary Journal,* March 1988.

3. Pough, Frederick. "Gilding the Lily: A Diamond on a Dop," *ibid.,* 43.

4. *cf.* Switzer, George. "Questing for Gems," *National Geographic,* December 1971; Goodavage, Joseph. "The Curse of the Hope Diamond?" Published article of undetermined source, NMNH.

5. White, John Sampson. "The Tell-Tale Glow?" *Lapidary Journal,* November 1994.

6. "Hall of Gems Lurks Like a Hidden Jewel In a Back Wing of Smithsonian Institution." Newspaper article, UPI, Washington dateline. NMNH.

7. Basinski, John E. Letter, October 14, 1985, NMNH.

8. Switzer, George, *op. cit.*

Additional references for the chapter include:

"Hind Horn," in Child, Francis. *English and Scottish popular Ballads.* Boston, New York: Houghton Mifflin company, 1904.

27 NATIONAL TREASURE

1. NMNH.

2. *ibid.*

3. *ibid.*

4. *ibid.*

5. Meetings the previous year were coming to fruition for the loan of major art objects. A state dinner at the White House was scheduled for May 11, and so the need to move quickly was apparent to him and to Mrs. Kennedy, if not to the Smithsonian. Baldrige, Letitia. Letter to John Walker, April 14, 1962. JFK.

6. NMNH.

7. *ibid.*

8. *ibid.*

9. *ibid.*

10. Switzer, George. "I Remember . . . Flying to Paris with the Hope," *Sun Magazine,* April 12, 1981.

11. *ibid.*

12. *ibid.*

13. *Dix Siècles de Joaillerie Française,* An exhibition at the Louvre, Paris, 1962.

14. NMNH.

15. Unattributed published article, September 8, 1963. NMNH. When President Kennedy was assassinated later in 1963, there were a few who blamed the curse of the Hope diamond given Jackie Kennedy's involvement in its exhibition in France.

16. Form of Procedure, December 1, 1962, for the planning of the transfer and exhibit. JFK.

17. NMNH.

18. Patch, *op. cit.*, 1976, 37.

19. Alexander, Ron. "The Honored Guests Were Jewels," *NYT,* December 1, 1982.

20. Many requests have come to the Smithsonian over the years, asking to borrow the diamond for exhibitions or commercial purposes. In the wake of the 1962 Louvre trip, U.S. Senator Symington asked the Smithsonian to lend the diamond to the Merchants Produce Bank for the opening of a new branch bank in Kansas City. The Smithsonian politely refused. Another Senator got the same result when in the wake of the South Africa trip he failed to persuade the Smithsonian to lend the diamond to the Texas State Fair. In July 1962 an advertising agency representing VO-5 hair spray wanted to do a commercial showing how their product would not dull the luster of the diamond. They offered the Smithsonian a $1,000 donation plus free publicity. They received a firm but polite refusal.

Susanne Patch used the examples of the 7-carat Blue Graff that sold for over $296,454 per carat and a 6.19-carat blue diamond that sold for $580,000 per carat in 1990 in order to provide an idea of the Hope's worth. *cf.* Patch, *op. cit.*, 1999, 88.

28 COLLECTION KEYSTONE

1. Post, *op. cit.*, 27. The Hope diamond provided an absolutely crucial impetus to the unprecedented growth of the Smithsonian's national collection. The museum simply lacked any large diamonds of great historical significance before its arrival. As George Merrill, the Smithsonian's gem curator, noted in the 1920s, the United States had no royal family nor crown jewels nor long-lived aristocracy to mine for such a collection.

2. "Illuminating the Hope Diamond," Absolute Action Fibre Optics, www.absolute-action.com/projects/hope.html.

3. Unattributed UPI newspaper article, NMNH.

4. Small, Lawrence. "The Gem of the Collection," *Smithsonian* magazine, April 2000.

Additional references for the chapter include:

"Harry Winston to Unite Dresden Green Diamond with Historic Hope Diamond for First Time Ever," press release, Harry Winston, Inc., June 2000.

Melson, William, Jeffrey Post, Michael Wise, Sorena Sorenson, Richard Fiske, James Luhr, Glenn MacPherson and Timothy McCoy. "Diamonds to Diamonds," *Geotimes,* December 1997.

"Mining Company Set to Buy Majority of Harry Winston," NYT.com, November 28, 2003.

"The Story of the Hope Diamond," Smithsonian Institution, www.si.edu/access/hopediam.htm.

Trescott, Jacqueline. "Gem Dandy: The Hope Diamond Has a New Home," *WP,* September 7, 1997.

Trescott, Jacqueline. "Smithsonian's Carat Patch to Host Green Giant," *WP,* June 21, 2000.

White, John Sampson. *The Smithsonian Treasury: Minerals and Gems.* Washington: Smithsonian Institution Press, 1991.

29 MISSING PIECES?

1. Attaway, Nancy. "The French Connection." *Lapidary Journal,* June, 2005; "Mysteries of the Smithsonian's Hope Diamond Solved with New Scientific Research: Discovery Channel Special Premieres Feb. 10," press release, Smithsonian National Museum of Natural History, February 9, 2005; *Unsolved History: Hope Diamond,* Discovery Channel. I had an intern, Nathaniel Gleicher, who had tried a computer simulation along the same lines several years before. Lacking the technology to develop accurate measures, that experiment was curtailed.

2. LOC, box 16.

3. McGlashan, Ian. "The Story of the Hope Diamond," *Lapidary Journal,* January 1980.

4. Ross, Nancy. "A Piece of the Rock," *WP,* January 31, 1997, C4.

5. Jewels of the Romanovs: Treasures of the Russian Imperial Court, Corcoran Gallery of Art, Washington, January 29–April 13, 1997.

6. There is an inventory of possessions from 1827 that mentions the pin. Additional materials include catalog entries. There is no other primary historical material on the provenance of the diamond. HSP. Additionally, Twining also catalogs the pin with the blue brilliant, *op. cit.,* 543.

7. Augusta is supposed to have suffered a gruesome death, mummified in an Estonian castle in 1788, well before the theft of the French Blue. But both the Duke and Caroline of Brunswick believed rumors and reports that she was alive for decades afterward.

Additional references for the chapter include:

Gorewa, Olga, Irina Polynova and Nikolai Rachmanov. *Joyaux du trésor de Russie.* Paris: La Bibliothèque d' Art, 1991.

Tillander, Herbert. "The Hope Diamond and its Lineage: A Challenge for Further Research. Presented at the 15th International Gemological Conference, Smithsonian Institution, 1975.

30 POP ICON

1. Cazan, Nancy. "The Hope Diamond Legend," www. Bsu.edu/teachers/academy/gems/activity12.html.

2. *Sex and the City,* 1985.

3. Hiaasen, Carl. *Stormy Weather.* New York: Alfred A. Knopf, 1995, 355.

4. McMurtry, Larry. *Cadillac Jack.* New York: Simon & Schuster, 1982, 144.

5. Klein, Richard. *Jewelry Talks: A Novel Thesis.* New York: Pantheon, 2001, 22.

6. Kornheiser, Tony. *WP,* August 28, 2003.

7. Posner, Richard. Hope Diamond. *High Performance,* Summer 1993, vol. 16, no. 2.

8. Newspaper advertisement, Washington, D.C., October 26, 1965. NMNH.

Additional references for the chapter include:

Brown, Janet Hubbard. *A History Mystery: The Curse of the Hope Diamond.* New York: Avon Trade Books, 1991.

"Hope Diamond." *Landscape Architecture.* December, 1993.

Life, op. cit.

"The Legend of the Hope Diamond," seedsnet.stark.k12.oh.us/np/hopediamond/hdlesson_frame.html.

INDEX